THE CHÁVEZ CODE

CRACKING U.S. INTERVENTION IN VENEZUELA

Revolutionary Hugs,

Caracas 2007

THE CHÁVEZ CODE
CRACKING U.S. INTERVENTION IN VENEZUELA

Eva Golinger

Editorial José Martí

Edition: Susana Díaz Alvarado
Correction: Maritza Vázquez Valdés
Design: Ernesto Niebla Chalita
Desktop Publishing: Diana Suárez Companioni
                              Adriana Vázquez Pérez

ISBN 959-09-0307-X

INSTITUTO CUBANO DEL LIBRO
Editorial JOSÉ MARTÍ
Publicaciones en Lenguas Extranjeras
Calzada No. 259 e/ J e I, Vedado
Ciudad de La Habana, Cuba
jmbf@icl.cult.cu

This book is dedicated to the memory of Danilo Anderson, assassinated in Caracas on November 18, 2004.

Table of Contents

FOREWORD
Cracking the Code of Lies / 11
ACKNOWLEDGMENTS / 27
INTRODUCTION / 29
CHAPTER ONE
Nicaragua and Chile: The Coup Cookbook / 37
The Nicaragua Model / 39
The National Endowment for Democracy / 40
The Nicaragua-Venezuela Connection / 42
U.S. Agency for International Development / 46
CHAPTER TWO
A President Denied a U.S. Visa / 48
Visa Denial / 52
CHAPTER THREE
From Vargas to Pre-Coup Premonitions / 54
FTAA Opposition and the U.S. Military Expelled / 57
A Fateful Flare-up / 59
CHAPTER FOUR
IRI Gives Birth to Primero Justicia / 62
IRI's Coup-Time Blooper / 63
Primero Justicia Assaults the Cuban Embassy / 70
CHAPTER FIVE
Decoding Venezuela / 74
"The Right Man for the Right Time in Venezuela" / 75
The Growing Coalition of Unlikely Friends / 78
The First Signs / 81
CHAPTER SIX
A Coup by Any Other Name / 84
Reich Comes onto the Scene / 85
Bogus Intelligence Reports / 87
The CIA Knows All / 89
"Another Piece Falls into Place" / 90
So Now More Pieces Are Falling into Place / 92
The Coup / 96

"No More Oil for Cuba" / 101
Venevisión's Contributions / 102
The U.S. Supports the Coup / 103
Carmona the Brief / 105
New York Police Department Connection? / 106
A Surprising Change of Events / 107
"Was the U.S. Involved in the Effort to Remove Venezuelan President Chávez from Power? Absolutely Not" / 109
Media Blackout / 110
More Money in the Pot / 111
CHAPTER SEVEN
    An Office for a Transitional Government / 116
    Development Alternatives, Inc. / 120
    Was Venezuela a "Worn Torn" Nation or "Otherwise Unstable"? / 120
CHAPTER EIGHT
    Paro Petrolero: An Oil Industry Sabotage / 125
    Million of Dollars Result in Billions in Losses / 125
    Media War against the People / 126
    "Democratic" Coordinator / 135
    INTESA: A Shoddy Deal / 136
    "Early Elections"—Constitution, What Constitution? / 138
CHAPTER NINE
    Electoral Intervention: The U.S.'s Last Hope / 141
    The Rise of Súmate / 141
    The Referendum / 142
    The Venezuela Terrorist Connection / 145
    "The Guarimba" / 147
    "Plan Consenso pa'Bush" (Plan Consensus for Bush) / 148
    The Petare Experiment / 151
    Penn, Schoen & Berland—U.S. Polling Firm of Choice / 154
    César Gaviria's Long Night / 156
CHAPTER TEN
    Up the Sleeve Strategies and Threats / 159
    The Súmate Case: NED on the Offensive / 159
    Miami: A Terrorist Hub /165
    Terrorist Camps / 167
    Future Relations / 168
EPILOGUE / 169
POST NOTE
The Chávez Code: A Model for Investigators / 173
APPENDIX / 177
GLOSSARY / 251

FOREWORD

Cracking the Code of Lies

The Chávez Code: Cracking U.S. Intervention in Venezuela begins with an almost detective-like description of how Eva Golinger and her collaborators discovered certain documents in the attics of the State Department, the Department of Defense and other unsavoury depths where U.S. foreign policy is concocted, and subsequently, the book becomes a meticulous essay about the National Endowment for Democracy (NED). Later, the book transforms yet again and returns in the guise of an intrepid melodrama full of pillage, robbery, political blackmail, a mercenary spirit and violence. After reading the last page, the reader might just as well ask himself or herself whether what he or she has read is really an incredible adventure novel or an imaginary game that has no connection to real life. However, there is not one line of fiction in this book. A large part is made up of documents obtained under the auspices of the U.S. Freedom of Information Act (FOIA), and it took Eva Golinger a great amount of time and effort to compile this material which is now at the disposal of her readers and, as stated in the first page, has implied gigantic risks for the author, including receiving death threats.

Even so, the reader should not forget that such a documentary testimonial comes into being not only because of the perseverance of the investigators, but because of the fickleness of employees who control access to U.S. secret archives, declassify at their own discretion, and conceal some of the most damning items. The author herself predicts that it will take decades before other documents are revealed. In other words, much more incredibly frightening evidence must still be censored and perhaps we may never know the most intimate details about the plans against Venezuela. As it is well known, it took more than thirty years and the *mea culpa* of Robert McNamara before we knew of the diabolical excuses that were invented to justify the U.S. invasion of Cuba, included in the design of the so-called *Operation Mongoose.*[1] When will we ever know the real story of what happened in Dallas on the day Kennedy was assassinated? When will we know what is now being hatched against Cuba, Venezuela and the world?

Thanks to this sample which the author and the independent journalist Jeremy Bigwood managed to dig up from the United States Government, it is possible to prove what the U.S. has repeatedly denied: the U.S. did know beforehand of the details of the coup d'état against Venezuelan President Hugo Chávez in April 2002, including plans to incite violence during public demonstrations, the arrest of the president and active participation in the coup itself.

"Dissident military factions, including some disgruntled senior officers and a group of radical junior officers, are stepping up efforts to organize a coup against President Chávez, possibly as early as this month," warned the CIA in a classified document known as the *Senior Executive Intelligence Brief,* dated April 6, 2002, five days before the attempted coup; this can be corroborated in *The Chávez Code,*[2] where we can read of new evidence about facts that are already known: the sense of relative morals espoused by professional U.S. politicians.

1. Fabián Escalante Font, *Operación Mangosta* (Havana: Editorial de Ciencias Sociales, 2002). "Operation Mangoose was the broadest subversive program undertaken by the Government of the United States against any foreign nation in the sixties; even today there are secrets contained in this operation that are considered to be among 'the jewels of the CIA,' in other words, maximum national security secrets. It was initiated in November 1961 as a result of the reflections of General Maxwell Taylor on the causes and conditions of the Bay of Pigs fiasco. It concluded by the end of 1962 as a result of the disastrous operations of the program by which the Kennedy's Administration had hoped to cause the destruction of the Cuban Revolution."
2. See Appendix, pp. 209, 210.

"To provoke military action, the plotters may try to exploit unrest stemming from opposition demonstrations," added the CIA. The document obtained by the lawyer and author of this book specifically refers to plans for the arrest of Chávez and of other ten high-ranking officers; this confirms the declarations printed in *Newsday* on November 24, 2004,[3] which were subsequently dissolved in the ocean of media coverage. Thanks to the testimony of a CIA spokesman, the newspaper revealed the existence of confidential documents that proved that the Agency never warned the Venezuelan Government of the impending uprising. To warn Chávez of the imminent coup, added the spokesman, "would suggest that we interfere in another nation's affairs."

Added to this magnificent certification of cynicism is the usual lie released by the Bush's Administration, something which the documents in this book leave perfectly clear. On April 16, 2002, five days after the attempted coup, the then White House Press Secretary, Ari Fleischer, was asked if the U.S. "had advance knowledge that something was in the works," such as a coup. "No," replied Fleischer, adding: "I think you have to be careful about advance knowledge of a specific act and general talk of unease in a nation like Venezuela."

While a poker-faced Fleischer was making these statements to the press, the entire subversive machine that the U.S. employed against a government that had been tacitly placed on its "enemy list" had been put into motion. Together with the NED's financial support of Chávez's hostile opposition, the CIA covert and not-so-covert actions had been unleashed. Evidence that appeared afterwards and that uncovered by the author is truly overwhelming.

Anyone who peruses press reports on those dates will discover much evidence that corroborates the eloquent CIA document presented in this investigation. In April of 2002 it was denounced before the Venezuelan National Assembly that "the

3. Bart Jones and Letta Tayler, "CIA Knew of Plot Against Venezuela's Chávez," *Newsday*, November 24, 2004. See also http://www.newsday.com/news/nation-world/world/ny-wovene244053424nov24,0,4856696,story.

arrest and subsequent delivery of two snipers, one from El Salvador and the other from the U.S., proved the effective participation of the Government of the United States in the coup d'état of April 11."[4] The newspaper *Últimas Noticias* published the names of two American officers who were in Fort Tiuna on April 11, together with the military coup plotters; this was confirmed by the Minister of Defense, Commander Jorge Luis García Carneiro, to the authors of the book *Chávez Nuestro.*[5] García Carneiro, on the day of the coup was on the fifth floor of Fort Tiuna, the headquarters of the General Staff of the Venezuelan Army; he saw them there, described how they were dressed and how they were armed. These two officers are Lieutenant Colonel James Rodgers, Assistant to the U.S. military attaché in Caracas—the author of the book refers to this individual—and Colonel Ronald McCammon, Intelligence officer.

The U.S. Ambassador in Venezuela, Charles Shapiro, was the first person to interview Pedro Carmona Estanga, the ipso facto president. Shortly thereafter, he spoke with Manuel Viturro, the Spanish Ambassador. The coup plotters were also advised by private consultants, the Phoenix Consulting Group, which employs former CIA agents.[6] According to Intelligence

---

4. Juan Vicente Gómez, "MVR and MAS Parliamentarians deliver proof," *La Fogata Digital,* April 25, 2002. See also http://www.lafogata.org/02golpe/golpe/v 11.html.

5. Rosa Miriam Elizalde and Luis Báez, *Chávez Nuestro* (Havana: Editora Abril, 2004), 176. García Carneiro confirms that "they were in civilian clothes, but armed. It struck me particularly because it was the first time I had seen grenade launchers. Later I found out that they were M-203 rifles."

6. Phoenix Consulting Group: According to its internet page (http://www.intell-pros.com), this firm "provides clients with competitive Intelligence consulting services for small, medium and large business in several industries. Its commercial services include: competitive Intelligence consulting services, professional development programs, executive seminars, and specialized security assistance. Its government services include field studies, training, special studies, and specialized security assistance. It also provides links to intelligence and counterintelligence organizations in the United States; competitive intelligence sites, related documents and reports, corporate and government counterintelligence sites, and other sites related to government intelligence in Europe, United Kingdom, Canada and Africa." Contrary to what Intelligence Online states, the name of this consulting group does not come from the Phoenix Program conceived during the Vietnam War, but instead it derives from the City of Phoenix in the State of Arizona, where it was founded.

information, Venezuelan territory was besieged by U.S. ships and planes, a completely irregular activity. "These ships were identified as NC1 3300, NC2 2027 and NC3 2132; they entered territorial waters at 9:00 A.M. on April 12, 2002, without due authorization. After 4:00 P.M. they headed towards the high seas," according to a report submitted by the Venezuelan Air Force to Carmona and found in the Miraflores Presidential Palace upon Chávez's return.[7]

On Saturday April 13, east of Los Roques and close to La Orchila, where the deposed President Hugo Chávez was being held, U.S. naval transport ships and several military helicopters were navigating Venezuelan territorial waters and air space. "After 12 noon, helicopters NC 11100 and NC 10107 had taken off from the deck of one of the ships, and returned after a short flight. A little later, a third plane, NC 20212, was seen approaching from the north-east, it circled the above-mentioned ship and flew off towards the north," added the report.

Alí Uzcátegui[8] assured the authors of *Chávez Nuestro* that while Chávez was being held at La Orchila "one of the plotters' plans was to send him to the United States. Carmona's Minister of Defense, Rear Admiral Héctor Ramírez Pérez, gave orders to Captain José Aguilera, the Commander of La Orchila Naval Base, to receive Chávez who was to be sent abroad from the island," said Uzcátegui.[9] On April 19, 2002, the English newspaper *The Guardian*[10] published declarations made by Wayne Madsen, former marine secret service agent saying: "The United States had been considering a coup to overthrow the elected Venezuelan President, Hugo Chávez, since last June," adding "the U.S. Navy aided the abortive coup which took place in

7. Report consulted by the authors of *Chávez Nuestro* and confirmed by the testimony of Jesús Suárez Chourio, who led the Miraflores Palace takeover in the afternoon of April 13, 2002 (unpublished testimony).
8. General Alí Uzcátegui, Chief of Army Staff, was the one who led the commando unit that rescued President Hugo Chávez in La Orchila on April 13, 2002, and subsequently took him to Miraflores.
9. Rosa Miriam Elizalde and Luis Báez, *Chávez Nuestro* (Havana: Editora Abril, 2004), 288.
10. Duncan Campbell, "American Navy Helped Venezuelan Coup," *The Guardian*, April 19, 2002.

Venezuela on April 11 with Intelligence from its vessels in the Caribbean to the key participants in the coup. I first heard of Lieutenant Colonel James Rodgers [the assistant military attaché now based at the U.S. Embassy in Caracas] going down there last June to set the ground," declared Madsen. "Navy vessels on a training exercise in the area were supposedly put on stand-by in case evacuation of U.S. citizens in Venezuela was required," he told *The Guardian*.

On April 16, 2002, the Venezuelan newspaper *Últimas Noticias* quoted Eliécer Otaiza, ex Director of the Information, Security and Protection Directorate (DISIP): "I understand that there is precise satellite information that shows U.S. military transport ships in territorial waters, close to La Orchila." He explained that the officers were commenting on the fact that it was possible that: "Marines were travelling on the ships and that an F 117 Phantom had been in the air that night."

Of course, money from the NED had been spread around and had helped to agitate public opinion in order to speed up these events. Instead of deterring the plotters, U.S. authorities offered logistic and political support to them. To back up a foreseeable direct U.S. military intervention, Rear Admiral Carlos Molina and Colonel Pedro Soto received $200,000 deposited to bank accounts in Miami. On February 18, 2002, these two men had demanded Hugo Chávez's resignation and accused him of having helped the Colombian guerrilla movement, FARC (Revolutionary Armed Forces of Colombia); this was an outright lie to justify the operations for the coup d'état in the context of a "war on terrorism." As Eva Golinger recalls, in those days "the NED had authorized an additional donation of 300 thousand dollars to the International Republican Institute so that it could continue 'strengthening political parties in Venezuela.'"

Yes, the coup failed, but all this wheeling and dealing —so similar to other projects of political subversion—reveals that in like circumstances, another attempt is not out of the question. The reason is simple: the true leaders of the remote-controlled conspiracy are in Washington and they continue demanding Chávez's head, with enough resources and incentives to orchestrate any violent manoeuvre, including the possibility of presidential assassination. Eva Golinger's investigations prove that U.S. secret and public services assisted the escape of many of the coup plotters—some were received with complete indiscretion in Miami by the arms dealer Isaac Pérez Recao—, and continue to pay and organize the opposition, especially those who led the "*firmazo*," the movement to call a referendum to remove Chávez.

Do As I Say, Not What I Do

Neither the media nor the politicians ever say that, according to U.S. laws, these events would be a flagrant violation of the Constitution. They would be judged in the United States for the crime of "treason," as stated in the U.S. Code, Title 18, Chapter 115, and Section 2381: "Whoever, owing allegiance to the United States, levies war against them or adheres to their enemies, giving them aid and comfort within the United States or elsewhere, is guilty of treason," and "shall suffer death, or shall be imprisoned not less than five years and fined under this title but not less than $10,000; and shall be incapable of holding any office under the United States."[11] The semantics used in Section 2383 of this same Code leaves no doubt as to the sanctions applied against whoever promotes, organizes or supports coup plotters: "Whoever . . . assists . . . in any rebellion or insurrection against the authority of the United States" is considered to be engaged in rebellion or insurrection. He/she "shall be fined under this title or imprisoned not more than ten years..." Also, the individual who conspires to overthrow the government—Section 2385—in other words: "Whoever knowingly or willfully advocates, abets, advises, or teaches the duty, necessity, desirability, or propriety of overthrowing or destroying the government of the United States . . . by force or violence, or by the assassination of any officer of any such government; or . . . prints, publishes, edits, issues, circulates, sells, distributes, or publicly displays any written or printed matter advocating, advising, or teaching

11. See http://www.lawresearchservices.com/firms/practice/ctcrime.html.

the duty, necessity, desirability, or propriety of overthrowing or destroying any government in the United States . . . shall be fined under this title or imprisoned not more than twenty years . . . ."

Even for someone who has just arrived from another planet, whoever examines the Venezuelan press before, during and after the events of April of 2002, will discover that this was a classical case of civic-military coup d'état "made in USA." An oligarchic and ultra-right-wing coup of that Holy Alliance: the Sword and the Power of Money. Add to that the "fourth power"—the written press and television—, both legitimizing and participating in the formula.

If, in retrospect, we draw a parallel with the coup d'état against Jacobo Arbenz in Guatemala, or against Salvador Allende in Chile, where the participation of the CIA is a given, we see an unbelievable similarity, besides being classified as crimes against humanity by any court or legislation on this globe, including that of the United States. Therefore, faced with so much proof—including that presented in this book— why is Venezuela being prevented from punishing the guilty parties? Why does the United States expects that no other nation has the right to apply, in their respective territories, the same sanctions that they grant themselves?

CODE CUBA

In January 2005 the National Endowment for Democracy officials were gathered to listen to a familiar speech, nothing surprising. In his last state of the Union address, Bush announced that U.S. foreign policy would focus on "renewed efforts to promote free elections, free trade, freedom of the press and trade union freedom in the world." In other words, they would direct new and generous funds to the organization which, since its public appearance in 1983, served as a blind for some of the murky undert-covert CIA activities meant to punish governments that dare disobey the commands of the Empire.

A couple of facts, with no apparent connection—CIA undert-covert activities and the consent of NED executives before Bush—, appear as a strategic jigsaw puzzle intending to change the geopolitical map of Latin America. Following an imaginary post-Iraq period, Venezuela and Cuba are the prime targets of Washington's Latin American agenda, one which has made use of all available means to destroy the revolutionary processes in those two countries and to cut off, at any cost, relations between the two governments.

Despite the fact that the efforts against the two rebel neighbours have been in vain, Bush has promised that during his next four year term the U.S. will continue in its efforts to overthrow Hugo Chávez and Fidel Castro. He is applying the same strategy that has already been tested in other countries —Chile, Nicaragua, Panama, the Philippines, Europe... —using all his arsenal to promote "democracy" and "liberty," words that have the power to virtually hypnotize the international press.

The NED is just that: empty verbiage and money. A lot of money. In Venezuela, as Eva Golinger points out, this organization "lubricated" the anti-Chávez faction with millions of dollars and re-ran the same scenario that it has been using against Cuba. There is enough information at the disposition of any investigative reporter to show that since its inception in 1983, this institution has devoted much of its efforts and money to Cuba, and even before that, when it was a mere embryo within the womb of the CIA.

The Cuban-American National Foundation (CANF) was, of course, a prime beneficiary of NED's financial generosity. From 1983 to 1988 it received $390,000 for its anti-Cuban activities. During that same period, the Political Action Committee (PAC), controlled by CANF's executives to finance its campaigns, donated an almost identical sum to the Florida Representative of the House, Dante Fascell, and to other political buddies, an evident compensation for the funds received from the NED.[12]

One should keep in mind that as early as the seventies, Congressman Fascell presented, for the first time, a bill to establish an

12. J.T., "¿Qué es la NED?, *La Jiribilla*, No. 14, August 2001. See also http://www.lajiribilla.cu/2001/n14 agosto/pueblomocho.html.

international institute that would pursue foreign policy tasks, based on the revelations of undert-covert work of the CIA in Latin America. He proposed that an open channel be approved for this same kind of actions. Though at that time his proposal was not passed, Dante Fascell became once again embroiled in the activities of the Democracy Project which the American Political Foundation (APF) launched, as soon as the political climate of the decade changed. The APF played a significant role in the design of the project which gave birth to the NED.

In his book *Rogue State: A Guide to the World's Only Superpower*,[13] William Blum assures us that in the eighties

> ... The Endowment donated a quarter-million dollars of taxpayers' money to the Cuban-American National Foundation, the ultra-fanatic anti-Castro Miami group. The CANF, in turn, financed Luis Posada Carriles, one of the most prolific and pitiless terrorists of modern times, who was involved in the blowing up of a Cuban airplane in 1976, which killed 73 people.[14]

In other words, one hand was washing the other, and the NED, as the CIA before it, referred to this kind of relationship as "supporting democracy."

In 1992, Carl Gershman, President of the NED, who, as the author tells us,[15] travelled recently to Caracas to rescue his grantees charged under the Venezuelan legal system, declared to *The Miami Herald* that "Cuba is our priority," because, "Cuban dissident groups could become political parties in post-Castro Cuba."[16] He knew what he was say-

---

13. William Blum, *Rogue State: A Guide to the World's Only Superpower.* (Maine: Common Courage Press, 2000).
14. Posada Carriles himself justified this crime and admitted his participation in it in an interview to *The New York Times* on July 13, 1998.
15. See Chapter Ten.
16. Arleen Rodríguez Derivet and Lázaro Barredo Medina, *El Camaján* (Havana: Editora Política, 2003).

ing. The NED's "efforts" were compensated with the passing on October 23, 1992 of the Law for Cuban Democracy —the Torricelli Law— which promoted support for individuals and organizations involved in program leading to "a democratic non-violent change in Cuba," via non-governmental organizations in the U.S. This was further encouraged with the passing, on March 12, 1996, of the Democratic Solidarity and Cuban Liberty Law, the Helms-Burton Act. After the enactment of these laws, the NED, the U.S. Agency for International Development (USAID) and the CIA (the latter, though never mentioned publicly undoubtedly played a role) intensified their program aimed at the so-called Cuban "civilian society."

Philip Agee, former CIA agent, who has evaluated the CIA-NED-USAID *troika*, has stated that these "participated in a continuous set of operations which could be financed against Cuba, while leaving the daily secret actions to CIA officials." The strategy was the following: pay mercenaries to do the dirty work under a blanket of fake political "legitimacy." CIA agents, affiliated to diplomatic missions, are in charge of controlling and reporting about the effectiveness of local operatives' activities. Agee assures: "In Cuba participation by CIA officers under cover in the U.S. Interests Section would be particularly useful, since NED and AID funding would go to U.S. NGO's that would have to find discreet ways, if possible, to get equipment and cash to recipients inside Cuba. The CIA could help with this quite well."[17]

Evidence about the quantity of money spent by these agencies in their Cuban projects is fragmentary. The CIA does not reveal its expenses, but information available on the NED and the USAID is quite interesting. The internet website of the USAID mentions $12 million pent on "Cuban programs" during 1996-2001 (an average of $2 million per year), but for 2002, the budget rose to $5 million, not to mention an

17. Philip Agee, "Terrorism and Civil Society: The Instruments of U.S. Policy in Cuba," *Counter Punch*, August 9, 2003. See also http://www.counterpunch.org/agee0809-2003.html.

additional non-allocated $3 million; in total, $8 million. The budget in 2003 for Cuba was $6 million, thus tripling the funds assigned since Bush was elected. For 2005, another $9 million appear on the books.

In 2004, as part of the interventionist Report of the Commission for Assistance to a Free Cuba,[18] advocating for a "fast and peaceful transition to democracy," $29 million additional were budgeted towards the fund of $7 million earmarked for the USAID Cuba Program—in effect this year— in order to accomplish the means to train, develop and strengthen the "opposition" and the "civilian Cuban society. . ." Moreover, another $5 million was included for, per the Bush's Administration "public diplomacy:" an attempt to buy anti-Cuban mercenaries throughout the world. A total of $41 million was directed towards openly overthrowing the Cuban Government. In the sixties, this was masked under Operation Mongoose and presented in a very undercover form; now it is public knowledge, with no sense of remorse. The Cuban case thus becomes the project of political interference and subversion that has increasingly and regularly received more funds. With Venezuela, as confirmed in *The Chávez Code*, they are following the same path.

THE NED AND THE CIA:
SAME DOG, DIFFERENT COLLAR

The NED is almost the same as the CIA, though not admitted by its Board of Directors: but the NED's dependence on the CIA was there right from conception. Under its alleged status of an "independent and private" entity, the organization functions as a financial arm of the Agency and tries to hide the true reasons for its creation. The most interesting thing about this entire story is that the CIA is able to censor or erase the contents of any document it desires, and totally exempt from the reach of FOIA, but it cannot hide funds. You can cross out words, but not what is bought with a check.

18. See http://www.state.gov/p/wha/rt/cuba/commission/2004/c12237.html.

Established in 1983, the NED was actually conceived about twenty years earlier, when in February 1967 it was revealed that the CIA was financing—through other "private and independent" foundations—U.S. civil society programs such as the National Association of Students, and foreign organizations such as the Congress for Cultural Freedom.

Contrary to what NED officials would like us to believe, the incestuous relationship with the U.S. Intelligence Service was not brought out into the open by "international Communist propaganda." On the front page of the March 31, 1997 edition of *The New York Times,* journalist John M. Broder declared: "The National Endowment for Democracy, created 15 years ago to do in the open what the CIA has done surreptitiously for decades, spends $30 million a year to support things like political parties, labor unions, dissident movements and the news media in dozens of countries."[19] The connection of its Executives with the CIA is no secret. Allen Weinstein, NED's first President in 1983, and the man who helped to pass the legislation that established the organization's goals, was quite explicit when he stated in 1991: "A lot of what we do today was done covertly 25 years ago by the CIA. In effect, the CIA has been laundering money through NED."[20]

In February of 2004, the NED named the notorious Frank Carlucci, an official of the CIA now heading the Carlyle Group—an arms contractor for the Pentagon—member of its Board of Directors. For more than fifty years, Carlucci served the CIA, toppling revolutions and helping to install right-wing regimes "supportive of the United States" on all continents. The payroll of the Board of Directors also includes retired General of the Army and former Supreme Commander of NATO, Wesley K. Clark, and Richard C. Holbrooke. Clark was in command during the war against Serbia: Holbrooke orchestrated the dismantling of Yugoslavia.

19. John M. Broder, "Political Meddling by Outsiders: Not New for U.S.," *The New York Times*, March 31, 1997. See the Spanish version at http://www.lajiribilla.cu/2002/n74octubre/1745_74.html.
20. *Ibid.*

We are incredibly fortunate that such a group of distinguished citizens will be supporting and helping to guide NED in its mission to promote democracy around the world," said the President, Carl Gershman who collaborated with Colonel Oliver North in the Iran-contra scandal, a criminal hybrid created to send funds and arms to the Nicaraguan counter-revolutionaries who attempted to overthrow the Sandinistas. The curriculum of Gershman in the government is made even more illustrious by his work as U.S. Ambassador Jeanne Kirkpatrick's Chief Advisor. He belonged to the right-wing institution Freedom House and served, in 1983, as Chief Consultant for the National Bipartisan Commission, better known as the Kissinger Commission. Today he is also on the Board of Directors of the Committee for a Free World, an ultraconservative entity. His strong links with the CIA are obvious to any objective observer who reads through his service record.

There is more evidence of this marriage in the documents that Eva Golinger obtained. In her web page on the internet, www.venezuelafoia.info, she publishes the letters exchanged between her colleague Jeremy Bigwood and officials of the CIA.[21] They refused to hand over the reports about the direct financing of the Agency to Súmate, a supposedly neutral organization "that promoted the referendum" against Hugo Chávez; notwithstanding, they voiced no objections in providing information about other institutions, with which, apparently, they had no close ties.

The only explanation for this denial—as the author points out in the letter she wrote to the directorship of the CIA's Office of Public Affairs—is that, in this case, the Agency had indeed allocated a budget to Súmate; therefore, according to the author's suggestion, besides the money that was received by this "neutral and non-profit" Venezuelan organization, there must have been another tidy sum arriving via the murky Intelligence channels; yet again, the two entities appear united in the subversive efforts of U.S. foreign policy.

21. See Appendix, p. 247.

No matter how you look at it, *The Chávez Code* is an enlightening book which reminds one of the warning made by "deep throat" to *The Washington Post* journalists who uncovered the Watergate scandal in 1972: *Follow the money.* Her testimony offers a series of documents that illuminate the truth about events that have moved the Venezuelan public in the last three years. The enormity of the U.S. interventions in Venezuela, bearing in mind the special sensitivity generated by a nation that is the prime supply-house of fuel in the hemisphere, is irrefutably demonstrated here, together with a warning about the range of variations used by the Empire to try to downplay the assassination attempts, the terrorism and the dirty war being waged against Venezuela.

This book shows us in detail how, in Venezuela, the U.S. has been carrying out its Plan A of intervention and subversion for Latin America. Its failure this time does not mean that the aggressor has given up. A short while after Eva Golinger wrote the last words of this book, evidence started to publicly appear which points to the fact that the Government of George Bush is initiating its Plan B: a flood of dirty propaganda and activities within international organizations destined to isolate the Venezuelan Government; without ruling out the possibility of assassinating or kidnapping the Head of State, something that is always the prelude to a military intervention.

Venezuela has denounced the fact that, in the first weeks of 2005, more than 50 articles have been published in major U.S. newspapers and programs shown on TV in the U.S., in which more than 85% of the consulted "experts" are connected to institutions or publications of the opposition. The most slanderous accusations have been supplied by "unidentified sources" within the Bush's Administration, all fanning the flames of a new definition made, at the beginning of the year, by Secretary of State, Condoleezza Rice, who said: "Hugo Chávez is a negative force in the region."

Starting with this war-cry, the U.S. has unleashed the CIA hounds and the media in its service, including the press and institutions such as the Organization of American States that once again intensify the heat and show different but very clear signs of a new crusade. It is possible therefore that within a year—maybe sooner—we will be reading a new book by Eva, or by some other daring investigative journalist, opening up a new chapter in this deadly saga that has been afflicting Cuba for more than forty years, and which just recently has been imposed upon the Venezuelans.

This is the secret harboured by *The Chávez Code*, and we should not be surprised to hear that its author has been threatened by the Venezuelan opposition and by the hostility of the U.S. authorities, country where she was born. The investigations of Eva Golinger, a courageous and committed woman dedicated to the truth, are a faithful allegory about the practice of State terrorism, painting a picture lacking in imagination but abounding in arrogance. *The Chávez Code* alludes to an experience that intimately concerns all the societies on this planet. It is an experience which leads us to a very simple question: if a government on this globe were to follow a path that deviated from the one chosen for humanity by Emperor Bush, is there any possibility that such a government could escape the crusade of "liberation" headed by the CIA and the NED?

ROSA MIRIAM ELIZALDE
ROGELIO POLANCO

Acknowledgements

Investigating United States intervention in Venezuela is not an easy task. There are risks and there are sacrifices. The overwhelming displays of love, solidarity and support that I have received from people around the world, especially in Venezuela, have guided me and encouraged me to continue on this obstacle-laden journey. The sincere and powerful embrace I have received from the determined people of Venezuela, and their heartfelt appreciation for revealing the information I have discovered, have made all the sacrifices and dangers encountered during this investigation worthwhile.

The risks have been many, the dangers always present. I have received numerous death threats from anonymous sources and my legal practice has diminished, due in part to client fears, political disagreements and my own dedication to this investigation, which in many ways has taken over a large part of my life.

Otto Reich referred to me as "an agent of the Chávez Government," unsure as to whether I was paid or unpaid for my work. This entire investigation has been conducted out of my own pocket and my bank records will verify. I even had to move from a beautiful duplex in Brooklyn, where I lived for three years, to an old family home out in Long Island because finances became so tight. So, Mr. Reich, if I am to be an "agent" of anyone, I am an agent of the people, a people struggling hard to achieve a more harmonious, just world.

This book would not have been possible without the love, support and expertise of many brilliant people who have entered my life over the past few years and decades. I am indebted to Jeremy Bigwood for his master FOIA skills; Andrés for genius ideas; Roselena for focus and clear thinking; Ángel for encouragement and brainstorming; Wendys for incredible photography and solidarity; Gustavo for standing by through really tough times; my mother, father and brother Jon for amazing, unconditional support and love; my furry little Lola who gave me company, love and warmth during late night research and writing; Rosa Miriam, Polanco, Abel, Iroel and all the members of the Cuba publishing team for their kindness, perfection and inconditional friendship; and to my family in Mérida, my friends Piki, Ernesto, Celia, Gretchen, Sarah, Lely, Gilberto, Temir, Mario Calderón, Samuel Moncada and other compañeros, without whom daily life would not be as pleasurable.

But most of all, I owe this book to the powerful, brave and *lindo pueblo venezolano* and their brilliant leader. I can only hope that the following pages aide true seekers of social justice.

All documents discussed in this book are available on my website, www.venezuelafoia.info.

Introduction

"What message do you have for my country?" General Rafael Oropeza had no answer for the United States military official standing before him on April 11, 2002 in the Fort Tiuna military barracks in Caracas. James Rodgers, a registered military attaché at the U.S. Embassy in Caracas, repeated the question. At the time of the coup d'état against Venezuelan President Hugo Chávez Frías, General Oropeza was in charge of the registry of all those entering and leaving Fort Tiuna, the base of Venezuela's Ministry of Defense and the nation's largest military fort.

Photographs of Rodgers driving around the fort during the days of the coup were later published in a national Venezuelan daily, *Últimas Noticias*.[1] The Department of State denied the existence of any James Rodgers despite the fact that he was found inscribed as a military attaché at the Embassy in Caracas.

When Rodgers realized General Oropeza had no answer to his encrypted question, he asked for Efraín Vásquez Velasco. Vásquez Velasco, a member at the time of the high military command of Venezuela's Armed Forces, was one of the leaders of the coup against President Chávez. From just his few words, it was clear that Rodgers was the U.S. liaison with the Venezuelan military officials executing the coup.

But the most incriminating moment the U.S. military had in Venezuela during the period of the April 2002 coup against

1. Eleazar Díaz Rangel, "Abril en Washington," *Últimas Noticias*, May 4, 2003, p. 19.

President Chávez was on April 8, 2002 at an exclusive farewell gathering for a Chinese military attaché at the elite Hotel Meliá in Caracas. It was on that evening that U.S. marine officer David Cazares mistook General Roberto González Cárdenas for General Néstor González González. It was an easy mistake. Both men were bald, about the same height and wore a military officer uniform, dressed with honors and a nametag that simply said "González." Cazares sidled up to General González and accusatorily asked, "Why haven't you contacted the ships that we have on the coast and the submarine submerged in La Guaira? What has happened? Why has no one contacted me? What are you waiting for?" General González had no idea what this U.S. naval officer was talking about, but before he could respond, a military attaché from Brazil approached him at the party to say goodbye. Cazares took advantage of the distraction to ask marine Captain Moreno Leal, standing nearby, if that was the General González, "the one who had been stationed at the border." Moreno responded: "That is General González, but I don't know if he was stationed at the border."

Cazares continued his interrogation of General González Cárdenas, insistently inquiring into why no one had yet contacted him or the three ships and the submarine standing by right off the Venezuelan coast. Prudently, González Cárdenas limited his response to a mere "I'll find out." The two met again in the elevator, leaving the gathering. "This has an operational cost. I await your answer," said Cazares firmly.

Venezuelan General Néstor González González was a key player in the April 2002 coup d'état against President Chávez. On April 10, 2002, General Néstor González González went on national television demanding the president step down, "or else." In a post-coup television broadcast on April 12, 2002, it was revealed that González González's statement was made purely for the purpose of keeping President Chávez from traveling to Costa Rica, where he was scheduled to participate in an Organization of American States General Assembly meeting that very same day. The plot had been successful. Chávez remained in Venezuela and the coup was executed as planned.

Yet the erroneous interaction between Cazares and González Cárdenas that April 8 was overlooked and dismissed by Venezuelan investigators after the brief ouster of President Chávez, and the U.S. just let it slide. Cazares' term in Venezuela was later cut short and he was shipped off to Chile once the *Últimas Noticias* article began to raise some eyebrows.

Other tidbits relating to movements of the U.S. military during the days of the coup that have been left hanging include a phone call from Colonel Donald F. McCarty, U.S. Air Force attaché, to the Intelligence Division of the Venezuelan Armed Forces on Friday, April 12, 2002, requesting authorization for the flyover of a Hercules C-130 that was transporting "diplomatic cargo," 5 kilograms of lithium battery, 5 kilograms of compressed oxygen class 2.2, 56 kilograms of ammunition, 40 kilograms of demolition cartridges and 2 kilograms of detonators. The request for flyover authorization was cancelled by Colonel McCarty via fax on April 15, 2002. It never took place.

On Saturday, April 13, 2002, while President Chávez was being held prisoner on La Orchila, a small island off the coast of Venezuela, a U.S. ship was detected nearby facilitating small airplanes engaging in flyover exercises. No authorization had been given by Venezuelan authorities for such activities and the U.S. Government later stated the exercises were "unrelated" to the situation unfolding in Venezuela and were just normal practices. Witnesses also attest to several Blackhawk helicopters landing at the Maiquetía airport outside of Caracas on April 11-12, 2002. The U.S. has denied such allegations.

U.S. submarines, naval ships, Blackhawk helicopters, flyovers, coup plotting... while many of these facts and rumors are semi-substantiated and still controversial, the full story of U.S. military involvement in the April 2002 coup d'état against President Chávez remains a mystery. But what has been uncovered and deciphered through a meticulous and ongoing investigation of U.S. involvement in the coup and other destabilization efforts in Venezuela is a very complex and sophisticated intervention crafted by a U.S. Government with decades of regime change experience.

The Chávez Code reveals by far the U.S. Government's most advanced form of intervention. By penetrating all sectors of civil society, political parties and the Venezuelan Armed Forces, the U.S. has been able to facilitate several attempts to overthrow Venezuela's democratic Government. Yet it has failed each time in these efforts despite multi-million dollar investments and complex, well-studied operations. We must remember that it took a decade to remove the Sandinistas from power in Nicaragua—that tiny, poor nation in Central America. President Reagan risked his presidency to prevent a socialist-oriented revolution from expanding throughout the hemisphere. When Congress denied him the funding for CIA covert operations with the "contra" armed forces, Reagan sold arms to Iran to raise the money. It was a scandal. But humans have a short memory span and Reagan successfully placed the blame on Colonel Oliver North, who withstood the wrath of the congressional hearings and investigations. Though humiliated, North's willingness to play the responsible party left Reagan with all the terrain and resources needed to continue efforts to impede the success of the Sandinistas.

The creation of the National Endowment for Democracy (NED) began a new period in U.S. intervention around the world and Nicaragua was the first application of this evolving interference in internal affairs of sovereign nations. More than one billion dollars were invested in Nicaragua in the decade of the 1980s to destroy the Sandinista Revolution.

Venezuela presents a new and more threatening challenge for the United States. As the top five supplier of petroleum in the world, Venezuela, the "port of South America," is a national security interest for the U.S. The Orinoco river region in southern Venezuela has substantial oil reserves, most of which have yet to be exploited. Up until 1998, Venezuela was a submissive player to U.S. policy, a collaborator of the most desired type. The U.S. was on the verge of being the number one benefactor of privatization efforts undergoing of the lucrative oil industry, nationalized since the 1970s. But then came Chávez.

President Hugo Rafael Chávez Frías was elected by approximately 60% of the vote in 1998, defeating Venezuela's traditional two parties, Acción Democrática (AD) and COPEI (Christian Socialist Party), by a landslide. He appealed to a cross section of Venezuelan society in that first election, primarily because he offered an alternative to the corrupt AD and COPEI parties that had ruled the nation for 40 years and had run the economy into the ground by the late 1990s. But Chávez's immediate implementation of his campaign promises, including a restructuring of the State-owned oil company Petróleos de Venezuela, S.A. (PDVSA), and a redrafting of Venezuela's young Constitution, proved too radical and abrupt for many Venezuelans accustomed to life under AD and COPEI, where promises were abandoned and structural change was spoken of but never implemented.

Despite shock from some sectors at the swiftness of the Chávez Administration's actions, more than 70% of the electorate participated in drafting and ratifying a new Constitution in 1999 that would authorize sweeping changes in Venezuelan society. As a result of new constitutional terms, presidential elections were held again in 1999 and Chávez won with a similar 60% margin.

With the authority of the 1999 Constitution behind him, Chávez was able to initiate a series of structural changes within PDVSA that would enable a more equal distribution of the company's profits, and in turn, provide income for social programs entended to decrease poverty and ensure social services for Venezuela's vast low and no income population.

During the period of 1998-2000, Chávez encountered a relatively indifferent U.S. policy towards Venezuela. It wasn't until George W. Bush arrived at the White House in 2001 that relations between Venezuela and the U.S. took a turn for the worse.

The Chávez Administration's policies did not sit well with the Bush Administration. The idea of a government in charge of one of the most important oil industries in the world that liaised closely and openly with Fidel Castro was a difficult pill to swallow for a republican administration that had again tightened the noose around the Cuban economy with the 40-year old goal of ousting Castro. Furthermore, Chávez's revitalization of the Organization of Petroleum Exporting Countries (OPEC), an entity the U.S. would have preferred muted, and his visits to fellow oil producing countries, such as Libya and Iraq, rubbed the Bush Administration the wrong way. Not to mention the Venezuelan's Government's focus on policies to reduce poverty and promote a participatory democracy, ideas repulsed by diehard market economists. Add in a very disgruntled and wealthy Venezuelan bussiness elite with friends in high places in the U.S. Government and corporate world, and a clear dislike for the Chávez's Government was clinched.

The overt statements and declarations made by U.S. Government officials indicating a tendency to break relations with the Chávez's Administration began in early 2001. After President Chávez expressed his disagreement and outrage to the bombings in Afghanistan post-9/11, relations between the Bush and Chávez Administrations quickly deteriorated. The Venezuela President was not playing by the "you are either with us or against us" rules and his country was too important to leave in the hands of such a disobedient actor.

Declassifying Venezuela

Utilizing the Freedom of Information Act (FOIA) in the U.S., independent journalist Jeremy Bigwood and I submitted numerous requests to various agencies and entities in the U.S. Government regarding different issues pertaining to Venezuela. The Freedom of Information Act is a body of U.S. law passed after the end of the Nixon's Administration that enables journalists and others to access and declassify secret U.S. Government documents. Information requested through the FOIA is first analyzed by the government agency possessing the relevant documentation, and then released or withheld in entirely, or a combination thereof.

There are many different entities within the U.S. Government. In order to find out how deeply involved the U.S. has

34

been in Venezuela it was necessary to file hundreds of requests with agencies ranging from the Department of State, to the Department of Defense, Department of the Army, Central Intelligence Agency, U.S. SOUTHCOM, Department of Agriculture, National Endowment for Democracy, U.S. Agency for International Development and others.

The investigation was initiated in 2003 and continues to the present time. Most likely it will extend for decades to come. Generally, the U.S. Government takes a long time to respond to FOIA requests and typically engages in delay tactics and censoring intended to prevent information from reaching the public at large. Often, documents or information withheld or unlawfully delayed can be appealed, but the appeals process can continue for an indeterminable period, therefore hampering critical information from reaching public scrutiny.

FOIA investigations generally occur years or decades after the U.S. intervention has ocurred, such as the case of Chile, often when it is too late to act in a preventative or precautionary manner.

This investigation, however, is occurring in "real time" and therefore has the privileged opportunity of effectuating change in U.S. policy on Venezuela. To date, the results of the investigation have already impacted U.S.-Venezuela relations and have also open the eyes of millions of Venezuelans who were unaware of the extent of U.S. meddling in their nation. The details of what the investigation has uncovered up to the present moment follow.

I must issue a disclaimer, however, because the investigation is not yet near completion. Due to the timeliness and importance of the information, I believe it is critical to conduct immediate analyses and make the documents available to the public domain as obtained. But it must be clear, that as more documents are acquired, more facts about the U.S. role in the events of the past few years in Venezuela are revealed and could alter the present understanding of this investigation. Also many of the documents have been heavily censored and appeals have been submitted when appropriate. The appeals process will delay the release of information for a longer, unpredictable period. Therefore I withhold from drawing any conclusions at this point regarding the extent of U.S. intervention in Venezuela.

CHAPTER ONE

Nicaragua and Chile: The Coup Cookbook

Present U.S. intervention in Venezuela has been implemented in three stages, each adapting to the circumstances presented by the failure of the previous attempt to garner any success. The U.S. strategy in Venezuela has followed a textbook outline of intervention in Latin America. The tactics used in Venezuela appear to be a metamorphosed version of those previously applied in Chile (1970s), Nicaragua (1980s) and Haiti (1990s), which all resulted in the ouster of democratically elected presidents, either through coup d'état (Chile and Haiti) or heavily influenced electoral processes (Nicaragua).

The past few years have shared common histories with Chile during the late 1960s and early 1970s. Distant cousins of the coup and strikes that plagued Chile have also beleaguered Venezuela, yet the latter was able to resist and overcome the attempts of the right-wing opposition movement financed and politically backed by the U.S. Government. The former, unfortunately, was forced to succumb to a violent takeover that resulted in the assassination of a democratically elected and popularly supported President, Salvador Allende and the installation of one of the most brutal dictatorships in Latin American history. The bloodied hands of the U.S. Government were stamped all over the 1973 coup d'état in Chile, and later, declassified documents attained by the National Security Archives revealed the intricate plots Henry Kissinger and his cohorts had enacted to crush the growth of Socialism in the region.

In Chile, the U.S. employed tactics that have subsequently proven successful time and time again. Before the coup, the U.S. had succeeded in funneling hundreds of thousands of dollars to labor unions, business associations and social organizations willing to band together to oppose Allende. The U.S. attempted to prevent Allende's election in 1970 by strengthening and supporting opposition parties and candidates, but the overwhelming popularity of the socialist leader left the U.S. Government with little choice but to go the violent route. Still, after Allende's election, the U.S. instigated acts of economic sabotage through massive strikes led by its financed counterparts and it attempted to isolate the Allende's Government from the international community. The U.S. also applied a strategy, later known as "Chileanization," which involved organizing internal right wing forces to destabilize the elected government. This concept ensured that as opposition forces incited violent confrontations with the government, international scandals and reactions would form over "Allende Crackdowns," the nation would spiral into civil disorder and instability and the government would be labeled a "human rights violator" or international pariah. It wasn't until all these efforts had failed three years later that the coup plan proceeded forward.

The tactics used in Chile were preserved for future use by the U.S. Government. The embarrassment of some members of Congress over the U.S. role in the overthrow of a democratically elected president and its unconditional support for a brutal dictator who went on to commit human rights atrocities for more than a decade merely affected the tone of future interventions, but not the substance. In Venezuela, the U.S. applied many of the same tactics it had used in Chile—the formation of a movement bringing together labor unions, business associations, political parties and social organizations, the economic sabotage and the strikes. And of course, the bloody coup. But the failure of this strategy to take root in Venezuela led the U.S. Government to alter its tactics, to merge together strategies it had successfully applied in other Latin American nations and to modernize its methodology.

During the 1980s, the U.S. Government was heavily envolved in Nicaragua. More than $1 billion[1] was invested into removing the Sandinistas from power, first through armed struggle and later through electoral intervention. The National Endowment for Democracy, the U.S. Agency for International Development and the Central Intelligence Agency shared terrain in that small Central American nation and these entities applied a series of methodologies that had been successful in prior interventions in Chile, the Philippines and Panama, to name a few.

The U.S. started a dirty war in the late 1970s in Nicaragua against the Sandinista's Government and decided to make that tiny nation the "test case" of its new strategic operations. Ronald Reagan's Administration created the "contras," a fifteen thousand-strong armed counterrevolutionary force that brutalized and terrorized Nicaraguan citizens at the behest of the U.S. Government. Alleging fears that Communism would "spread throughout the region," the Reagan's Administration justified the widespread human rights abuses and atrocities committed at the hands of its CIA-trained counterrevolutionaries. However, after several years of armed combat that resulted in strengthening, rather than weakening, the Sandinista's Government, the U.S. Government had become so desperate that it had to sell arms to Iran illegally in order to support its billion-dollar conflict in Nicaragua. Seeing its own failure in Nicaragua, officials in the Reagan's Administration proposed a change in the U.S. policy—a move towards a "democratic" solution rather than an armed conflict.

Coming out of the 1970s, the U.S. Congress was hesitant to finance covert operations in Latin America after the harsh

1. *Congressional Record* (House), October, 4, 1989, p.H 6642. George Miller (D- CA), stated that figure was $1 billion: "We are going into this election process [spending] $1 billion dollars. We funded the Contras, we have destroyed [Nicaragua's] economy, we have taken Mrs. Chamorro and we pay for her newspaper to run, we funded her entire operation, and now we are going to provide her the very best election that America can buy."

revelations of the U.S. role in the overthrow of Allende in Chile were made public through congressional investigation.[2] The Congress had imposed substantial restrictions on CIA funding and support of private groups and organizations in other nations, therefore hampering the capacity of the U.S. Government to covertly build networks that supported U.S. interests abroad. The Iran-contra scandal made financing of such groups even more difficult and it became obvious that a new approach was necessary.

THE NATIONAL ENDOWMENT FOR DEMOCRACY

In the late 1970s, the American Political Foundation (APF), a coalition of labor, business, political and academic leaders, formed with the objective of seeking new methods of achieving U.S. foreign policy goals abroad despite the congressional restrictions in place. The APF, funded by Congress and componed of ultra-conservative think tanks such as the Center for Strategic and International Studies and the American Enterprise Institute together with representatives from the National Security Council (NSC) and the United States Information Agency (USIA), the propaganda office of the U.S. Government, proposed the creation of an institution funded by Congress to provide financial and political support to groups and organizations working for U.S. interests abroad. The institution would focus on "promoting democracy" abroad through financial support intended to foster the "infrastructure of democracy" that would enable a free press, unions, political parties, universities and social organizations to function in the interests of U.S. foreign policy.

In 1983, resulting from APF recommendations, the National Endowment for Democracy was established by congressional legislation, the National Endowment for Democracy Act (P.L.98-164), and congressional funding was

2. U.S. Congress, *The Church Commission Report,* 1975. See also Patricia Verdugo, *Allende. Cómo la Casa Blanca provocó su muerte* (Santiago de Chile: Catalonia, 2004), 25-41.

authorized to ensure its success. At the time of the NED's creation, the APF had also recommended the formation of "core grantees" to act as funnels for congressional funds to reach political parties and partisan groups in other nations. The core grantees, which included the Center for International Private Enterprise (CIPE), the National Democratic Institute (NDI), the International Republican Institute (IRI) and the Free Trade Union Institute, overseen by the AFL-CIO and later denominated the American Center for International Labor Solidarity (ACILS), were all connected through an interlocking Board of Directors that shared influences within the NED and the U.S. Congress.[3]

The NED was created to serve as the perfect conduit for U.S. Government funds to provide international political aid that would support its interests abroad and influence foreign and domestic policy in nations of strategic importance. Established during the Cold War, the NED's objectives reflected a neoconservative agenda that prioritized its global struggle against Communism over democratic notions of sovereignty and self-determination. Hence, the NED's premiere in Nicaragua provided a major dose of U.S. intervention on a political and electoral level and its technique was perfected over the course of nearly a decade.

The NED's leadership clearly reflects its goals. Carl Gershman has been the President of the NED since 1984. A former member of the Socialist Party USA who split off to lead a right wing faction, Social Democrats USA, Gershman is linked to the old-school hawks network. Known as a "neocon," Gershman worked in the early 1970s with several key neoconservatives figures, including Richard Perle, Elliot Abrams and Paul Wolfowitz.

In Nicaragua, the CIA had originally been the principal conduit for financing the anti-Sandinista movement (the

3. Council on Hemispheric Affairs and the Inter-Hemispheric Education Resource Center, *National Endowment for Democracy: A Foreign Policy Branch Gone Awry,* 1990. Today, Republican Senator John McCain and Democrat Madeleine Albright oversee the International Republican Institute and National Democratic Institute, respectively.

"contras"), but after their failure to unseat the Sandinistas during the 1984 elections, the NED was employed to ensure success in the 1989-90 ballot. In fact, during the 1984 elections, the U.S. was so sure of their defeat that they advocated widespread voter abstention on the opposition side in order to discredit the elections, which, despite U.S. power and influence, still failed. The second time around the U.S. decided to take a thoroughly proactive role in the electoral process. Through the formation and crafting of an opposition movement comprised of social organizations, political parties and NED affiliates, the U.S. Government was able to foment and control the outcome of the Nicaraguan elections.

The U.S. pushed for the unification of the various political parties and social organizations that opposed the Sandinistas, many of which were far right and shared conservative agendas with the Reagan and Bush Administrations. The U.S. made financing through the NED to these organizations contingent upon their formation of a unified group, the Coordinadora Democrática Nicaragüense (CDN), capable of winning the 1989-90 elections. The CDN was comprised of four conservative political parties, two trade union groupings afiliated with the AFL-CIO, and a private business organization, COSEP, that had close links to influential U.S. corporations and figures in the business community.

Closer towards the elections, the NED blackmailed the fourteen opposition parties in Nicaragua into forming one party, the Unión Nacional Opositora (UNO), that would endorse the U.S.-chosen candidate, Violeta Chamorro, for the presidency. By threatening to deny all funding sources to these parties, the NED was able to achieve its goal. Chamorro became the leading candidate, with full opposition support, to confront Sandinista President Daniel Ortega.

THE NICARAGUA-VENEZUELA CONNECTION

The U.S. could not afford another loss in Nicaragua against the Sandinistas and this time around, the effort was a "no holds barred" full-edged electoral intervention to ensure the U.S.-selected candidate would assume the presidency. The CIA had been financing Nicaragua's main newspaper, *La Prensa*, during the Sandinista-"contra" war, and passed on the baton in large part to the NED and its international afiliates during the late 1980s. Control of media was a major tool in the propaganda war entended to not only win over supporters internally in Nicaragua, but also to filter news and information to the international press with a guaranteed anti-Sandinista and pro-U.S. spin. The Venezuelan Government, then headed by Carlos Andrés Pérez (in his second term), played a major role in the funneling of funds and support from the U.S. Government to the CDN, UNO and *La Prensa*.

Carlos Andrés Pérez had developed close ties to the Chamorro family while in exile in Costa Rica during the Pérez Jiménez dictatorship in Venezuela. He also had ties to other influential Nicaraguans developed during his first presidential term from 1976 to 1980. Carlos Andrés Pérez was eager to offer Venezuela's support for the U.S. efforts to oust the Sandinista Government through the strengthening of an anti-Sandinista civil opposition.

Beginning in 1989, the CIA rerouted a minimum of $200,000 monthly through Venezuelan private foundations destined to fund *La Prensa* and campaign materials for the UNO. Carlos Andrés Pérez maintained close contact with President Bush during the electoral process in Nicaragua and even appointed his Secretary of the presidency, Beatriz Rangel,[4] as his personal representative in his contacts with Bush. According to one source, Rangel was observed carrying a suitcase "stuffed with secret funds from Washington

---

4. Beatriz Rangel currently works with the Cisneros Group of Companies in New York and Miami, which is the multinational corporation owned by media mogul Gustavo Cisneros, a Cuban-Venezuelan slated to have been involved in the April 2002 coup attempt against President Chávez. Up until mid-2004, Rangel was also a Board Member of the Inter-American Dialogue, a Washington, D.C. think tank that has been highly critical of the Chávez's Administration.

and Miami to Caracas" destined for the Nicaraguan opposition's campaign.[5]

Venezuela's largest union, the Confederación de Trabajadores Venezolanos (CTV) worked in connection with the NED and the AFL-CIO to establish ties with workers and unions in Nicaragua, with the goal of incorporating them into the opposition movement.[6]

Carlos Andrés Pérez also recommended the use of the U.S. polling firm, Penn and Schoen Associates, to conduct a polling program in Nicaragua as part of the electoral intervention agenda. Penn and Schoen had done polling for Carlos Andrés Pérez's presidential campaign together with the Venezuelan firm DOXA and had also been used successfully as part of U.S. electoral intervention in Panama.

Penn and Schoen later became the polling firm of choice for these types of interventions and has subsequently been used in the former Yugoslavia during the elections that ousted Milosovic from power and most recently, in Venezuela, during the recall referendum against President Chávez on August 15, 2004. In fact, in Venezuela, Penn and Schoen came under international scrutiny for allegedly producing fraudulent exit poll results conducted with Venezuelan NED-grantee, Súmate, that were intended to discredit the official results of the referendum.[7]

The Venezuela connection to the NED and the CIA intervention in Nicaragua in the late 1980s evidences the strong bond that was formed between those entities and politicians involved in the actions of that period. Such relationships have clearly been integral in the recent interventions the U.S. Government has pursued in Venezuela during the Chávez era.

5. William Robinson, "A Faustian Bargain: U.S. Intervention in the Nicaraguan Elections and American Foreign Policy in the Post-Cold War Era," *Westview Press*, 1992, p. 93.
6. The CTV continues to be one of the NED's major recipients in Venezuela, as well as a clear instrument of U.S. policy, evident through the union's key role in the 2002 coup d'état against President Chávez and the subsequent illegal oil industry strike in winter 2002-2003.
7. See Chapter Nine of this book.

Carlos Andrés Pérez particularly has played an interesting role in the three different interventions the U.S. has engaged in ultimately in Venezuela and has served as a liaison between old-school officials and other influential individuals in the U.S., as well as a facilitator of funds to those who led the coup against Chávez and as an international propagandist spreading harsh critiques of the Chávez's Administration. In Nicaragua, the U.S. utilized a variety of tools and methodologies to remove the Sandinistas from power. First armed conflict was exploited then a skillfully crafted electoral intervention plan that involved the formation of a capable opposition movement, the selection and molding of an opposition candidate, the unification of diverse opposition parties, the buying of media to win the propaganda war,[8] the financing of the opposition's electoral campaign and the use of international networks to covertly funnel additional funds to the opposition and media in Nicaragua and ensure regional support for the U.S. selected candidate. The U.S. intervention scheme also envolved the use of U.S. selected polling firms to influence opinions on the electoral process and the creation of a "neutral" Nicaraguan non-profit entity dedicated to "electoral education" during the campaign.

Vía Cívica, as it was denominated, was created at the behest of the NED to function as a conduit for funds to finance the electoral process directly. Since Nicaraguan law prohibited the direct financing of political parties and campaigns, as does U.S. law, the NED had to seek alternative routes to channel its funds. NED's "core grantees" were used to finance the opposition parties, as were the pathways provided by the Carlos Andrés Pérez's Administration in Venezuela, but the creation of Vía Cívica offered an overt and direct channel. As the elections neared in late 1989, the U.S. Government actually trapped the Nicaraguan Government into permitting the financing of the opposition's campaign

8. The U.S. Government did not just use *La Prensa* as its only conduit of information. It also provided funding through the NED, USAID and the USIA, the U.S. Information Agency, to finance radio stations and local television outlets in Nicaragua.

to the tune of $9 million, despite the prohibitions in place by law.[9] Vía Cívica, an alleged "non-partisan civil society" organization, was additionally utilized to influence the electoral process in favor of the opposition by preparing and distributing electoral material and conducting "electoral education" workshops and conferences that clearly showed bias towards the opposition.

The major U.S. investment and intervention in Nicaragua was successful. In 1990, Violeta Chamorro was declared the winner of the elections and the Sandinistas were oficially removed from power. As a result of the layers and networks the U.S. had built to cover its influential role in the electoral process, the elections were widely viewed as "transparent and democratic" and were accepted internationally. The U.S., satisfied with the outcome of its efforts, proceeded to expand and implement its new "democratic intervention" model in other nations.

U.S. AGENCY FOR INTERNATIONAL DEVELOPMENT

There was another entity that existed prior to the Nicaragua intervention that was also utilized to enable financing of U.S. interests abroad. The United States Agency for International Development (USAID), an international funding entity officially established by the U.S. Congress in 1961, was originally entended to aid humanitarian development around the world. Similar to the NED, USAID had large portions of its funds diverted to support foreign political movements aligned with U.S. interests. Though USAID was created to separate military aid from humanitarian and development aid, it merely became an additional fund for the CIA to dip into as cover for covert interventions. USAID is overseen and directed by the Department of State, which exercises "make or break" authority over its actions.

---

9. The U.S. Government accomplished this by promising not to covertly finance the opposition through the CIA. However, this promise was promptly broken.

One of the first documented misuses of USAID funds was during the early 1960s in Brazil. The CIA was heavily envolved in attempts to thwart João Goulart from succeeding in the Brazilian presidency because he was viewed as "leftist-leaning" and supported "social and economic reforms" that in the eyes of the CIA had Communism written all over them. The CIA and USAID spent approximately $20 million to support hundreds of anti-Goulart candidates for gubernatorial elections in 1962. USAID was used as a cover to invest heavily in the Brazilian labor movement. The funds were filtered through the international branch of the AFL-CIO, then American Institute for Free Labor Development (AIFLD), now known as the American Center for International Labor Solidarity (ACILS), and were controlled on the ground by the CIA. In 1964, President Goulart was overthrown by a CIA-backed coup that resulted in a brutal U.S.-sponsored dictatorship extending approximately 20 years. [10]

In the 1980s, as part of the move towards "democratic intervention" models, the Department of State established the USAID Office of Democratic Initiatives, with the goal of supporting and "strengthening democratic institutions." From 1984 to 1987, USAID utilized the Office to filter more than $25 million into electoral processes in Latin America. Although the NED later assumed similar operations, USAID has continued to use the Office, now known as the Office of Transition Initiatives (OTI), to intervene in nations involved in crises that "threaten democracy." USAID and NED also overlap in funding initiatives for the International Republican Institute and the National Democratic Institute, both core NED grantees. A large portion of USAID and NED funds are channeled into electoral intervention efforts and civil society penetration. In the case of Venezuela, more than $20 million has been invested by USAID and NED since 2001 to foment conflict and instability in the name of "promoting democracy."

---

10. William Blum, *Killing Hope: U.S. Military and CIA Interventions Since World War II* (Maine: Common Courage Press, 2004), 163-172.

CHAPTER TWO

A President Denied a U.S. Visa

Venezuela shares a history of corrupt governments, dictatorships, U.S. intervention and stark economic divisions with much of Latin America.[1] Venezuela's democratic political system was born in 1958, after a popular uprising overthrew the dictatorship of General Pérez Jiménez.[2] The country's first democratic constitution was ratified in 1961 and granted vast rights that had been denied under years of dictatorship rule. Throughout the 1960s and 1970s, Venezuela's oil wealth greatly enriched the nation, and despite ample corruption in the ruling elected governments, the populus was relatively unengaged in political discourse since the administrations throughout those decades provided for substantial basic infrastructure needs and social services.

The 1980s saw the first decline in Venezuela's booming economy and poverty levels began to rise. The leading political parties AD and COPEI, that had held tight reign on the country's politics since the overthrow of Pérez Jiménez in 1958, were beginning to be seen as corrupt and blame was placed on them for the changes in the distribution of the oil wealth, caused primarily by the institution of a neo-liberal economic agenda. Venezuelans distrust in the government slowly began to rise.[3]

---

1. Noam Chomsky and Edward S. Herman, "The Washington Connection and Third World Fascism," in *The Political Economy of Human Rights,* Vol. I (Cambridge: South End Press, 1980).
2. Richard Gott, *In the Shadow of the Liberator: Hugo Chávez and the Transformation of Venezuela* (London: Verso, 2000).
3. "Report on Venezuela." *NACLA Report on the Americas,* Vol. XXVII, No. 5, March/April, 1994.

In 1988, AD candidate Carlos Andrés Pérez was elected based on a platform of returning the country to its 1970s wealth and economic distribution, a promise Venezuelans believed based upon Pérez's successful prior presidential reign in the 1970s. It was during Pérez's first term in the 1970s that the oil industry was nationalized and PDVSA, the State-owned oil company, was born. But soon after assuming office in 1989, Pérez backtracked on his campaign promises and instituted a neo-liberal economic "packet" that was set to increase domestic gas prices by 100 percent in the first quarter of 1989, as well as significantly affect other social and economic issues throughout the nation.[4] In reaction, transportation prices immediately rose, and an enraged citizenry reacted violently and angrily. The result was the "Caracazo," the worst incident of violence in contemporary Venezuelan history, which left thousands dead. Human rights abuses were rampant and became the norm and constitutional guarantees and rights were suspended on an indefinite basis.

Nevertheless, as a result of the neo-liberal free-market reforms instituted by Carlos Andrés Pérez and based on International Monetary Fund and World Bank doctrines, during 1990 to 1992, Venezuela had the highest rate of economic growth in the Americas, as well as its sharpest increase in economic inequality ever and record levels of poverty and malnutrition.

On February 4, 1992, Lieutenant Colonel Hugo Rafael Chávez Frías led a military rebellion, which although failing, was widely supported throughout the country and gave Chávez and his growing Bolivarian Revolutionary Movement 200 (MBR-200)[5] national media attention and sympathy. Chávez was detained and imprisoned as a result of the rebellion but he left a permanent mark on the majority of Venezuelans.

---

4. *Ibid.* See also Richard Gott, *In the Shadow of the Liberator: Hugo Chávez and the Transformation of Venezuela* (London: Verso, 2000).
5. The 200 stands for the year-long celebrations taking place in 1983 when Chávez formed the MBR, to remember the 200th anniversary of the birth of Simón Bolívar.

For the first time in history, a political figure had taken responsibility for his actions. Chávez had been given two minutes on national television on the day of his arrest and his famous statement, "por ahora" ("for now"), became imbedded in Venezuela's history. Chávez had left Venezuelans with the hope that he and his revolutionary movement would return someday, and stronger.

Later that same year, on November 27, 1992, another rebellion against Carlos Andrés Pérez's Administration was led by members of the Bolivarian Revolutionary Movement 200 while Chávez was imprisoned, yet it also failed. Several months later as fate would have it, in May 1993, Carlos Andrés Pérez was indicted and impeached on charges of corruption by his own political party, and was given home detention until 1996, when he abandonded Venezuela and took up residency in New York and Santo Domingo.

After a brief interim government following Pérez's impeachment, new elections in 1994 brought one of the founders of COPEI and a former president in the 1970s, Rafael Caldera, to the Presidential Palace. During those elections, more than 40% of the voting population abstained. Though Caldera won only 30% of the votes, he had won the highest percentage of votes in comparison with the other three candidates. The level of interest and trust amongst Venezuelans in government had drastically declined. Caldera was supported by a broad anti-neoliberal coalition, yet once in office, continued the same neo-liberal policies instituted during the Pérez regime, aligned with International Monetary Fund and World Bank policies and commitments. During Caldera's presidency, the economic divisions throughout the country skyrocketed, and the Venezuelan currency, the bolívar, rapidly devalued. Poverty levels grew to an all-time high and the country's national debt reached over $23 billion dollars.

During his first year as president, Caldera pardoned Hugo Chávez, and his fellow compatriots, for their roles in the 1992 rebellions against Carlos Andrés Pérez and they were released from prison. During his two-year prison term in San Francisco de Yare, Chávez had solidified his political party and found supporters. Upon his release from prison, Chávez began strengthening his party, changing its name to the Movimiento V República (Fifth Republic Movement) (MVR) because Venezuelan law prohibits the use of patriotic names for political parties, and aligning with Movimiento al Socialismo (MAS) and new leftist party called Patria Para Todos (PPT) to create the Polo Patriótico (Patriotic Pole) (PP) a populist multiparty alliance. By the 1998 presidential elections, Chávez, backed by the Patriotic Pole, was the leading candidate. The traditional parties that had long dominated Venezuelan politics, AD and COPEI, lost significant support throughout the country, based on charges of corruption and failed policies. As a result, despite last minute dirty political maneuvers and corrupt campaigning by the other candidates, Chávez won the 1998 presidential elections by a substantial majority, 56.20%, considering the rest of the votes were split amongst three other candidates.[6]

Chávez's Fifth Republic Movement had pledged to make substantial and significant economic and social changes within Venezuela. The movement was well received by the majority of Venezuelans during a time in which they had been experiencing declining living standards and drastic drops in the price of oil, the country's principal export commodity.

Chávez, a former military Lieutenant Colonel, had based his movement in large part on the philosophies and ideology of Simón Bolívar, the great Liberator of South America, who had attempted to unite the continent to become a major power against imperialist forces. Chávez's movement sought to implement similar ideas by encouraging the political unification of Latin America through the creation of a sovereign and powerful economic block. These concepts were highly applauded by a citizenry that was suffering the effects of a neo-liberal agenda that had crippled the economy and drastically raised poverty levels.

6. The votes were split as follows: Chávez – 56.20%, Henrique Salas Römer – 39%, Irene Sáez – 4%, Alfaro Ucero less than 2%.

In 1998, in the early days of the presidential campaign, a Peruvian journalist invited Chávez to be interviewed on a Miami television program. Just like any other citizen, Chávez applied to the U.S. Embassy in Caracas for a visa to enter the U.S. His request was denied on the grounds of "prior terrorist activity" due to the 1992 rebellion against Carlos Andrés Pérez. Chávez had been placed on the U.S. Government's "terrorist watch list." In addition to denying his visa request, the U.S. Embassy made a public statement regarding the reasons for the rejection, clearly evidencing their distaste for his candidacy. Chávez was not surprised. Soon after, during a local Venezuelan news interview, a reporter made a condescending remark about the visa denial. Candidate Chávez responded humorously: "What do you mean? I have a visa," as he pulled out a visa credit card from his wallet.

The day after he won the presidential elections in December 1998, President Chávez was dining with his family when he received a phone call from the U.S. Embassy in Caracas. The Ambassador, John Maisto, had authorized an immediate issuance of his U.S. visa. It was hand delivered.

Before his inauguration on February 2, 1999, President-elect Chávez had planned an international tour to Spain, France, Germany, Italy, Canada, Cuba, the U.S. and the Dominican Republic. In Washington, D.C., he was to meet with President Bill Clinton on January 27, 1999, at the White House. During his meeting in Spain, he received an unexpected phone call from a State Department official. To Chávez's surprise, the official had called to urge him to cancel his visit to Cuba before arriving at the U.S. The official claimed that it would not be in Chávez's interests to meet with President Fidel Castro in Cuba before coming to the White House. He even threatened to cancel the Washington visit if Chávez did not comply. It was at that moment that Chávez made the decision to preserve the sovereignty and right of self-determination of the nation he had been chosen to lead. President Chávez firmly told the U.S. representative that he had no intention of canceling his Cuba visit, despite the cost in Washington's eyes.

From Canada he traveled to Havana and met with Fidel. From Havana he traveled to Washington and met with Clinton. But not officially. Clinton had decided not to receive Chávez in an official capacity, but rather through the "back door." According to President Chávez, Clinton met with him in an informal room in the White House with no press or photographers allowed. Dressed in jeans and a tee shirt, Clinton received the Venezuelan President with a soda in hand and an intentionally casual attitude. The meeting lasted about fifteen minutes and it went unannounced to the world. There was no protocol envolved. Chávez had been treated as though he was an unimportant visitor and not the president of one of the most important nations in the Western Hemisphere.

Clinton later sent his Secretary of Energy, Bill Richardson, to lead the U.S. delegation at Chávez's inauguration ceremony. Clearly, this was a sign of how the U.S.' view of Venezuela was clouded with thick petroleum.

The grounds had been set for his relationship with the U.S. Government. Chávez, a student of Simón Bolívar and a meticulous orator of Bolívar's mantras believed the Liberator's premonition that ". . . the United States is destined to plague the Americas with misery in the name of liberty."[7]

---

7. "...los Estados Unidos [que] parecen destinados por la Providencia para plagar la América de miserias a nombre de la Libertad" are Simón Bolívar's original words sent to Colonel Patricio Campbell, Secretary of Business of the United Kingdom in Colombia, on August 5, 1829.

CHAPTER THREE

From Vargas to Pre-Coup Premonitions

Relations between the U.S. and Venezuela were relatively uneventful in the first year of Chávez's Administration. After the initial visa quandary, things had settled down, and Washington had taken a more "wait and see" approach to the new Venezuelan Government. But in December 1999, things got a little tense.

December 14, 1999 started out as a normal day in Caracas and its costal regions. But by the afternoon, torrential rains had begun to fall that seemed as though they would never cease. The State of Vargas, which is located to the northwest of Caracas on the coast and is home to the main airport in Venezuela, Maiquetía's Simón Bolívar International Airport, saw the worst of the rains. Massive flooding and mudslides invaded the State and tragedy broke out. Homes of Venezuela's majority poor, built with herat and tin, were washed away in the downpour, along with hundreds, if not thousands of residents.

Tens of thousands of Vargas residents lost their homes and all of their belongings. Hundreds were killed by the rains and flooding, trapped in mountainsides, crushed by mudslides and drowned by the forceful floods. The airport was flooded and shut down for more than a week. The National Guard and Army were called in to rescue whoever and whatever was rescue-able. It was Chávez's first tragedy as president, and it was of major importance.

The rains were so powerful and intense that they washed away part of Venezuela's geography. After the Vargas floods, new maps had to be drawn up reflecting the changes in Venezuela's territory. A majority of those who survived but lost their homes and belongings lived in a state of homelessness and desperation for months while Chávez's Plan Bolívar built the Vargas residents new homes in other parts of the country.

International assistance was offered from many nations around the world, the U.S. amongst them. Venezuela was open to receiving financial assistance to rebuild the area devastated by the tragedy and to construct new homes and lives for the survivors. But the Venezuelan Government was startled when the U.S. announced it had sent in naval ships and helicopters to aide in the rescue—despite the fact that no request had been made by the Chávez's Administration for military assistance. Chávez told U.S. Ambassador John Maisto "no thanks," declaring that while Venezuela would accept financial assistance it was not about to open its coasts and borders to U.S. military teams for an unspecified period. President Chávez, fully aware of U.S. interventions throughout Latin America considered that Washington was trying to pull the wool over his eyes. The U.S. had been eager to get its military on Venezuelan terrain and saw the Vargas tragedy as a prime opportunity.

The rejection of U.S. aid was exploited by a growing private media industry in Venezuela opposed to President Chávez's policies. National papers and television stations declared it an "outrage" that Chávez had denied foreign aid in a time of need. An *El Universal* article carried a political cartoon portraying two workers carrying a statue of a hand giving the middle finger with the caption: "Where do we put this new international aid?" But despite the media's siding with the U.S. Government on the issue, the State Department was concerned about repercussions. After all, it had rushed in military ships with no authorization, under the guise of "humanitarian aid." Chávez had caught them before they could make ground, literally.

A cable from the U.S. Embassy in Caracas on January 20, 2000 revealed a level of concern regarding the situation. In order to distract attention from the naval ships scandal, the Embassy engaged in a media ploy to bring favorable coverage to U.S. intentions in Venezuela. According to the cable:

A highly-successful 1/19 media trip arranged by the Embassy and the joint task force has significantly shifted coverage to a different topic: U.S. efforts to bring water to affected areas. The Ambassador accompanied a group of eight international and national journalists on visits via land and Blackhawk helicopter to four separate water purification sites . . . coverage was immediate and highly favorable.[1]

And luck behold, the naval ships incident became a distant memory. In any case, Venezuela had its hands full with the worst natural tragedy in history to ever hit the nation.

In July 2000, Ambassador Maisto was removed and Donna Hrinak was sent in as the new U.S. Ambassador to Venezuela. Hrinak joined the Foreign Service in 1974. She served as Embassy diplomat in Caracas, Sao Paulo, Bogotá, Poland and Mexico City up until 1991, when she was named Deputy Assistant Secretary for Inter-American Affairs, responsible for overseeing relations between the U.S., Mexico and the Caribbean. Prior to her appointment at the U.S. Embassy in Venezuela, she held posts as the Ambassador in Bolivia and the Dominican Republic. Hrinak was to remain up to the weeks before the coup in 2002.

Relations between the two nations became shakier just one month after Ambassador Hrinak's arrival.

Venezuela was one of five founding members of the Organization of Petroleum Exporting Countries in 1960, along with Iran, Iraq, Kuwait and Saudi Arabia. Currently, OPEC has eleven member countries that are heavily reliant on oil revenues as a main source of income. In addition to the founding five, other members include Indonesia, Libya, Nigeria, Qatar, the United Arab Emirates and Algeria. OPEC had a significant decline in power and influence during the 1990s and by the time President Chávez came to office in 1999, oil was selling for about

1. Cable from the U.S. Embassy in Caracas to the Secretary of State in Washington, D.C., January 2000. Available through the author. See http: www.venezuelafoia.info.

$8/barrel. Venezuela was elected as the president of OPEC in June 2000 and through its Representative, Alí Rodríguez Araque, began a series of measures intended to boast oil prices and control production output. Venezuela aided in bringing the price of oil up to approximately $30/barrel.

As the new Head of OPEC, President Chávez decided to embark on an international tour visiting fellow OPEC nations. The trip included visits to all other ten member countries, including Iraq. Chávez was to become the first democratically elected Head of State to visit Iraq and its leader, Saddam Hussein, since the Gulf War Part One in 1990. The U.S. was up in arms. The State Department threatened the Chávez's Administration in the days proceeding the Iraq visit, suggesting that the trip "contravened United Nations political sanctions, as the Venezuelan leader had not sought advice from the UN sanctions committee before his visit . . . It's Venezuela's obligation, as a UN member State, to observe all the Security Council resolutions regarding Iraq and the sanctions regime," claimed State Department spokesman Richard Boucher in early August 2000.

Right after Chávez's trip to Iraq, Secretary of State Madeleine Albright omitted Venezuela from a tour of South American nations. The U.S. denied any connection between the two matters.

The remainder of the Clinton's Administration was fairly uneventful with regards to Venezuela. Ties were beginning to be built between a growing opposition movement in Venezuela and sectors of the U.S. Government, but nothing too noticeable. Nevertheless, when George W. Bush took office in 2001 the relations starting rapidly going downhill.

FTAA OPPOSITION AND THE U.S. MILITARY EXPELLED

In April 2001 at the Summit of the Americas meeting in Quebec, Canada, President Chávez manifested his opposition to the Free Trade of the Americas Act (FTAA), a hemispheric trade bloc proposed by the United States. He began advocating for a South American regional trade organization capable of negotiating with the powerful United States economy. The FTAA would create the world's largest "free trade zone" and would encompass 34 nations in the Western Hemisphere including 800 million people. Corporate rights would become a hemispheric priority, leaving sovereign nations and governments with little or no say in decisions affecting internal politics and issues.

Chávez became, alongside Fidel Castro of Cuba, the most outspoken Head of State opposing the FTAA throughout the region and was championed by anti-globalization activists and movements for his posture. His position clearly endangered the possibility that the U.S. proposed agreement would take root immediately and even threatened its future implementation. The drift widened between the countries.

In September 2001, before the attacks on the World Trade Center in New York City, the Venezuelan Government announced that it would not renew a 50-year old bilateral military cooperation agreement with the U.S. Ambassador Donna Hrinak made no comments to the press on the decision. The Venezuelan Defense Minister at that time, José Vicente Rangel, also requested that the U.S. military mission in Venezuela vacate the space they had been occupying on the Fort Tiuna Defense Ministry headquarters.

The news was a blow to U.S. foreign military policy in Venezuela, which had enjoyed a guaranteed influential infiltration into Venezuela's Armed Forces and Defense Department. But despite the abrupt decisions of the Venezuelan Government, the U.S. still had other roads of access into the Venezuelan Armed Forces.

A cable from the military section at the U.S. Embassy in Caracas dated June 2000 revealed the true intentions behind the International Military Education and Training (IMET) program the U.S. had been running in Venezuela: "Expand United States government access and influence at all levels of the Venezuelan Armed Forces . . . Increase the number of Venezuelan Armed Forces Officers at all levels receiving instruction in U.S. military schools. . ."[2]

2. Available through the author.

Furthermore, the cable revealed the training program was contingent on the U.S. requirements that the Venezuelan Government place IMET graduates in "key positions as general staff officers or as commanders of key tactical units." This placement would guarantee the U.S. access to the Venezuelan Armed Forces at the highest levels. The program had been going on for years and Venezuela boasted a military force with the highest percentage of officials trained in the School of the Americas and other U.S. military institutions.

The State Department cable cited to an example of "one of the biggest supporters of adopting U.S. proposals..." the U.S. trained Major General (retired) Raúl Salazar Rodríguez.

Salazar Rodríguez was Chávez's first Minister of Defense and also commanded the Armed Forces. At the time of the April 2002 coup, he was the Venezuelan Ambassador in Spain. The retired Major General was one of the key figures involved in the coup plotting from that Iberian nation, which had also been fingered in the coup.[3]

Regardless of Venezuelan Government demands, the U.S. took its time. It wasn't for another three years that it finally withdrew its military commando from Fort Tiuna. But the U.S. IMET training program survived, although President Chávez did suspend the training of Venezuelan military at the Georgia-based School of the Americas.

A FATEFUL FLARE-UP

On October 29, 2001, President Chávez went on national television and deplored the U.S. bombings in Afghanistan that had been initiated as part of the Bush-declared "war on terrorism." At a time when most nations were expressing allegiance to the United States, Venezuela was the first democratic nation to demonstrate disagreement with the Bush's Administration tactics. Showing photographs of Afghani children killed

---

3. Manuel Fernández, "Investigación realizada por Izquierda Unida acerca de la participación de España y los Estados Unidos en el golpe de Estado en Venezuela," May 23, 2002. See http://www.izquierda-unida.es.

in U.S. bombing attacks, Chávez defiantly stated: "Terror cannot be fought with more terror . . . This has no justification, just like the attacks in New York didn't either."[4]

The U.S. did not hesitate in its response. Ambassador Donna Hrinak was called immediately to Washington for "consultations," which in government lingo means a problem is brewing. On November 2, 2001, State Department spokesman Richard Boucher afirmed the U.S. Government growing concern about Chávez:

> I think a lot of things are going on down there. We have seen comments by President Chávez that we, frankly, found surprising and very disappointing. And I think we want to look at the relationship, because we do believe this relationship is an important and longstanding one between the United States and Venezuela.[5]

After Hrinak returned to Caracas, she requested a meeting with President Chávez. In that closed-door meeting, the nervous Ambassador read from a document addressed to the Venezuelan leader. The text was a request sent from Washington demanding Chávez officially and publicly retract his statement about the bombings in Afghanistan. Before the Ambassador could get even a quarter of the way through the document, President Chávez interrupted her. "You are speaking to the Head of State of this nation. You are an Ambassador in my country. You are out of line. Please leave my office now."[6]

Hrinak was shocked. She did not expect such a firm and defiant reaction from the Venezuelan President in light of the request she was making on behalf of the most powerful nation in the world. Embarrassed and uneasy, Hrinak apologized and requested, humbly, that the president allow her to

4. See http://www.analitica.com/biblioteca/hchavez/cadena20011029.asp.
5. State Department, *Daily Press Briefing*, November 2, 2001.
6. Author's unpublished interview with President Hugo Chávez.

at least read through the entire text, then she would go. Chávez agreed, but dismissed her once she was done.

It was becoming clearer that the relationship the U.S. Government had once enjoyed in Venezuela prior to Hugo Chávez Frías was over. The new Venezuelan Government had no plans on being subservient to U.S. interests and this did not sit well in Washington.

It was around that time that the National Endowment for Democracy quadrupled its funding in Venezuela and the opposition began to grow aggressively.

CHAPTER FOUR

IRI Gives Birth to Primero Justicia

In Fiscal Year 2001, the International Republican Institute received a whopping $340,000 grant from the National Endowment for Democracy for its work in Venezuela to "train national and/or local branches of existing and/or newly created political parties on such topics as party structure, management and organization, internal and external party communications and coalition building."[1]

During the year 2000, IRI's grant from the NED for its work in Venezuela was a mere $50,000. The amount from 2000 to 2001 was almost sextupled.

The National Endowment for Democracy, which had maintained a minimal presence in Venezuela during the previous years, all of a sudden began investing heavily in political party strengthening and civil society "political" education and orientation. IRI, known officially as the international branch of the Republican Party, became a major player in Venezuela. During 2000-2001, its Venezuela funds appeared to come exclusively from the NED, although IRI also received substantial funding from USAID.

IRI's work in Venezuela during 2000 had been focused on an organization by the name of Fundación Participación Juvenil (Youth Participation Foundation), but IRI canceled the program due to its determination that the "goals for the youth program in Venezuela can be better achieved if IRI ad-

1. See Appendix, p. 181.

ministers the program directly."[2] IRI had clearly decided that it needed a more "hands-on" approach in Venezuela.

In 2000, a new political party was inscribed in Venezuela's Consejo Nacional Electoral (National Electoral Council) (CNE). Primero Justicia (Justice First) had previously been a non-governmental organization (NGO) focused on judicial reform. The International Republican Institute must have been attracted to its majority young adult membership and its conservative politics. The switch from IRI's work with the Fundación Participación Juvenil to its focus on Primero Justicia was effortless, as the two entities shared many of the same members and goals.

Run by a Board of Directors that reads like a right-wing parade, IRI is headed by former National Security Advisors, Corporate Executives, State Department officials, former Ambassadors and Directors of conservative think tanks such as the American Enterprise Institute. At the time of the increase in financing for its Venezuela programs, Georges Fauriol, a former colleague of Otto Reich, a staunch anti-Chávez Bush Advisor, was in charge of IRI's Latin America Program.

IRI's Coup-Time Blooper

Although it pledged to be non-partisan, IRI's objective in Venezuela was clearly to support and build the opposition movement with the goal of removing President Chávez from office. This was evidenced on April 12, 2002, during the coup d'état against President Chávez, when IRI President George Folsom issued a public statement applauding the illegal overthrow of Venezuela's democratically elected Government:

2. IRI-NED grant 00-030/6279. See http://www.venezuelafoia.info.

IRI PRESS RELEASE

To: National and foreign editors

IRI PRESIDENT FOLSOM PRAISES VENEZUELAN
CIVIL SOCIETY'S DEFENSE OF DEMOCRACY

Washington, April 12, 2002
George A. Folsom, President of the International Republican Institute (IRI) praised the Venezuelan people in their efforts to bring democracy to the country. The following is a statement from President Folsom concerning last night's events.

Last night, led by every sector of civil society, the Venezuelan people rose up to defend democracy in their country. Venezuelans were provoked into action as a result of systematic repression by the Government of Hugo Chávez. Several hundred thousand people filled the streets of Caracas to demand the resignation of Lt. Col. Hugo Chávez. Chávez responded with sharpshooters and his paramilitary Bolivarian circles killing more than 12 civilians and wounding more than 100 others. In contrast, IRI commends the patriotism of the Venezuelan military for their refusal to fire on their countrymen.

IRI also applauds the bravery of civil society leaders—members of the media, the Church, the nation's educations and school administrators, political party leaders, labor unions and the business sector—who have put their very lives on the line in their struggle to restore genuine democracy to their country. IRI will remain engaged for the long term with political parties and our civil society partners to help rebuild Venezuela's fractured political system and restore elected democracy to the country.

IRI has promoted the strengthening of democracy in Venezuela since 1994 and recognizes that Venezuela's future is not a return to its pre-Chávez past, but instead the development of accountable, non-corrupt, and responsive government.

Today, the National Assembly is expected to meet to lay the groundwork for the transitional government to hold elections later this year. **The Institute has served as a bridge between the nation's political parties and all civil society groups to help Venezuelans forge a new democratic future, based on accountability, rule of law and sound democratic institutions. We stand ready to continue our partnership with the courageous Venezuelan people.**

IRI is a nonprofit organization dedicated to advancing democracy worldwide. IRI's programs span the globe and include training on civic responsibility and the legislative process, and strategies for building political parties and election campaigns. IRI is a nonpartisan organization, federally funded through the National Endowment for Democracy (NED) and the U.S. Agency for International Development (USAID), as well as privately funded by donations from individuals, corporations and foundations."[3]

After April 14, 2002, once it was clear that President Chávez had been returned to power and a coup had occurred, Carl Gershman, President of the National Endowment for Democracy, wrote a scathing memo to George Folsom, stating: "By welcoming [the coup]—indeed, without any apparent

3. The words in bold mean an emphasis added by the autor. See http://www.prnewswire.com/cgibin/stories.pl?ACCT=PRNI2&STORY=/www/story/04-12-2002/0001705053&EDATE=www.prnewswire.com.

reservations—you unnecessarily interjected IRI into the sensitive internal politics of Venezuela."[4] Gershman's statement to Folsom was rather ironic, considering the NED had been funding IRI to train and build the opposition movement during the prior year, clearly an interjection into "sensitive internal politics." What Gershman meant, of course, was that Folsom had made that interjection public unnecessarily. In any case, Gershman's remarks to Folsom were mere puffery. Instead of cutting back financing to IRI, NED increased it right after the coup.

Based on IRI's disagreement with the Chávez's Administration policies and its desire to find a counterpart in Venezuela, it was logical that the right wing organization would find solace and potential in an emerging conservative youth party willing to be shaped and directed as determined by its financiers. In early 2001, IRI began intensive training programs for opposition parties in Venezuela. The sessions were not limited to Primero Justicia leaders and members. Other opposition parties, such as the traditional AD and COPEI, and MAS, Proyecto Venezuela and lesser-known parties had also been invited.

One of the first IRI training sessions in March 2001 brought the Executive Director of the Mississippi Republican Party, George Fondren, to Venezuela to teach these failing opposition parties about "political communication." Mr. Fondren preached to anti-Chávez leaders such as Francisco Arias Cárdenas, Henrique Salas Römer, Governor Enrique Fernando Salas Feo, William Ojeda, Julio Borges, Governor Eduardo Lapi, Liliana Hernández, Antonio Ledezma, William Dávila and Sergio Omar Calderón, about the fundamentals of campaign communications, "how to connect with people to convince them to vote for you, and how to relate with them on an emotional level."[5] The IRI helped to

---

4. Joshua Kurlantzick, "The Coup Connection: How an Organization Financed by the U.S. Government Has Been Promoting the Overthrow of Elected Leaders Abroad," *Mother Jones,* November/December 2004. See http://www.motherjones.com/news/outfront/2004/11/11401.html.

5. See http://www.venezuelafoia.info.

set up training programs and party strategies that could be implemented throughout the country by the party leaders themselves—Strengthening Political Parties as the NED grant was aptly titled.

It was clear that IRI's initial focus was on rebuilding these traditional parties that had dropped the ball during the 1998 presidential elections and had truly lost power. IRI's objective was to provide the fundamental base for these parties to spring back into the political sphere, with the ultimate goal of reassuming the national government. After all, Venezuela's largest oil exporting company was owned by the State. Whoever was in power held control over a multi-billion dollar oil industry with limitless reserves. Hence, the need for a sextupling of IRI's funding in Venezuela.

After a scandal arose resulting from the financing of political parties in Panamá, in 1984 the United States Congress passed an amendment to the NED regulations that prohibited it from funding political parties or individuals engaged in political campaigns or elections.

"The Declaration of Principles and Objectives of the NED, adopted in 1984, affirms that NED funds cannot be used to finance the political campaigns of candidates aspiring for political positions."[6]

Just as financing political parties abroad is prohibited, the U.S. also does not permit, by law, foreign governments or entities to finance political parties or campaigns in the U.S. Title 2, section 441e, of the U.S. Federal Penal Code, states: "It is illegal for a foreignor, directly or indirectly, to contribute money or any other valuable instrument to anyone in connection with a federal, state or municipal election. Or to contribute to any committee or political party."[7]

Early on in 2000, IRI hand selected the newly formed Primero Justicia as its prime counterpart in Venezuela and began crafting and forming this young political party into

6. David Lowe, "De la idea a la realidad: NED a los 20 años." See http://www.ned.org/abort/nedhistory.html. David Lowe is NED's Vice-President.
7. See http://www.uscode.house.gov.

becoming one of the most vocally opposed to the Chávez's Government. Taking advantage of the lack of leadership and popularity of the traditional parties in Venezuela, Primero Justicia successfully landed itself key political positions in the 2000 regional elections, including five National Assembly seats in Miranda State, twenty-three municipal council member seats in Miranda State and two key municipal mayor offices in the wealthier sectors of Caracas.

In the early days of December 2001, IRI brought Mike Collins, the former Press Secretary for the Republican Party, to train Primero Justicia and other opposition parties, such as anti-Chávez metropolitan Caracas mayor Alfredo Peña's growing movement, the new Unión por el Progreso and the two traditional parties, AD and COPEI, on communications strategies. In the case of Primero Justicia, Mike Collins gave sessions focusing on "crafting a message for the party, finding a target audience and developing an image that will attract that target."[8] In sum, the republicans came in to develop Primero Justicia's image and party message, essential aspects of a successful political party.

The IRI training sessions were not just limited to political parties. On December 5, 2001, just five days before the first opposition "general strike," Mike Collins directed a session with the Centro de Divulgación del Conocimiento Económico (Center for the Dissemination of Economic Information) (CEDICE), a "free market think tank similar to the CATO Institute in Washington, D.C." The IRI training was directed towards local journalists and focused on reporting on politicians and political movements.[9] By that period in Venezuela, the private media (non-State channels) had banned together to take an open opposition stance to the Chávez's Administration. IRI's training sessions enhanced this position, as media coverage subsequently became more biased, inaccurate and subjective.

8. See http://www.venezuelafoia.info.
9. See http://www.venezuelafoia.info.

In 2001, IRI underwent substantive changes in its Venezuela team in the Washington headquarters. Stanley Lucas, who had been the Senior Program officer for Venezuela, moved to the IRI Strategic Planning team. Former NED officer Elizabeth Winger Echeverri took over the Senior Program officer position for Venezuela and Ecuador. Stanley Lucas was also simultaneously running IRI's Haiti program, which had been financing activities to seek removal of Haitian President Jean Bertrand Aristide.

USAID funded IRI more than $3 million from 1998-2003 to destabilize Haiti under the guise of "promoting democracy," the usual term put forth by such programs as a cover. Lucas, a wealthy Haitian-born, was hired by IRI in 1992 to run their Haiti program. Similar to IRI's work in Venezuela, Lucas and IRI hosted training sessions for Aristide's most virulent opponents. IRI's millions and Lucas' genius applied the U.S. intervention model formerly used in Nicaragua: unification of opposition parties.

In Haiti, IRI crafted and built the Democratic Convergence, a grouping of the disparate opposition parties, social organizations and groups in the country. The Democratic Convergence was elemental in provoking the ongoing tension and violence in the nation, eventually leading to the illegal and violent overthrow of President Aristide. IRI's role was beyond pivotal.

Back in Venezuela, Lucas was encouraging the same tactics and strategies to be implemented through IRI's programs. IRI sessions promoted dialogue and compromise between the opposition parties as a way of converging disparate viewpoints to craft a solid opposition to the government. But the Venezuela circumstances were different from those in Haiti. Venezuela's traditional parties had flopped, but they were still breathing, and IRI saw the potential for resuscitation. And with the protagonist positions of most Venezuelan political parties, IRI had decided initially to work on strengthening them all.

Primero Justicia has been the most successful of IRI's endeavors in Venezuela. As a party comprised primarily of young professionals with little or no political experience, IRI has been able to form and mold party leaders and determine and shape the party goals, strategies and platform, essentially building the party from scratch. With the hundreds of thousands of dollars IRI has pumped into Primero Justicia from NED and USAID funds, the new conservative party has left the traditional political parties in Venezuela in the dust. Primero Justicia has become the number one opposition party and by far the most outspoken. Its leaders and members have played key roles in the major destabilization attempts against the Venezuelan Government, and one of its most powerful figures, municipal mayor of Baruta, Henrique Capriles Radonski, was even formally charged by Venezuela's Attorney General for aiding and abetting in the assault against the Cuban Embassy in Caracas that occurred on April 12, 2002 during the coup.

PRIMERO JUSTICIA ASSAULTS THE CUBAN EMBASSY

A vicious aggression, anti-Chávez extremists from both Venezuela and Cuba (residing in Venezuela) stormed the Cuban Embassy in the Baruta section of Caracas, destroying property, automobiles and cutting off access to electricity, gas and water going into the Embassy. Live on television, the aggressors threatened to kill Embassy diplomats by "starving them" and forcing them to "eat carpet," depriving them of water and food supply. Mayor Capriles Radonski, in charge of the municipal police, made no effort to stop the assault and in fact encouraged it by arriving at the scene and interacting with the aggressors.

Capriles Radonski also violated diplomatic law by forcing entry inside the Embassy, where he attempted to persuade Cuban Ambassador Germán Sánchez Otero to turn in Vice President Diosdado Cabello and other Chávez's Government's officials the opposition believed were taking refuge in the Cuban Embassy. Though Ambassador Sánchez Otero permitted Capriles Radonski on the premises to engage in dialogue, he made clear that the actions were violating diplomatic law. The Primero Justicia mayor attempted to force a search of the inside of the Embassy by threatening the Ambassador that the situation would only worsen if a full search were not allowed. Dissatisfied, Capriles Radonski left the Embassy. If it hadn't been for the growing pro-Chávez demonstrations appearing all over Caracas and the rapid fall of the coup government, the Cuban Embassy would have suffered substantially more damage and injury. Capriles Radonski denied that his actions were unwarranted and illegal and claimed Ambassador Sánchez Otero "invited" him inside the Embassy. He was later charged by the Attorney General's Office for the assault and detained for four months. The case was subsequently dismissed by a sympathetic judge.

During the actions leading to the coup d'état on April 11, 2002, municipal mayor of Chacao, Leopoldo López, a leading Primero Justicia party member, played a key role. As revealed on the Venevisión morning program, 24 Horas with Napoleón Bravo on April 12, 2002, Leopoldo López, hand in hand with coup leader Rear Admiral Carlos Molina Tamayo, led the opposition march on a illegal route to the Miraflores Presidential Palace, where violence broke out. On that morning program, López spoke in detail of his important role in those events.

López, Capriles Radonski and other leading Primero Justicia members, such as Coordinator Gerardo Blyde and National Coordinator and Assembly member Julio Borges, made frequent trips to Washington during the pre-coup period to visit IRI headquarters and meet with officials in the Bush's Administration. The National Endowment for Democracy was a frequent host to these ultra-conservative Venezuelans, as was the Colombian Ambassador in Washington, informally.

Primero Justicia National Assembly members Julio Borges and Liliana Hernández have generally been the most outspoken critics of all legislation proposed by government party lawmakers.

IRI's training has been relatively successful, though it has still failed to consolidate national support for the party. Primero Justicia is viewed as more of a "Caracas" party than one with national reach.

IRI went through a series of trial periods with opposition parties in Venezuela to determine which was worth the most investment. Apparently, Primero Justicia won. But, early on in its grant program in Venezuela, IRI engaged in an interesting collaboration with another new political party, Unión por el Progreso (Union for Progress), led by Francisco Arias Cárdenas.

Arias Cárdenas was involved in Hugo Chávez's rebellions in 1992 against the Government of Carlos Andrés Pérez. An old friend of Chávez, he shared many of the same objectives and ideas as the Bolivarian leader. But he also had deep political aspirations. In 1995, he was elected Governor of Zulia State, the most important State in Venezuela. Zulia is home to the heart of Venezuela's oil industry, built around Lake Maracaibo, a huge lake right in the center of the State. When Chávez was elected president in 1998, Arias Cárdenas stood by his side. But his loyalty did not last long. Just one year later, after the new Constitution had been ratified by popular vote and new elections had to be held, he decided Chávez was incapable of governing the nation and ran against him. Thus began the train of betrayal Chávez was to face from those close to him, even inside his government.

Arias Cárdenas' abrupt and public departure from the Chávez ranks made headlines. And they must have been international, because IRI heard them loud and clear. Immediately, IRI began working with Arias Cárdenas and his newly formed party, Unión por el Progreso, shaping and molding it in preparation for the upcoming presidential elections. It was an interesting choice for IRI, because Arias Cárdenas claimed to be a progressive far from a right-wing republican. Clearly, IRI was ready to back any party capable of beating Chávez.

IRI could boast relative success. Arias Cárdenas, while losing the elections, garnered a near 38% of the vote, despite his fairly last minute decision to challenge the popular president. IRI had tapped into a part of the populace that was looking for a way out of a future Chávez's Administration planning to implement more radical changes.

72

But Unión por el Progreso and Arias Cárdenas lost ground and credibility after those elections and momentum within the opposition again dropped. It was around that time that IRI received a $340,000 grant from NED for "Strengthening Political Parties." It was clear that COPEI, AD, MAS, Proyecto Venezuela, Unión por el Progreso and Primero Justicia needed a big boost. And though the other parties still had lingering potential, Arias Cárdenas' party had suffered a big defeat as had Proyecto Venezuela, which posted its leader, Henrique Salas Römer as a candidate against President Chávez in the 1998 elections. AD and COPEI were getting support in the single digits.

Primero Justicia, which had garnered important seats in the 2000 regional elections, appeared to be IRI's, and the U.S. Government's, Venezuelan hope.

CHAPTER FIVE

Decoding Venezuela

In September 2001, the U.S. Embassy in Caracas began sending signs up to Washington that a change in government was soon likely and the man to fill the president's shoes was Pedro Carmona, President of Fedecámaras, Venezuela's Chamber of Commerce. In a September 2001 cable from the Embassy in Caracas to the Secretary of State, Department of Commerce and Department of Energy in Washington, Ambassador Donna Hrinak notified of an upcoming visit to be made by selected members of the Consejo de Empresarios Venezuela-Estados Unidos (Council of Venezuelan-U.S. Businessmen) (CEVEU) to Washington. Pedro Carmona, one of the selected members, was labeled as "a highly regarded and influential business leader who has consistently played a critical role in advancing U.S. commercial interests in Venezuela."[1]

The Embassy cable strongly recommended the Department of State arrange meetings between the CEVEU representatives and the Under Secretary of Commerce for International Trade, the Assistant Secretary for Policy and International Affairs, Department of Energy and the Assistant Secretary of State for Economic and Business Affairs. Ambassador Hrinak also requested appointments be arranged between Carmona and his fellow travelers and U.S. Representative Cass Ballenger, U.S. Representative Gregory Meeks, U.S. Representative Mark Souder and U.S. Senator Bob Graham. With an endorse-

1. See Appendix, p. 201.

ment from the Embassy and State Department, Carmona was sure to be received in Washington with open arms.

After Ambassador Hrinak returned from consultations in Washington in early November 2001 and relations were still brittle between the two countries, she sent a cable up to Washington informing the Secretary that the Carmona-led Fedecámaras had announced the suspension of dialogue with the Venezuelan Government. Hrinak mentioned the possibility of a nationwide work stoppage to be announced on November 28, 2001. In the cable, the Ambassador sided with Carmona's version of events, justifying the harsh reaction from the business community:

> Carmona, only recently elected as President of Fedecámaras, had been attempting to establish a dialogue with the Chávez Government. The cut-off of communication and the threat of a national work stoppage are a strong reaction to what is widely perceived to be a disregard for the views of the private business sector by President Chávez and his cabinet. While discontent with Chávez has been widespread in the private sector since his election, Chávez's October 29 speech coupled with the GOV's[2] failure to respond to private sector concerns over the new laws appears to have brought the discontent to a head.[3]

Hrinak's frame made it sound as though the growing conflict was all Chávez's fault.

"THE RIGHT MAN FOR THE RIGHT TIME IN VENEZUELA"

In a highly censored and classified cable from the U.S. Embassy in Caracas at the end of November 2001, Ambassador Hrinak reported on the decision made by Fedecámaras to declare a national strike as of December 10, 2001. But in the few areas

2. GOV is Government of Venezuela.
3. Cable from the U.S. Embassy in Caracas to the Secretary of State, Washington, D.C., November 1, 003392, 191150Z, priority 2985.

left uncensored, the cable made clear that the U.S. Government shared the opposition's views entirely on the driving issue behind the strike: the 49 laws President Chávez had enacted under the "Enabling Act" earlier that month. "President Chávez acted beyond his enabling act authority in decreeing certain laws," wrote Ambassador Hrinak. "The Land Law is an attack on the right of private property," she further enumerated.

A few days later, Frederick Cook, an Embassy official sent another cable, this time addressed to the State Department, the CIA, Defense Intelligence Agency, National Security Council, and other U.S. Embassies in Bogota, Quito, La Paz, Lima, Mexico, Buenos Aires, Brasilia and the U.S. Interests Section in Cuba, referring to Pedro Carmona as "statesman-like" and "the right man for the right time in Venezuela."[4]

Clearly, the stage was being set for a U.S.-backed change of leadership in Venezuela.

In the months that followed, Carmona and fellow union leader Carlos Ortega took several trips to Washington accompanied by other prominent opposition leaders, such as Leopoldo López and Gerardo Blyde of Primero Justicia and other NED grantees.[5] But it was during that first "strike" on December 10, 2001, that a solid bond was formed between two traditional opponents, Fedecámaras and the Confederación de Trabajadores Venezolanos (CTV), historically the leading workers union in the nation.

In 2001, the NED grant to the American Center for International Labor Solidarity (ACILS), the international branch of the AFL-CIO, was tripled. Though ACILS had an ongoing relationship with the CTV since the early 1990s, its average grant for work with the Venezuelan union was about $60,000. But in 2001, this amount was increased to $154,375 with the goal of defining "a new mission and role for the union movement in the development of the nation."[6]

---

4. Cable declassified by our FOIA requests. See http:// www.venezuelafoia.info. Available through the author. See Appendix, p.
5. On February 13, 2002, Carlos Ortega met with Otto Reich in Washington, D.C. See http://www.state.gov/r/pa/prs/dpb/2002/8034.html.
6. See Appendix, p. 182.

This new role and mission, it seemed, was a joint venture with the bosses organization, Fedecámaras, to build a movement capable of ousting the Chávez's Government. In order to achieve this goal, the NED was the number one financier.

As 2001 came to a close, the NED had pumped up its spending in Venezuela to a whopping $877,435. In addition to ACILS' tripled budget with the CTV and IRI's sextupled grant for its work with Primero Justicia, et al, the National Democratic Institute (NDI) had jumped on board. While NDI had been absent from the 2000 NED-Venezuela budget, it received a $210,500 grant to work with the social organization, Momento de la Gente (The People's Moment) to "engage citizens in the policy-making process" and to focus on "government accountability and transparency." Momento de la Gente was one of the leading civil society groups in the growing opposition movement to President Chávez. The generous $210,500 grant was sure to boost their national projection and mission.

Momento de la Gente was also a direct NED-grantee in 2000. Headed by the well-connected, wealthy Mercedes de Freitas, Momento de la Gente had received a mere $16,747 from the NED in 2000. But by 2001, as their political efforts to oppose Chávez were gaining ground, NED increased their direct grant to $40,000, almost four times what they were previously receiving just months before. The grant specifically noted that the NED funding would be "used to cover core institutional costs." So basically, NED was funding the functioning of the organization as it was taking on a leadership role in the opposition coalition forming between labor, business and civil society. Together with the NDI-NED grant, more than $250,000 was made available to Momento de la Gente in 2001—almost twenty times what they had been granted the year before.

Momento de la Gente's Mercedes de Freitas made a plea to NED Program Director Christopher Sabatini during the days of the coup against Chávez to accept the Carmona Government and dismiss any notions that a coup had occurred. At that time, her organization had just received an additional $64,000 grant in the months before the coup.[7]

7. David Corn, "Our Gang in Venezuela," *The Nation,* August 5, 2002.

By the end of February 2002, Fedecámaras and the CTV, along with opposition-aligned political parties and social organizations, were calling for massive marches in the streets of Caracas.

THE GROWING COALITION OF UNLIKELY FRIENDS

Months before the April 11, 2002 coup, the U.S. Government had put into action a skillfully devised plan to aid the anti-Chávez movement in its objectives. An opposition to Chávez had been loosely formed between unlikely allies that included Venezuela's largest labor union, the Confederación de Trabajadores Venezolanos, the Chamber of Commerce, Fedecámaras and leaders from the traditional political parties, AD, COPEI, Movimiento al Socialismo and others, as well as new parties, Primero Justicia and Proyecto Venezuela. Despite their differences, these entities shared a common disagreement with the Chávez's Administration policies based on their own loss of political and economic power, resulting from the change of government. This opposition, including the CTV, was primarily comprised of individuals and organizations stemming from Venezuela's elite, or as commonly referred to in Venezuela, the "oligarchy." Although tension and animosity were stirring amongst Venezuelan elites soon after President Chávez won his second term under the newly ratified Constitution in 1999, it wasn't until 2001 that the opposition coalition began solidifying and making its voice heard. History shows that this wasn't the first time this alliance between the CTV, Fedecámaras and the traditional political parties had been formed. In the late 1980s, during Carlos Andrés Pérez's generous collaboration with the U.S. Government, these same entities came together to form the National Democratic Foundation, which was used to funnel NED monies from the U.S. to Nicaragua. So once again, labor, business and political parties were unified to promote U.S. interests in Latin America.

The NED had been present in Venezuela, though minimally, since the late 1980s when they began financing the CTV.

78

But from 2000 to 2001, the NED's budget in Venezuela quadrupled and funding began flowing in to large and small organizations that all shared one common characteristic: a public aversion to President Chávez. Of the more than $877,000 that NED gave out in Venezuela in 2001 to "promote democracy" many of the recipients of the money included several Venezuelan organizations that were awarded direct grants from the NED with no intermediaries. Numerous other organizations were given funding through the four NED core grantees, IRI, NDI, CIPE and ACILS. Some of the entities directly funded by NED in 2001-2002 included the Asamblea de Educación (Education Assembly), Asociación Civil Comprensión de Venezuela (Venezuelan Civil Association for Understanding) and the Asociación Civil Consorcio Justicia (Justice Consortium). All of these organizations were aligned with the opposition movement.

The Asamblea de Educación worked on opposing all Chávez-promoted legislation involving education reform. Its leader, Leonardo Carvajal, was a staunch Chávez opponent who disagreed with Chávez's educational goals and vowed to do his best to prevent the proposed changes from being enacted. By 2001, the Chávez's Government had already built more than 1000 new "Bolivarian" schools in neighborhoods and areas with traditionally little or no access to quality education. The government was also promoting the implementation of a new "Bolivarian curriculum," which would alter the previous school curriculum to include more accurate historical information on Venezuelan and Latin American history, as well as change the Eurocentric approach to education for a more South American one.

So, in addition to providing $55,000 of funding for Mr. Carvajal's and his organization's opposition activities and attendance at marches, the NED grant was also funding efforts to oppose legitimate legislation being lawfully debated and enacted by Venezuela's National Assembly. In fact, Carvajal admitted later that the NED funding was the primary source of income for his organization. He even received a salary from the NED grant to finance his lifestyle.

The grant to Asociación Civil Comprensión de Venezuela in the amount of $57,820 from the NED came at a peculiar moment. The focus was on "initiating a national debate on the newly changing role of the military in the country." President Chávez is a former military Lieutenant Colonel. A large percentage of his cabinet members and top-level government officials are retired or active military officers. While the NED grant to ACCV may have seemed timely, it was also rather unusual. As NED was financing efforts to raise awareness on the negative aspects of military involvement in government, Venezuela had just elected, twice, a military-strong government. It doesn't seem odd then that around the time of the ACCV-NED project, dissident military officers began aligning themselves with the opposition movement.

In the years 2000, 1999 and prior, the primary recipients of NED funds in Venezuela were the ACILS for its work with the CTV, CIPE for its work with counterpart Centro de Divulgación del Conocimiento Económico (CEDICE) and the IRI for its ongoing training and shaping of political parties in the nation. Direct NED grantees in Venezuela during those years included groups such as Centro al Servicio de la Acción Popular (Center for the Service of Public Action) (CESAP), Programa para el Desarrollo Legislativo (Program for Legislative Development) (PRODEL), Fundación Momento de la Gente and Sinergia, an organization dedicated to strengthening other social organizations aligned with the opposition. All of these entities had leanings towards the opposition, some more than others. Even so, the NED role in Venezuela was relatively minor prior to 2001. Then the Bush's Administration authorized an increase in spending on organizations capable of forming a solid opposition movement to Chávez.

These contributions are couched in high minded terms of "strengthening political parties," coming from "The National Endowment for Democracy," appearing to be nothing more than well intentioned efforts to help democracy take root. But imagine being subjected to an equivalent amount of "aid" from a foreign country, shoveling billions of dollars into the U.S. to build parties and educate candidates who are sympathetic to that government's interest. Such an effort would be immediately exposed for what it was, an attempt to subvert the democratic process, not to build it. When reading of these high-minded efforts, it is a simple matter of consistency to hold them in the same jaundiced light as if they were being applied to the U.S.

THE FIRST SIGNS

On December 10, 2001, the first "general strike" was called by the loose coalition of the CTV, Fedecámaras, private media, NED-funded social organizations and opposition political parties with the objective of opposing the Chávez's Government proposal of a set of 49 laws that would implement many of the new rights represented in the 1999 Constitution. Prior to the strike, high-level officials of the U.S. Government, including Colin Powell, George Tenet and Roger Noriega, had made statements indicating a possible break in relations with the Chávez's Administration, basing such attitudes on Chávez's overt opposition to the bombing of Afghanistan in October 2001. The call to consultations of the U.S. Ambassador in Venezuela, Donna Hrinak, in early November 2001, was an indicator of a change in relations.

The December 10th opposition-led strike "paralyzed" the nation for a day and set the stage for the months to come. The opposition organized multiple protests and acts of civil disobedience and a faction of senior military officers began to "defect" and publicly declare a state of rebellion. The private media upped its tone of aggression towards the government and overtly gave 100% coverage to the opposition, rarely presenting balanced news accounts. The private media channels ran continuous advertisements promoting the strike and calling on citizens to participate in marches and demonstrations against the government.

The U.S. Department of State Office of Inspector General report on *U.S. Policy Toward Venezuela: November 2001-April 2002,* completed after the April 2002 coup at the request of Senator Christopher Dodd (D-CT), concluded that:

. . . during the six month period [November 2001-April 2002], NED, the Department,[8] and DOD[9] provided training, institution building and other support programs totaling about $3.3 million to Venezuelan organizations and individuals, some of whom are understood to have been involved in the events of April 12-14. Further, the federal assistance programs involved numerous contacts between NED, the Department, and DOD and these organizations and individuals during the six months period.[10]

In fact, the Inspector General report affirmed that NED funding for programs in Venezuela during that same six-month period totaled over $2 million. The report also evidenced something that NED's own internal documents released under FOIA had attempted to cover up: an additional $622,000 NED had funneled into ACILS for its work with the CTV during the period February 2001-January 2002, approximately $150,000 every three months. On top of the $622,000 NED had given another grant to ACILS in the amount of $154,400 to support the CTV.

The $2 million figure was astonishing. The year before, NED's total grant program in Venezuela was just a little above $200,000. Twelve months later, it was ten times that amount.

And those receiving the financing—all of it—were building an opposition movement to the democratically elected and popularly supported Venezuelan Government. Democratic or not, popular—who cares?—the U.S. Government wanted Chávez out and through financial and political support for

8. The Department refers to the U.S. Department of State.
9. DOD is the U.S. Department of Defense.
10. U.S. Department of State and Broadcasting Board of Governors Office of Inspector General, *A Review of U.S. Policy Toward Venezuela: November 2001-April 2002*, July 2002, report no. 02-OIG-003. Redacted for public use.

the growing coalition of business, labor, political parties and social organizations, they thought his demise would be plausible.

U.S. Public Funds for "Promoting Democracy" in Venezuela

Years	NED/U.S. Dollars	USAID/U.S. Dollars
2000	232,831	—
2001	877,435	—
2002	1,698,799	2,197,066
2003	1,046,321	8,903,669
2004	874,384	6,345,000
2005	*	5,000,000
Total Public Funds: $27,175,505		

*. The NED has still not made public its 2005 Venezuela funds.

CHAPTER SIX

A Coup by Any Other Name

On February 25, 2002, Charles Shapiro was officially sent to Caracas as the new U.S. Ambassador to Venezuela. But Washington's decision to replace Hrinak with Shapiro had been made back in December 2001, as the opposition consolidated and showed potential, yet clearly needed some experienced support and guidance. Shapiro's history with the State Department provided evidence as to the tone the U.S. Government now chose to set with Venezuela. A 24-year veteran of the Foreign Service in Latin America, Shapiro worked in the U.S. Embassy in El Salvador for five years during the tumultuous 80s when U.S. intervention was at an all time high and an attaché of the U.S. Embassy in Chile[1] during the coup d'état against the Salvador Allende's Government. From 1999 to 2001, he held the capacity of Coordinator of the Bureau of Cuban Affairs Office in Washington, responsible for monitoring and overseeing U.S. policy toward Cuba and upholding U.S.-imposed restrictions on travel and comerce between the two nations. The Chávez's Administration was known as an open ally of Fidel Castro and Chávez made no attempt to conceal or alter his relationship with Cuba despite Washington's insistent requests and demands. Sending Shapiro to Caracas was a clear sign that the U.S. was losing patience with Chávez and his Castro-friendly policies.

---

1. Carlos Fazio, "Venezuela un país singular," *La Jornada,* July 1, 2002. Note Fazio's statement: "Shapiro was an attaché in Chile [the Embassy] during Salvador Allende's constitutional Government."

Ambassador Shapiro wasted no time at all acclimating to the Venezuelan political scene and getting Venezuela in tune with the U.S. agenda. By the time he officially was installed in the U.S. Embassy in Caracas, three top-ranking Venezuelan military officers had publicly denounced President Chávez and threatened a military rebellion. On February 7, 2002, Venezuelan Air Force Colonel Pedro Sota demanded Chávez's resignation. Colonel Sota's call was followed the next day by National Guard Captain Pedro Flores, who claimed the majority of Venezuela's Armed Forces was ready to rebel against the government. Then, on February 18, Rear Admiral Carlos Molina Tamayo accused President Chávez of "seeking to impose a totalitarian regime in Venezuela and placing the nation in danger by soliciting closer ties to Cuba and distancing itself from the United States." Rear Admiral Molina Tamayo demanded Chávez's resignation and spoke of a "rising military rebellion in the armed forces."

Earlier that month, the opposition had staged several large protests, gathering hundreds into the streets to demand President Chávez's resignation. On January 31, 2002, the Catholic Church had declared its opposition to Chávez, refusing to engage in dialogue with the government and instead, expressing support for the growing opposition movement. The public military rebellion, and in particular the position of Rear-Admiral Molina Tamayo, was a clear indicator that the situation was becoming more instable each day. Rumors of a possible coup began circulating around the country.

REICH COMES ONTO THE SCENE

Towards the end of February 2002, Carlos Ortega, then President of the CTV, which had become one of the leaders of the opposition movement, led a small delegation of AFL-CIO and CTV members up to Washington to meet with top-level officials. Particularly noteworthy, a meeting had been arranged between Ortega and Otto Reich, who at the time had just been named the Assistant Secretary of State for Western Hemisphere

Affairs.[2] Considering that Reich had been a key player in the decade-long intervention in Nicaragua, later serving as Ambassador in Venezuela, during which he was implicated in securing the release and entry into the U.S. of one of the most notorious terrorists in Latin America, Orlando Bosch, the relations between Ortega and Reich were no surprise. Reich had a history of aiding overthrows of democratic governments or those governments not working in U.S. interests. A vehement anti-Castro Cuban-American who had long worked to support the ousting of Fidel Castro, Reich considered Chávez's Government on the path to "Castro-communism" and therefore it needed to be stopped at all costs.

During the Reagan's Administration, Reich headed the Office of Public Diplomacy for Latin America, a Reagan creation that was declared illegal after a 1987 investigation by the U.S. General Accounting Office. Reich's Office was charged with disseminating "black propaganda," covert misinformation designed to influence public opinion against Nicaragua's Sandinista Government. The Office attempted to influence U.S. reporters and mainstream media to portray the Sandinistas in a negative light and to run deceptive Op-Ed articles drafted by Reich and his Office, but signed by university professors and anti-Sandinista Nicaraguans.

The Senate Foreign Relations Committee blocked Reich's appointment in January 2002 as Assistant Secretary of State for Western Hemisphere Affairs. But President George W. Bush exercised his right of Executive Privilege and appointed Reich on an interim basis for a one-year period. Subsequently, failing Senate confirmation, Bush named Reich as his Special Advisor on Latin American Affairs. Reich resigned on June 16, 2004 to return to the private sector, after leaving a career of intervention and regime change behind him. But back in early 2002, he was frequently meeting with opposition leaders and emanating the U.S.'s desire for a change in Venezuelan Gov-

2. Email from Lourdes Kistler at ACILS to Mary Sullivan at the Department of State, confirming the Ortega delegation visit and meeting with Otto Reich on February 11, 2002. Obtained under FOIA. Available through the author.

ernment. Reich also met frequently with Pedro Carmona, the Head of Fedecámaras, already well on the radar screen of the U.S. Government since 2001. Reich's role was only to increase as the coup rumors gained credibility.

In March 2002, the International Republic Institute was given an additional $300,000 grant from the NED to continue its work "strengthening political parties" in Venezuela. NED granted ACILS another $116,001 for its work with the CTV, despite the labor union's public calls for President Chávez to resign. In fact, NED gave out grants totaling $1,098,519 to organizations and projects in Venezuela in 2002, a $200,000 increase over 2001. Now, the jump from financing in 2000 was five-fold. In addition to the above, groups receiving direct NED financing in Venezuela during the 2002 pre-coup period included the Consorcio Justicia, which received two grants, one for the amount of $84,000 and another for $11,000; Acción Campesina, $35,000; Asamblea de Educación $57,000; Centro al Servicio de la Acción Popular (CESAP), $63,000; Momento de la Gente, $64,000; CIPE-CEDICE, $90,000, $66,266 and $116,525; Instituto Prensa y Sociedad, $25,000; Asociación Civil Justicia Alternativa, $10,000; Fundación Justicia de Paz del Estado Monagas, $11,000; and NDI, $50,000.

All of the groups receiving NED monies were involved in the opposition movement in early 2002. Most were spending the majority of their time marching in the streets calling for Chávez's resignation and focusing their energies on seeking out ways to force regime change. Such activities are a far cry from where U.S. taxpayer dollars should be spent.

BOGUS INTELLIGENCE REPORTS

On March 20, 2002, a Secret Intelligence Assessment was prepared by the U.S. Southern Command Joint Intelligence Center entitled, *Venezuela: Growing Evidence of an Insurgent Partnership.*[3] While heavily censored in old-style black marker, the report analyzed the alleged connections between the

3. Available through the autor. See http://www.venezuelafoia.info.

Chávez's Government and the Colombian guerrilla organizations, the FARC[4] and the ELN,[5] considered by Washington as terrorist organizations. The assessment made reference to an agreement between Chávez and the FARC to provide free access to Venezuelan territory in exchange for a FARC promise not to kidnap or extort Venezuelan citizens. The source for this hardcore intelligence was the Bogotá daily, *El Tiempo*. No other credible source was provided.

The Intelligence Assessment further cited a letter published in Venezuela's daily, *El Universal*, from the dissident military officers calling for Chávez's resignation, charging that the Venezuelan Government had allowed the FARC to establish two large camps on Venezuelan territory in the Perija Ridge, and that additional FARC camps were under construction in San Joaquín de Navay. The only source provided was *El Universal*.

The U.S. Southern Command Intelligence report further cited multiple accounts of Chávez's collaborations with the FARC and the ELN, including an alleged channeling of $1 million into a FARC-ELN front company, Cootraguas, from the Chávez's Administration. The sources? *El Universal* newspaper, Globovisión television station and *El Nacional* newspaper. What do all these media outlets share in common? An open and explicit dislike and opposition to the Chávez's Government and a notorious manipulation and distortion of information. Maybe Otto Reich's Office of Public Diplomacy had been re-hatched.

The "Intelligence" report even claimed that according to *El Universal*, $2 million were used to purchase weapons "through Nicaragua's Sandinista Front in order to arm the members of the Bolivarian Circles and to create a special military force to defend the regime."[6] The Bolivarian Circles are

---

4. Fuerzas Armadas Revolucionarias de Colombia (Colombia Revolutionary Armed Forces).
5. Ejército de Liberación Nacional (National Liberation Army).
6. U.S. Department of Defense Southern Command, Joint Intelligence Center, *Intelligence Assessment*, March 20, 2002. Obtained under FOIA. Available through the author.

community and neighborhood based grassroots organizations formed to coordinate local issues and to foster community relations. No concrete evidence has ever been provided to prove claims that the Venezuelan Government has armed such organizations.

Despite the lack of credible sources, this Intelligence Assessment prepared by the Department of Defense, Southern Command, was sent up to Washington and circulated around Congress to influence opinion on Venezuela. It was no wonder that soon after, U.S. Congress members were declaring they had evidence of Chávez's collaborations with the FARC and the ELN. However, not one single Congress member has ever presented any evidence to prove such claims.

In any case, the bogus intelligence report was offered as a justification for increasing U.S. Government's is efforts to support an illegal ouster of President Chávez. Surely if a link was made between Chávez and a terrorist group, his removal from office, however conducted, would be accepted.

THE CIA KNOWS ALL

On March 5, 2002, CIA operatives in Venezuela prepared and sent a Senior Executive Intelligence Brief (SEIB) to approximately 200 top-level representatives at the Defense Intelligence Agency, the National Imagery and Mapping Agency, the Central Intelligence Agency, the Department of State and the National Security Agency. The SEIB was labeled "Top Secret " and "Not for Foreign Dissemination." The top secret brief detailed how ". . .opposition to President Chávez is mounting . . . Calls for his resignation by public officials and private-sector leaders are becoming daily occurrences . . . The military is also divided in its support for Chávez . . . A successful coup would be difficult to mount."[7]

The SEIB also mentioned, "opposition leaders are not unified and lack a singular strategy for replacing Chávez." Clearly, the CIA was well aware of the opposition's downfalls,

7. Available through the author. See http://www.venezuelafoia.info.

hence the need for more than $1 million in NED funding to "strengthen political parties" and anti-Chávez NGOs. And it was just around that time that NED gave IRI that extra $300,000 to "strengthen political parties." ACILS also received that additional $116,001 to back the CTV. Leaders of those very same political parties and labor unions were precisely the ones the CIA was referring to as "not unified" and "lack[ing] a singular strategy for replacing Chávez." So the U.S. believed that a substantial influx of U.S. taxpayer dollars into these groups could aid them in unification and strategizing.

"ANOTHER PIECE FALLS INTO PLACE"

On March 5, 2002, something happened that pleased the U.S. Government. A cable sent by the U.S. Embassy in Caracas up to Washington, CIA, DIA, NSC and others, carried the subject line: LABOR, BUSINESS AND CHURCH ANNOUNCE TRANSITION PACT. The summary of the cable read:

> With much fanfare, the Venezuelan great and good assembled on March 5 to hear representatives of the Confederation of Venezuelan Workers, the Federation of Business Chambers and the Catholic Church present their "Bases for a Democratic Accord," ten principles on which to guide a transitional government . . . This accord represents an important step for the opposition, which has been quick to condemn Chávez but had so far offered no vision of its own .[8]

An assumption could be made by reading this cable that the U.S. Embassy considered the Venezuelan great and good to be everyone but the "Chavistas" since those assembled to hear the opposition leaders present their "transitional govern-

---

8. Cable from the U.S. Embassy in Caracas to the Department of State, Washington, D.C., March 2002, R 052151Z. Available through the author. See Appendix, p. 203.

ment" pact were all in the anti-Chávez crowd. But bias aside, on March 5, as the CIA was sending briefs to top intelligence and government officials about the difficulties of mounting a coup and the divisive opposition, the leaders of the CTV, Fedecámaras and the Catholic Church were doing their best to come together and agree on what to do after they got Chávez out of office. According to the cable, Carlos Ortega, CTV President, stated: "This accord is a pact for us . . . to guide us through the transition and to establish a Government of Democratic Unity."

If it had any doubts before, as of March 5, 2002, the U.S. Embassy must have been absolutely clear that the opposition was planning to get rid of Chávez. While the U.S. Government may have liked this idea on its premise, they also knew full well that Chávez's constitutional term was not up until December 2006, four years away. Therefore, unless they truly believed Chávez was just going to step down, despite the fact that he gave no signs whatsoever to make anyone believe he would voluntarily resign, the only other option was a coup d'état. Considering that high ranking military officers, such as Molina Tamayo were threatening military rebellion, it was not far fetched for the U.S. Government to think a coup was on the rise.

In fact, the U.S. Government appeared to have been pleased by the March 5 accord reached by the opposition, considering that it had already invested nearly $2 million in trying to strengthen and unify the opposition parties. A comment in the Embassy cable revealed such satisfaction: "Another piece falls into place," wrote Embassy official Cook, "This accord . . . may well form the frame of reference and code of conduct for a transitional government . . ."

The "another piece falls into place" comment should raise some eyebrows, lots of eyebrows. If the opposition agreement of a post-Chávez transitional government is another "piece" in the plan, then completion of the scheme must be the ouster of Chávez. The U.S. had been ranting and raving about the lack of unity amongst the opposition, which is why via the NED, it was pumping in a couple of million dollars to strengthen opposition parties and aid them in strategizing. The March 5th accord showed that the investment was paying off — "another piece" was falling right into place and the day when the final goal would be reached was getting closer.

If on March 5, the U.S. Government still believed Chávez's removal would come through resignation, then on Monday, March 11, 2002, they no longer could sell that story. Another SEIB was sent by the CIA folks in Venezuela up to the five intelligence agencies in Washington, this time in the form of a warning. The warning was prepared by the DCI Strategic Warning Committee, a highly secretive and top level group chaired by the National Intelligence Officer for Warning and comprised of representatives from the Directors of the National Security Agency, the Defense Intelligence Agency and the National Imagery and Mapping Agency, as well as the Assistant Secretary of State for Intelligence and Research and the Deputy Director for Intelligence of the CIA. The top secret warning was more specific: "There are increased signs that Venezuelan business leaders and military officers are becoming dissatisfied with President Chávez . . . the military may move to overthrow him."[9]

SO NOW MORE PIECES ARE FALLING INTO PLACE

The military is preparing a coup and the opposition leaders have agreed on a post-Chávez transitional government agenda. The highest levels of the U.S. Government knew this in early March 2002. Despite the fact that coups against democratic governments are illegal, the U.S. did nothing to persuade the plotters from acting. In fact, their actions were encouraged. No threats were made to cut NED financing to its grantees, despite their open ties with coup plotters. Moreover, the monies were increased during the period when the conspiring was at a head.

Furthermore, the U.S. military had substantial control and influence over the Venezuelan Armed Forces, particularly those

9. See http://www.venezuelafoia.info.

officers who had declared rebellion, all of who had received training in the U.S. academies such as the School of the Americas. Yet, no attempts were made to dissuade the officers from coup plotting. By April 1, 2002, the U.S. Government knew the coup was coming soon. A CIA SEIB of that date, again from the DCI Strategic Warning Committee, stated: "President Chávez is facing continued strong opposition from the private sector, the media, the Catholic Church and opposition political parties . . . Reporting suggests that disgruntled officers within the military are still planning a coup, possibly early this month."[10]

Ten days before the coup, the U.S. Government was aware of who was planning it—the private sector, the opposition parties, the Church, and now the media were involved too—and that the dissident military officers would be the ones most likely to carry it out.

Within five days, the U.S. Government knew how the coup was going to be played out, in detail. A top secret CIA SEIB from April 6, 2002, headlined "Conditions Ripening for Coup Attempt" and informed: "Dissident military factions, including some disgruntled senior officers and a group of radical junior officers, are stepping up efforts to organize a coup against President Chávez, possibly as early as this month . . . the level of detail in the reported plans—targets Chávez and 10 other senior officials for arrest . . ."

The "level of detail in the reported plans" implies that the CIA had the "reported plans" in their possession on April 6, five days before the coup actually took place, which could only mean that they were in close contact with the plotters.

The April 6 CIA SEIB further revealed that: "To provoke military action, the plotters may try to exploit unrest stemming from opposition demonstrations slated for later this month or ongoing strikes at the state-owned oil company PDVSA."[11]

10. See http://www.venezuelafoia.info.
11. See http://www.venezuelafoia.info.

So far, as of April 6, 2002, the U.S. Government knew the following:

WHAT: A coup d'état against President Chávez was be ing planned.
WHEN: Early April 2002.
WHO: The private sector, the media, the Catholic Church, opposition political parties and dissident military officers.
WHERE: Venezuela.
HOW: Exploit violence in the opposition march, provoke military action and arrest Chávez and other top-level officials.

That's a lot of detail and in-depth information.
Lets look at what happened after April 6th.
On April 7, 2002, President Chávez announced the firing of seven PDVSA managers, the forced retirement of twelve managers and the removal of an additional five from their positions. The workers were dismissed largely due to mismanagement of the industry, embezzlement of finances and a difference in policy from the Chávez's Government. Since PDVSA was a State-owned company, the Executive had full decision-making authority over its operations and employees. The decision sparked immediate protest from the opposition. The CTV called for a "general strike" starting on April 9, also supported by Fedecámaras. The fired PDVSA workers called for an "indefinite strike."

By April 10, the PDVSA workers had shut down several operations within the State-owned oil industry, placing the life-blood of the nation in danger. The shutdowns were directed mostly at operations affecting the internal Venezuelan markets for fuel and gas, intended to induce panic and unrest amongst Venezuelans and encourage protest. All activities related to fuel production at the Puerto La Cruz refinery were halted. An "Operación Morrocoy" (Turtle Operation—slow down) was implemented in the José Complex near Puerto La Cruz and affected liquefied petroleum gas production. Several refineries near Puerto Cabello were stopped, including the largest fuel distribution plan in Venezuela, Yagua, and El Palito refinery, which provided fuel to most of the Venezuelan market. PDVSA Caracas was closed down.

To say the least, the country was in a state of turmoil and the "pieces were falling into place," as planned.

On April 10, Pedro Carmona and Carlos Ortega announced in a televised press conference that the "general strike" would be "indefinite." The U.S.-financed opposition leaders also declared the "immediate establishment" of a "coordinating committee for democracy and liberty" intended to "rescue Venezuela's freedom and liberty and coordinate all opposition activities." The political parties comprising the committee included AD, COPEI, MAS, Proyecto Venezuela, Primero Justicia and Alianza Bravo Pueblo, all NED and IRI-funded parties. They announced an opposition march scheduled for 9:00 A.M., April 11, from Parque del Este in the eastern side of Caracas, to the PDVSA headquarters in Chuao.

A lot happened, or was supposed to happen on April 10, 2002 and the days to come. On that date, a NED sponsored conference to "promote democracy" in Venezuela had been planned by grantee Consorcio Justicia. One of the headline speakers programmed for the conference was Pedro Carmona, President of Fedecámaras, outspoken oppositionist, coup plotter and favorite of the U.S. Government. But the conference, which was financed by Consorcio Justicia's $84,000 NED grant, never took place due to the strikes and protests occurring throughout Caracas that day.[12]

Evidencing an increasingly tense situation, the private media channels aired a high-level General, Néstor González González,[13] declaring rebellion and publicly calling for President Chávez to "step down." Two days later, on live television, it was revealed that General González González had pre-fabricated and recorded that media moment in order to prevent

12. David Corn, "Our Gang in Venezuela," *The Nation*, August 5, 2002.
13. This is the same General González González referred to in the Introduction. U.S. military attaché James Rodgers had mistaken General González Cárdenas for this General González González at a social gathering and revealed part of a mysterious collaboration between U.S. military and dissident Venezuelan military officers during the days preceding the coup.

Chávez from attending an Organization of American States (OAS) Assembly meeting in Costa Rica, so that the President would remain in the country and the coup plan could be activated. General González González had succeeded in his efforts.

THE COUP

On April 11, 2002, CTV, Fedecámaras and the NED-supported opposition parties held one of the largest rallies and marches Venezuela had ever seen.

The night before, Ambassador Shapiro had cabled to Washington:

> Five to seven thousand opposition supporters held a loud and jubilant rally at PDVSA headquarters until late in the evening . . . Virtually all prominent opposition figures including Pedro Carmona, Alfredo Peña and Carlos Ortega gave impromptu speeches . . . Carmona seemed particularly energized by the size and mood of the crowd . . . It was a celebratory atmosphere, not unlike after Venezuela defeated Paraguay in world cup qualifying.[14]

Shapiro's likening of the opposition rally in preparation for a coup d'état to a soccer game demonstrates the patronizing and belittling attitude the U.S. had assumed in the face of the overthrow of a democratic government in South America.

About midday on April 11, speakers at the opposition rally, including Carmona and Ortega, began calling for supporters to march on the Presidential Palace, Miraflores, to demand Chávez's resignation. No official permit or authorization had been requested or given for this change in route. Caracas mayor Freddy Bernal appeared on the state television channel, Channel 8, pleading with Carmona and Ortega

14. Cable from the U.S. Embassy in Caracas to the Secretary of State, Washington, D.C., April, 2002, 01110482. Available through the author. See Appendix, pp. 211-212.

96

to not direct marches towards the palace, fearing violence would ensue.

A pro-Chávez rally was occurring in front of Miraflores Palace and thousands of Chávez supporters became alerted to the opposition's movements and objectives. The Presidential Guard was called out to ensure the two sides, now riled up, would not clash. Before the opposition marchers even reached the side of Miraflores where the pro-Chávez supporters were gathered, two anti-Chávez marchers were shot. The bullet wounds showed the shots came from within the opposition march itself. But no warnings were given to other marchers that violence had erupted from within their own crowd.

Instead, the march continued aggressively towards the palace. Led by Rear Admiral Carlos Molina Tamayo, who had publicly denounced the president just weeks before and threatened a military rebellion, the crowd managed to pass through several Metropolitan Police barriers that had been set up to prevent the march from reaching Miraflores. The Metropolitan Police were under the control of greater Caracas mayor Alfredo Peña who just minutes before had been addressing the anti-Chávez rally, calling for marchers to head to the palace. Joined by ex-President of PDVSA, retired General Guaicaipuro Lameda, Molina Tamayo was able to break another police barrier that had been set up in the El Calavario section of Caracas, close to the palace and the pro-Chávez rally. The National Guard came out to prevent a confrontation between the two groups and eventually, Molina Tamayo and Lameda ceased their call to raid the pro-Chávez rally. Unfortunately, the plan had already been set into motion and the resulting violence could no longer be impeded.

At 2:15 P.M. the high military command was broadcast on national television, attempting to diffuse rumors of violence that were circulating throughout the country. Earlier that day, in the eastern part of town, ten high level military officers had summoned CNN correspondent Otto Neustald to a residential location to record a prepared statement for subsequent broadcast. Read by Rear Admiral Héctor Ramírez Pérez, who was subsequently named Minister of Defense by the Carmona coup government, the testimony deplored the massacre of innocent civilians, announcing that a macabre conspiracy had been implemented by Chávez, resulting in the death of six Venezuelans, killed at the hands of government forces. Ramírez Pérez called for a military insurrection, citing the violence as justification. Neustald had to do two takes of the Rear Admiral's testimony. It was recorded before any violence had erupted in the opposition or pro-Chávez demonstrations.[15]

A few months later, Neustald, participating in a forum entitled Journalism in Times of Crisis at the Bicentennial University of Aragua in Venezuela, revealed that "On the 10th at night they called me on the telephone and said, Otto, tomorrow the 11th there will be a video of Chávez, the march will go towards the presidential palace, there will be deaths and then 20 military officials of high rank will appear and pronounce themselves against the government of Chávez, and will request his resignation. They told me this on the 10th at night."[16] The media's involvement in the coup had clearly been premeditated.

Venevisión, the most popular station in the country, had installed a correspondent on the rooftop of a building nearby the palace, with a view of Puente Llaguno, the area where the pro-Chávez rally was concentrated. Nevertheless, throughout the greater part of the day, the private media had been exclusively broadcasting images from the opposition demonstration and march. The lack of balanced coverage appeared to be part of the plan.

Remember, according to a CIA SEIB, the media had also joined in the coup plotting.

By about 3:00 P.M. violence had erupted in various areas along the outskirts of the palace. It was around that time that Molina Tamayo, Guaicapuro Lameda, Pedro Carmona and Carlos Ortega were called to a meeting at the Venevisión head-

15. Otto Neustald testified months later at a university conference that he had been called by the military officials to pre-record their message in a private residence. He affirmed that at the time of the recording, which specifically cites deaths caused by Chávez forces, no violence had occurred.
16. See the documentary film, Crónica de un Golpe de Estado, Venezolana de Televisión, 2002.

quarters. In fact, most of the opposition leaders disappeared, one by one, from the march, leaving the masses to confront the planned massacre on their own. Shortly after, shots began ringing out from atop buildings surrounding the palace and from the Metropolitan Police, stationed on Avenue Baralt, right beneath Puente Llaguno. The first to fall were in the pro-Chávez concentration. Twelve people were killed in that sector. After 3:10 P.M. more than twenty deaths and injuries occurred in a lapse of thirty minutes. But no television stations were reporting the events.

Soon, innocent victims from both concentrations were hit and before it was clear as to what was happening on the ground, the private stations began to broadcast the pre-recorded Ramírez Pérez's statement, blaming the deaths on Chávez and calling for a military insurrection.

Just as the call for military rebellion began, at 3:44 P.M., President Chávez initiated a broadcast on national television, on "cadena."[17] But as he was speaking, the private television channels illegally captured alternative transmitters and were able to split the television screens to show the president on just half a screen and the opposition on the other side, or in some cases, block the president's cadena all together and broadcast the military call for insurrection.

The images taken by the Venevisión cameraman and correspondent stationed on a rooftop nearby Puente Llaguno had been manipulated back at the studio. The full scene of the Metropolitan Police below and snipers on rooftops above the bridge was cut and the only footage left was that of the pro-Chávez demonstrators firing at targets below the bridge. The Venevisión reporter recorded a voiceover claiming Chávez supporters stationed on Puente Llaguno were firing on peaceful, unarmed opposition marchers at the orders of President Chávez. The video failed to pan the full image to show that no opposition marchers were even in that area. The manipulated footage was picked up and broadcast over and over again

17. A "cadena" is when the government broadcasts on all airwaves in the country, per decree.

by all the private channels, and even sent around the world to justify the ouster of President Chávez.

The author of the video, Luis Alfonso Fernández of Venevisión, won the top journalism prize in Spain (Premio Rey 2003) for that same news video. He later admitted to the newspaper *Panorama* that "in reality, that day I did not see the Chávez supporters firing at the opposition march." Journalist Ricardo Márquez of *Últimas Noticias* wrote that Luis Alfonso Fernández stated he could not see who the Chávez supporters were firing at and that the voiceover on the video was added after the events. Another journalist from a private channel, Del Valle Canelón of Globovisión, initially affirmed that in the video, the group of civilians were seen firing, but against the Metropolitan Police.[18]

At the time, the video served its purpose. Utilizing the manipulated images as justification, the military officers who had already declared rebellion, together with opposition leaders, stormed Miraflores and attempted to force President Chávez's resignation.

The discussion about the Avenue Baralt and Puente Llaguno violence in a cable on April 11 sent by Ambassador Shapiro to Washington is completely censored. But the cable did remark that:

"On the morning of April 11th, the opposition's Coordinating Committee for Democracy and Liberty decided to go for broke—to seek the immediate departure of President Chávez by popular acclamation . . . The following opposition rally held in front of PDVSA headquarters in Chacao was an overwhelming success. . ."[19]

Apparently, Shapiro considered it an "overwhelming success" that the coup was occurring as planned and the opposition was actually accomplishing its objective.

Meanwhile, President Chávez, refusing to resign, was detained and imprisoned in Fort Tiuna. The palace was taken over by opposition leaders and the State-owned television

18. See *Panorama*, August 31, 2003.
19. Cable from the U.S. Embassy in Caracas to the Secretary of State, Washington, D.C., April 11, 2002, 0120341Z. Available through the author. See Appendix, p. 213.

channel 8, which had broadcast a substantially different account of events than the private media, was shut down by force. Pedro Carmona, the Fedecámaras Chief, was named by an unknown party as "interim president" later that day and to the understanding of most, a transition team was to be named to govern through the following weeks.

Wasting no time at all, the PDVSA Board and Managers were reinstated to their positions.

"No More Oil for Cuba"

One of Ambassador Shapiro's first cables up to Washington after the intense events of the day began: "Televised scenes of joy have marked the return of Petroleos de Venezuela (PDVSA) employees to their La Campiña headquarters building . . . PDVSA executives underline that the company should return to normal operations by early next week. Shipments are expected to resume today. PDVSA spokesperson stated publicly that no oil will be sent to Cuba . . ."[20] Evidently, the least of the U.S. Government's concerns was the harsh disruption of constitutional order instigated by a coup d'état led by its benefactors. The primary preoccupation of the U.S. Government appeared to be its guaranteed oil flow. As one of the top five exporters of oil in the world, Venezuela is also the closest major oil supplier to the United States. Venezuela also owns eight oil refineries in the U.S. and the Citgo gas chain, which has franchises across the country.

The U.S. was also rather concerned about the flow of oil to Cuba. Under the Chávez's Administration, Cuba and Venezuela shared an amicable trade relationship. Venezuela provided oil to Cuba at specific tariffs and Cuba provided medical doctors, sports trainers and other expert services at special rates. The U.S. Embassy cable referencing the cut off of oil supply to Cuba is heavily censored under the heading "Cuba Connection to End?" The only piece left uncensored was a quote from reinstated PDVSA

20. Cable from the U.S. Embassy in Caracas to the Department of State, Washington, D.C., April 11-12, 2002. See http://www.venezuelafoia.info. See Appendix, p. 217.

worker Edgar Paredes: "We are not going to send even one barrel of oil to Cuba, which drew thunderous applause."

VENEVISIÓN'S CONTRIBUTIONS

Several accounts indicated that in the course of events on April 11, multinational media mogul and close Bush family friend Gustavo Cisneros, hosted Carmona, CTV Head Carlos Ortega and other opposition leaders and media owners at his Venevisión television headquarters for briefings and meetings throughout the day. Also, several phone calls and visits were made between Otto Reich, Elliot Abrams, Ambassador Shapiro and Pedro Carmona, along with other coup participants. All of these contacts were verified later, but excused as merely "normal communications" during a time of heightened risk.

On April 12, Venezuelans awoke to television personality, Napoleón Bravo, host of Venevisión's "24 Horas" morning show declaring: "Good morning, Venezuela. We have a new president." During this extraordinary television moment, the guests thanked the private media channels for their integral role in making the coup happen and explained in detail the plans leading up to the coup.[21] They specifically underlined the key role of the private media in broadcasting the images that would justify the coup. On that same program, in an interview with Rear Admiral Carlos Molina Tamayo and Víctor Manuel García, President of Cifras Encuestadoras CA (CECA), television presenter Napoleón Bravo of Venevisión confessed to having facilitated in his own house the recording of the call to military rebellion by General González González on April 10.

It was later on that same program that Bravo hosted Rear Admiral Carlos Molina Tamayo, Leopoldo López, Víctor Manuel García and other coup participants, giving an in depth account of the coup plotting and plans against Chávez. García revealed that he had headed a civilian commando at Fort Tiuna

---

21. See the documentary footage from the 2003 film The Revolution Will Not Be Televised, which captured this television broadcast where the hosts thank Venevisión, Globovisión and RCTV for the success of the coup.

that was in constant contact with the two military commandos, also on the Fort, led by General Efraín Vásquez Velasco
and General Néstor González González. García spoke of his
constant contacts with Rear Admiral Molina Tamayo and their
close coordination during the opposition march. García's live
commentary, though reckless, made clear that the events the
day before had been meticulously planned.

But the U.S. Government already knew that. Five days
before, the CIA had prepared a brief informing top level government officials about the detailed plans of the coup, the
provocation of violence in the opposition march and the detention of the president. The What, When, Who, Where, and
How that were known and reported on April 6 had come to
fruit, exactly as planned.

THE U.S. SUPPORTS THE COUP

But the U.S. role was not to just sit back and remain dormant
in this conspiracy. Which is why on the morning of April 12,
President Bush's spokesman Ari Fleisher publicly announced
the U.S. Government's support for the "Carmona Administration" and its condemnation of "Ex-President" Chávez for
inciting the violence that forced him to "resign." In fact, the
White House, the State Department and the U.S. Embassy in
Caracas all issued similar statements blaming Chávez for the
massacre and recognizing Carmona as a legitimate leader:

Let me share with you the administration's thoughts
about what's taking place in Venezuela. It remains
a somewhat fluid situation. But yesterday's events in
Venezuela resulted in a change in the government
and the assumption of a transitional authority until
new elections can be held.

The details still are unclear. We know that the action
encouraged by the Chávez government provoked
this crisis. According to the best information available, the Chávez government suppressed peaceful

103

demonstrations. Government supporters, on orders from the Chávez government, fired on unarmed, peaceful protestors, resulting in 10 killed and 100 wounded. The Venezuelan military and the police refused to fire on the peaceful demonstrators and refused to support the government's role in such human rights violations. The government also tried to prevent independent news media from reporting on these events.

The results of these events are now that President Chávez has resigned the presidency. Before resigning, he dismissed the vice president and the cabinet, and a transitional civilian government has been installed. This government has promised early elections.

The United States will continue to monitor events. That is what took place, and the Venezuelan people expressed their right to peaceful protest. It was a very large protest that turned out. And the protest was met with violence.[22]

The U.S. role also seemed to be convincing the world that Chávez was the instigator of the violence that had occurred, therefore justifying his overthrow. In fact, according to the White House and the State Department, there was no ouster, Chávez had resigned, and he had even dismissed his entire cabinet beforehand. Considering the CIA had reported to the State Department, the National Security Agency and other top level officials in Washington, that a detailed coup plan existed at least five days prior, the U.S. reaction on April 12 rings of conspiracy. The White House knew the opposition and dissident military officers were planning to overthrow Chávez by exploiting violence in an opposition march and arresting the president. The fact that the coup events played out almost identical to the plan shows the U.S. had premeditated its response in order to legitimize the coup government.

22. See http://www.whitehouse.gov/news/releases/2002/04/20020412-1.html.

The U.S. was also in charge of pressuring other nations in the region to recognize the Carmona's Government as legitimate. The U.S., backed by Colombia and El Salvador, attempted to convince other nations gathered at a Rio Summit to issue a statement recognizing Carmona as Venezuela's new President. Not only did other nations in the region refuse to succumb to U.S. pressure, they decided to issue a statement condemning the illegal ouster of President Chávez, "Venezuela's constitutional and legitimate president" and rejecting the Carmona's Government as "a disruption in Constitutional order." The Organization of American Status followed suit.[23]

The U.S. was one of the only countries in the world to rush to judgment on the muddled events of April 11 and to openly laud and recognize Pedro Carmona as a legitimate president. Considering that officials of the U.S. Government had been prepping Mr. Carmona for this moment for months explained the immediate level of confidence they had in him. Also, the fact that they had advance knowledge of the coup plans further explained their preparedness.

CARMONA THE BRIEF

Soon after, Pedro Carmona, the Fedecámaras Chief, was sworn in as "interim president." To the surprise of many, during a sweeping first act on April 12 in the Salón Ayacucho in Miraflores Palace, he issued a decree dissolving all of Venezuela's democratic institutions, including the National Assembly, the Supreme Court, the Public Defender's Office, the Attorney General, the Constitution and the 49 laws Chávez had decreed in December. Carmona also reverted the name of

23. On November 23, 2004, Spain's Foreign Minister, Miguel Ángel Moratinos, declared that the previous Spanish Ambassador in Venezuela received instructions from his Foreign Minister to support the coup against President Chávez. Just a few days later, Mexico's ex-Foreign Minister, Jorge Castañeda, accused the ex-Presidents of El Salvador and Colombia of backing the coup against Chávez. Castañeda affirmed that in the Rio Summit on April 12, 2002, Spain and the U.S. tried to convince the other nations to back the Carmona's Government. When that proposal was rejected, El Salvador and Colombia spearheaded another.

the country from the Bolivarian Republic of Venezuela back to the Republic of Venezuela.

The reading of the "Carmona Decree," which instituted those undemocratic changes, as the text was later referred to, was broadcast by the private media and endorsed by more than 395 Venezuelans present in the palace. In the meantime, pro-Chávez legislators, such as Tarek William Saab, and other supporters, were brutally attacked and detained by the Caracas police force, under the control of opposition leader and mayor Alfredo Peña. An April 13 cable from Shapiro to Washington confirmed: "To date, several members of Chávez's MVR party have been detained by police forces. These include MVR Deputy William Tarek Saab and former Interior Minister Rodríguez Chacín. We have also heard reports that Táchira Governnor Ronald Blanco La Cruz and Mérida Governor Florencio Porras, both of MVR, were being held. We do not know what charges, if any, have been filed against them."[24]

Yet despite the U.S. Government's clear knowledge that former Chávez Government officials, Governors and Congress members were being politically persecuted, no statement was issued to condemn such human rights violations or call for the immediate release of those detained. Instead, the State Department and White House publicly lauded Carmona.

NEW YORK POLICE DEPARTMENT CONNECTION?

More than 60 Venezuelans were killed in the violence that ensued after the coup, primarily at the hands of the Metropolitan Police. The IRI had worked closely with Peña during 2001 to "shape his image" and the NED-funded Liderazgo y Visión organization had received a $42,207 grant to work with the Caracas Metropolitan Police, several members of which were later charged with the homicides of pro-Chávez supporters killed during the events of April 11, 2002.[25]

24. See Appendix, p. 222.
25. See http://www.venezuelafoia.info.

106

In 2000, Peña entered into a contract with ex-New York Police Department (NYPD) Chief William Bratton, who was brought to Venezuela by the NED-funded opposition group, CEDICE, to train and improve the capacity and quality of the Metropolitan Police. Bratton, known for cleaning up New York City during the years Rudolph Giuliani was mayor, was the creator of the "quality of life crime." Bratton's success in New York was due in large part to his harsh treatment of the Big Apple's immense homeless population and street culture. Under Bratton's direction, the NYPD became notorious for human rights violations and multiple brutal killings of innocent victims. Bratton's contract was renewed by Peña at the end of 2000.

A Surprising Change of Events

The events of the following 48-hours drastically altered the old-school coup plan that had at first appeared successful. Millions of Chávez supporters filled the streets on April 13 demanding his return to office. At the same time, President Chávez was being held captive in La Orchila, where allegedly a plane was set to take him outside of the nation. The Presidential Guard, along with other factions of the military that had remained loyal to Chávez, swiftly forced Carmona and his advisors into detention and returned the palace grounds to the Chávez cabinet members, who then initiated the rescue of the constitutional President, Hugo Chávez.

There are many different versions of the events that occurred on April 11-14. According to a CIA Spot Commentary issued at 2:00 A.M. on April 14, 2002:

> Escalating public protests and signs that his military support was flagging prompted interim President Pedro Carmona to resign late Saturday night . . . Carmona's support unraveled quickly yesterday as political parties, labor unions and the military sensed he was moving too quickly and without their consultation. Disbanding Congress and scrapping the

constitution left Carmona operating without a legal framework and ruling by decree—a move condemned by many regional leaders and the international community.

That is, except the United States, which had hastily expressed its approval of the Carmona regime, despite its blatant illegality.

Shapiro's cables to Washington also confirmed the disagreement within the opposition as to how the coup government should function. The Embassy Political Office (POLOFF) stated:

> POLOFF has received several phone calls from party members who are concerned about the new government's course of action, especially the dissolution of Congress. They resent not being included in the new government, and fear that the Carmona government is proceeding undemocratically. Although many party representatives were involved in the decision to name Carmona interim president, the party representatives who are now expressing concern say that the party leaders themselves were not consulted.[26]

The concern within the opposition parties and the U.S. Government was not about the disruption in constitutional order that had just occurred—the ouster of a democratically elected president via force. The opposition political parties were resentful that they were not playing a bigger role in the coup government. The concern over the dissolution of Congress was not because it represented a highly undemocratic act, but rather because many of their own Congressional Representatives had been deposed by the measure. So Carmona's actions in many ways provoked his own failure—not because

---

26. An urgent cable from the U.S. Embassy in Caracas to the Secretary of State, Washington, D.C., April 13, 2002, 0131803Z. Available through the author. See Appendix, p. 223.

of their undemocratic nature, but rather because of his self-ishness.

"Was the U.S. Involved in the Effort to Remove Venezuelan President Chávez from Power? Absolutely Not"

Ambassador Shapiro visited Carmona several times during the course of the coup. He claimed that his visits to Carmona on April 12 were intended to persuade him to reactivate the Congress and other institutions he had dissolved. But Shapiro's responses to questions about his relations with opposition leaders and coup participants were highly crafted and thought out.

Not by him of course.

Shapiro received a cable from the Department of State in Washington on April 16, 2002, containing *Western Hemisphere Affairs Press Guidance* drafted by a L.S. Hamilton in the State Department and approved by Richard Boucher, State Department spokesman.

When asked the question: "Did U.S. Officials meet with Venezuelan opposition officials prior to the April 11 removal of President Chávez from power?" The answer to memorize was: U.S. Officials have met with a broad spectrum of Venezuelans over the past several months both in Caracas and in Washington. U.S. Officials met with business community representatives, labor union officials, catholic church leaders, opposition political leaders and a wide array of Venezuelan Government officials.[27]

Referring to questions on meetings with Carmona, the *Press Guidance* then stated: "If Asked," which meant, don't offer any information if not asked. The extended response was:

In the course of normal diplomatic contacts, U.S. officials met with Pedro Carmona, the President of the Venezuelan Federation of Chambers of Commerce (FEDECÁMARAS). Our message to all Venezuelan

27 See Appendix, p. 230.

contacts has been consistent. The political situation in Venezuela is one for Venezuelans to resolve peacefully, democratically and constitutionally. We explicitly told all of our Venezuelan interlocutors on numerous occasions and at many levels that under no circumstances would the United States support any unconstitutional, undemocratic effort, such as a coup, to remove President Chávez from power.[28]

So one message saying "no coups" was being relayed "explicitly" while the U.S. Government at the same time was funneling a couple million dollars into the pockets of the coup plotters and meeting with them on a regular basis to discuss their plans.

It was no surprise that the response to the question: "Was the United States involved in the effort to remove Venezuelan President Chávez from power?" was "ABSOLUTELY NOT."

MEDIA BLACKOUT

Chavez's return to power in the early morning hours of April 14 came too late to stop the headlines and editorials in the *The New York Times, Chicago Tribune* and other international press which all praised the Venezuelan president's undemocratic ouster in the same tone as the Bush's Administration.[29] The Venezuelan papers had become remarkably silent, though some car-

---

28. See Appendix, p. 230.
29. Fairness in Accuracy and Reporting issued a Media Advisory, "U.S. Papers Hail Venezuelan Coup as Pro-Democracy Move," explaining that papers such as *The New York Times* triumphantly declared that "Chávez's 'resignation' meant that 'Venezuelan democracy is no longer threatened by a would-be dictator.'" *The New York Times* went so far as to blindly write that Chávez "stepped down after the military intervened and handed power to a respected business leader." After Chávez was returned to power on April 13-14, *The New York Times* ran a second editorial on April 18, 2002, seemingly apologizing for their April 13th celebratory tone, which stated: "In his three years in office, Mr. Chávez has been such a divisive and demagogic leader that his forced departure last week drew applause at home and in Washington. That reaction, which we shared, overlooked the undemocratic manner in which he was removed. Forcibly unseating a democratically elected leader, no matter how badly he has performed, is never something to cheer." April 18, 2002.

ried outdated coup praising headlines such as *El Universal's* "A Step in the Right Direction!" After multiple outbursts of joy and elation for Carmona's takeover and Chávez's forceful removal, the media was silent on April 13 and 14, imposing a blackout on information and news about developing events.

Andrés Izarra, former Managing Producer of "El Observador", a news program on the private station RCTV, testified to the Venezuelan National Assembly that he received clear instructions from Marcel Granier, the owner of RCTV on the day of the coup and the following days to air: "No information on Chávez, his followers, his ministers, and all others that could in anyway be related to him." Furthermore, Izarra confirmed that on the day of the coup, RCTV had a report from CNN that Chávez had not resigned, but had been kidnapped and jailed, yet the stationowner refused to report the story.[30] In fact, all the private channels disseminated the news that President Chávez had resigned, despite their knowledge to the contrary.

The very same private stations that had just provided 24-hour coverage to the opposition broadcast Tom and Jerry cartoons with the occasional movies such as Pretty Woman in between as Chávez supporters piled into the streets to demand his return. The media did not cover the popular uprisings all around the country in support of Chávez. The blackout was intentional. The media was in mourning.

MORE MONEY IN THE POT

As calm and normalcy were established in Venezuela in the following days, the U.S. Government was forced to issue a statement minimally recognizing the legitimacy of the Chávez's Government. But, the U.S. has never backtracked on its statement about the version of events that took place on April 11, 2002. It stood by the claim that Chávez ordered the violence

---

30. Naomi Klein, "The Media Against Democracy: Venezuela Highlights the Threat to Freedom from Corporate Control," *The Guardian*, February 18, 2003. See also http:www.asambleanacional.gov.ve.

against "peaceful opposition marchers," despite ample evidence proving otherwise, including declassified U.S. Government documents.

Even on April 17, 2002, when it was clear that the majority of Venezuelans supported President Chávez and that an illegal coup had occurred, the U.S. Government still stuck to its "story." In remarks to the North-South Roundtable at the Carnegie Endowment for International Peace, then Principal Deputy Assistant Secretary for Western Hemisphere Affairs, Lino Gutiérrez, stated:

> We know that supporters of President Chávez fired on anti-government protestors resulting in more than 100 people wounded or killed ... We know that the government prevented five independent television stations from reporting on events . . . President Chávez allegedly resigned the presidency . . . The roots of the present crisis lie, we think, with the polarization that occurred under President Chávez and his confrontational policies. President Chávez has attacked freedom of the press, interfered in labor union elections, criticized the Church, stacked the judiciary and attempted to cow any opposition . . . Let me say now, categorically: the United States did not participate in, inspire, encourage, foment, wink at, nod at, close its eyes to, or in any way leave the impression that it would support a coup of any kind in Venezuela. The record is crystal clear ...

The CIA SEIB reports show not only that the U.S. knew about the detailed plans of the coup, but it also augmented the financing of the opposition—and those specifically involved in coup plotting—in the months and weeks prior. Clearly, such support qualifies as participating in, encouraging, fomenting and closing its eyes to the coup. Furthermore, its subsequent endorsement of the Carmona's Government and its attempts to induce other governments to recognize Carmona as a legitimate leader constitute clear "support" for the coup.

Gutiérrez's statement that "supporters of President Chávez fired on anti-government protestors resulting in more than 100 people wounded or killed" was intentionally inaccurate. It was quite clear during and after the coup that the majority of those killed and injured were in the Chávez camp.

Footage shot by independent journalists in the area at the time clearly got the procession of victims on tape. Most that fell during the violence on April 11 were in the pro-Chávez demonstration. In the days subsequent to the coup, more than 60 Chávez supporters were killed by Metropolitan Police officers during rebellions in the barrios, in protest to Chávez's arrest. Police records, morgue reports and witness testimony affirm this fact.

But no evidence was ever provided to support claims that "supporters of President Chávez fired on anti-government protestors," except a manipulated video image, later discovered to be a complete farce. The tape, filmed and produced by Venevisión, owned by ardent anti-chavista and billionaire Gustavo Cisneros, intentionally cut footage and added a voice-over recorded in the studio, well after the events had occurred. The narrator claimed the Chávez supporters were firing on "peaceful" opposition protestors when in reality, those "Chavistas" who fired guns that day were shooting back at the Metropolitan Police and snipers firing at them.

The Metropolitan Police, under the authority of opposition mayor Alfredo Peña, were major players in the coup. It was later discovered through forensic investigations that snipers had fired from the roofs of building surrounding Puente Llaguno and the presidential palace.

The U.S. Government was forced at this point to admit that Chávez was the "legitimate leader" of Venezuela. However, it also warned that the U.S. was "keeping close watch on him." But that did not hinder the continued efforts to oust Chávez through other means.

In April 2002, shortly after the failed coup, the U.S. Department of State issued a grant of $1 million in "Special Venezuela Funds" to the NED.

If the NED really was set up to foster democracy, it seems odd that they would receive these extra funds for Venezuelan opposition groups. At this moment in time, Venezuelans have just shown they are masters of democracy—they reversed a coup. That is an Olympian feat in the annals of democracy. But instead of recognizing Venezuela's tremendous advances in democracy and ceasing the U.S.-imposed "promotion of democracy," the U.S. Government augmented its presence in Venezuela.

The fact that the NED gets sizable new funding at this juncture clearly shows its real objectives don't match the spin. Moreover, NED's choice of benefactors of the extra funds clearly evidenced its disinterest in promoting democracy.

The NED proceeded to distribute these extra funds to the very same groups that had just played key roles in the coup against President Chávez. Asamblea de Educación, whose President Leonardo Carvajal had been named Education Minister by Carmona, was given a new grant of $57,000. Fundación Momento de la Gente, whose Director Mercedes de Freitas had tried her best to explain to the NED that a coup never took place by claiming that Carmona was a "legitimate leader placed by civil society" was awarded $64,000. Asociación Civil Liderazgo y Visión, a group dedicated to promoting alternative models to the Chávez's Government and providing leadership trainings, at the time directed by Oscar García Mendoza, who not only published two congratulatory declarations to the Carmona's Government in the national newspapers on April 12, but also signed a civil society decree recognizing the legitimacy of Carmona as president, received $42,207.

CEDICE, through NED core grantee CIPE, was awarded $116,525, despite the fact that its Director, Rocío Guijarro, was one of the first signers and endorsers of the "ill-fated" Carmona Decree. And the International Republican Institute, which had issued a laudatory statement in favor of the coup and Carmona's takeover on April 12, was given $116,000 to continue its work with Primero Justicia, despite the fact that several of the parties' leaders had signed the Carmona Decree and one, Leopoldo Martínez, had even been named Minister of Finances under Carmona. The ACILS was given an additional $116,525 to finance the CTV, despite the union's visible participation in the coup.

The NED's bias against Chávez was quite clear. In a June 2002 memorandum written by Christopher Sabatini, program Director for NED in Latin America, he stated:

> Chávez has done little to demonstrate his good faith or desire for a mediated solution and has continued to infame popular passions and class tensions . . . There are rumors . . . that the government has distributed Uzis to the Bolivarian circles . . . most people I spoke to recognize that the government is anti-democratic and is driving the country to ruin through a misguided revolutionary plan and sheer incompetence. . .

Sabatini also admitted the groups financed by NED were in the opposition camp: "My general impression is that the NED's program is working with some of the most serious civic groups in the country . . . many of them have very clear oppositionist positions toward Chávez. . ."[31]

The failure of the coup resonated uncomfortably with the U.S. Government. The $1 million special grant from the State Department for NED projects in Venezuela clearly was not going to cover future efforts at regime change in Venezuela. A new strategy was necessary that could adapt to the peculiar circumstances in that South American nation. Therefore, just a few months after the coup, the State Department ordered the placement of a USAID Office of Transition Initiatives (OTI) in Venezuela.

31. See Appendix, pp. 195-197.

CHAPTER SEVEN

An Office for a Transitional Government

"We don't need an Office for Transition Initiatives because this is not a government in transition," stated Tarek William Saab, then National Assembly member from the MVR party regarding the news that an Office for Transition Initiatives was being established in the U.S. Embassy in Caracas, July 2002.

The concept of the OTI was established by USAID in 1994 "to respond to countries experiencing a significant and sometimes rapid political transition, which may or may not be accompanied by a social and/or economic crisis." The OTI "assesses, designs and implements programs that have characteristics of being fast, flexible, innovative, tangible, targeted, catalytic and overtly political, focusing on the root causes of the crisis."[1] According to USAID annual reports, OTIs have been used previously in Kosovo, Haiti, Indonesia, Peru, Guatemala, the Philippines and Colombia, amongst other nations.

In Bolivia, the OTI was set up to "support Bolivia's fragile democracy" and to "promote a peaceful and informed dialogue between the government and the people." In Haiti, the OTI was set up in February 2004, "in response to the political turmoil resulting in, and from, the resignation of President Jean-Bertrand Aristide."

1. Taken from USAID's own background description of its OTI in a contract between USAID and Development Alternatives, Inc. for $10 million for projects in Venezuela during August 2002-August 2004. See http://www.venezuelafoia.info. See also http://www.usaid.gov/our-work/cross-cutting-programs/transition-initiatives.

While these efforts may appear noble at first sight, in the case of Haiti, it was widely known and accepted that Aristide did not "resign," but rather a coup d'état took place, supported and facilitated by the U.S. Government. The fact that OTI would come to the rescue right afterward based on claims that Aristide's "resignation" had sparked a political crisis clearly evidences bias. If the OTI were truly dedicated to promoting democracy, it would have aided Aristide's return to his constitutional position, instead of facilitating the "transition" to an unelected, coup government.[2]

USAID generally engages its OTI to establish on the ground relationships with political organizations, media and NGOs and to provide necessary funding and training to obtain desired results. As a rapid response operation, OTI falls under the special authorities of the International Disaster Assistance account funding. "Time is always of the essence" in an OTI operation and its general timeframe is two years. Venezuela was no different. Ronald Ulrich, Head of the OTI in Venezuela at its commencement afirmed publicly: "This program will be finished in two years, as has happened with similar initiatives in other countries, the office will close in the time period stated."[3]

According to OTI's calculations, its closing date was August 2004, two years after its official inauguration. Despite President Chávez's transparent electoral victories on August 15, 2004 in a recall referendum on his mandate and again on October 31, 2004 when his party, MVR, won 21 out of 23 governorships in regional elections and the majority of mayoral offices throughout the nation, confirming democratic stability in the nation, the OTI in Venezuela has extended its stay indefinitely.

The OTI's continued presence in Venezuela was not made public. In fact, OTI and USAID's operations in Venezuela have

2. See http://www.africaspeaks.com/haiti2004/.
3. Karenina Velandia Rosales, "EE.UU. invertirá 7 millones en programas para fortalecer la democracia en Venezuela," *El Nacional,* March 2, 2003. See http://impresodigital.elnacional.com/archivo/result.asp?file=e%3A%5C-www%5Celnacional%5Chome%5Carchivo%5C2003%5CO3%5C02%5Cnl-2n2.htm&rest.

been relatively secretive. Venezuela is the only country program on the OTI website that has no links or information about its objectives, activities or projects at all. The extension of OTI in Venezuela was revealed on OTI's budget for 2005, which had an authorized $5 million for Venezuela. When the U.S. Government sees a need to spend millions in taxpayer dollars to fund a "transition office" in a country that has overseen nine electoral processes in the past five years that have all ratified the authority of its current government, it could be read as an ominous signal that more U.S.-backed efforts to topple the government are in the works.

Ambassador Charles Shapiro wrote a press bulletin explaining the OTI's purpose back in 2002. He brushed off the meaning of the name "Office for Transition Initiatives" and wrote:

> I know, I know—the name of this office has created a controversy . . . I could explain that we never had the intention of using this name formally in Venezuela, knowing full well that the word "transition" could result in misunderstandings . . . Some will believe me, others won't . . . So I make just one request: forget about the bureaucratic name used in Washington, and in its place, concentrate on what our efforts represent.[4]

So here was Ambassador Shapiro appealing to Venezuelans to ignore the fact that the U.S. had just set up a transition operation in their nation, like the kind reserved for nations in crisis, such as the former Yugoslavia, the Congo and East Timor, and instead, to accept the "intentions" of the office with open arms.

What exactly were those intentions? A document establishing OTI's operations in Venezuela clearly outlines the feelings of those impelling its creation:

4. Charles S. Shapiro, "La Oficina," *Press Briefing of the U.S. Embassy in Caracas Informative and Cultural Office*, 2002.

In recent months, his popularity has waned and political tensions have risen dramatically as President Chávez has implemented several controversial reforms. The tensions came to a head in April when protesters were shot outside the presidential palace . . . The current situation augers strongly for rapid U.S. government engagement.[5]

Note that the word "coup" is not mentioned. And according to this statement, which is consistent with all others made by the U.S. Government, the coup and resulting violence were all Chávez's fault. But more revealing is the blatant remark that Venezuela is in need of "rapid U.S. government engagement." There is no other term for that than "intervention."

"These programs exist where there are conflicts, like in Burundi and the Congo," affirmed Ronald Ulrich and Jack McCarthy, Representatives of the OTI program in Venezuela.[6]

Apparently the Program Directors didn't have any problem with exposing the true intentions or origins of the office.

Since a real crisis didn't exist in Venezuela that rose to the level of the horrors occurring in the Congo where thousands were being massacred, the U.S. Government had to aide in its creation.

By now, entire opposition organizations and leaders were living off the millions the U.S. was pouring in to "promote democracy" and the only assurance that these funds would keep rolling in was to agitate the conflict and ensure an ongoing crisis. U.S. interests believed this ongoing conflict and "crisis situation" would chip away at the Chávez Government's credibility and support and eventually result in the president's ouster.

The OTI was a way to penetrate civil society even further than the NED was capable of with a budget five times as high.[7] Its arrival in June 2002—post-coup—was no coincidence. The OTI had been originally programmed for Venezuela

5. Contract between USAID and Development Alternatives, Inc. Obtained under FOIA. Available through the author.
6. See note 3 of this Chapter.
7. See table of U.S. funding in Venezuela, p. 83.

in March 2002, but the coup prospects put its establishment on hold. If the coup had succeeded, the OTI would have been unnecessary, as its ultimate goal had always been to facilitate the removal of President Chávez from office.

But Shapiro's plea seemed to find resonance in the majority of Venezuelans and the government, including President Chávez, who accepted the OTI and its proposal at face value.

DEVELOPMENT ALTERNATIVES, INC.

The OTI set up shop in the U.S. Embassy in Caracas in June 2002. The program was closely coordinated with the U.S. Embassy and in fact, the OTI program Director fell under the authority and supervision of the U.S. Ambassador. With $7 million dollars allotted for the 2-year project, during it's first six months the OTI's was given a budget of $2,197,066 —more than double that of the NED's and for just half a year. Soon after its founding in Venezuela, the OTI awarded Development Alternatives, Inc., a private U.S. consulting company, with a $10,061,062 contract to establish and monitor a $7 million grant fund and program in "direct response to increasing political polarization in Venezuela."

OTIs often use contractors to provide additional support and administration of funds. As a protective measure, the contractor sets up a parallel office, hires staff, establishes communications systems and selects and monitors grantees. According to USAID, contractors are "critical to the success of OTI programs because they are expected to overcome the significant challenges posed by 'war torn' or otherwise unstable countries in which OTI operates."[8]

WAS VENEZUELA A "WAR TORN" NATION OR "OTHERWISE UNSTABLE"?

Despite the contractor's separate status from the OTI, all of its operations and employees fall under the authority of the OTI

8. See note 5 of this Chapter.

field officer and the U.S. Ambassador. According to the contract, "the field representative will maintain close collaboration with other Embassy offices in identifying opportunities, selecting partners and ensuring the program remains consistent with U.S. foreign policy." In other words, the U.S. Embassy was intimately involved in the decision-making process and operations of the OTI and its private contractor.

Development Alternatives, Inc. (DAI) quickly moved to establish its office in the swanky El Rosal sector of Caracas, right down the road from the International Republican Institute's Venezuela headquarters. DAI also promptly complied with its contractual obligations and announced the creation of the Venezuela: Iniciativa para la Construcción de Confianza (Venezuela: Construction of Confidence Initiative) (VICC). DAI claimed its purpose, along with the OTI, was to step in "to assist Venezuelans in fostering political conditions that would preclude violent conflict and systemic breakdown."[9]

But OTI, USAID's and DAI's operations were highly secretive. Though word of the OTI had resonated in the political sphere in Venezuela when it was first established, no one had ever heard of DAI before. For that matter, the Venezuelan Government was also completely unaware that NED and USAID were financing political activities in the country. This is an astonishing fact considering that USAID has invested more than $20 million in Venezuela since mid-2002, and NED has given out more than $4 million—exclusively to opposition groups—since 2001.[10]

The relationship between USAID and DAI was peculiar. At the time the contract was made between the two organizations, USAID had already designated all the top-level program directors and officers DAI was to employ in Venezuela. DAI was subject to the determinations made by USAID and therefore the choice of employees was non-negotiable. Other lower levels employees who were to be hired by DAI before project

9. Joel M. Jutkowitz, "Building Confidence out of Discord in Venezuela," *DAI News*. See http://www.dai.com/dai_news/text_only_fall_confidence_in_venezuela_text_only.html.
10. See table, p. 83.

commencement had to first be approved by the OTI field officer at the U.S. Embassy in Venezuela. USAID has an inordinate amount of control over its private contractor.

The designated employees were listed by first initial and last name only in the contract:

J. McCarthy: Chief of Party
H. Méndez: Program Development Officer
L. Blank: Program Development Officer
G. Díaz: Program Development Officer
G. Fung: Financial Management Specialist
J. Jutkowitz: Local Program Manager

The assignment and selection of these individuals by a government agency for employment with a private contractor was quite unusual. Obviously, they had to be highly trained and knowledgeable of Venezuela's political situation and the U.S. foreign policy objectives in the region. Most likely, the individuals chosen were former or current USAID or U.S. Government employees specializing in this type of operation.

From the requirements listed in the forty-page contract with DAI, it was clear that USAID had an intrinsic interest in protecting its OTI employees and its private contractor, as well as its assets in the country. The contract obligated DAI to lease offices and residences for employees that met OTI standards: "the required setback from public thoroughfares; rebar grates on first floor windows, and a fenced perimeter or compound and secure parking with flood lighting for vehicles." Before leasing offices or residences and purchasing security equipment, DAI was obligated to consult with the OTI officer and seek inspection and documented prior approval. Furthermore, DAI was required to supply its employees with global positioning systems (GPS) technology and other high tech security equipment as instructed by OTI. Such requirements seem a bit extensive and unusual for a private contractor charged with dispensing grants to local groups working to "promote democracy and support dialogue."

But if the OTI's requirements revealed a heightened security interest in its operations with DAI, the actual grant-making procedures seem oddly easygoing and unrestricted. "For those who request our help, it is only necessary to bring a proposal that meets one of the two objectives of the program . . . the requirements are not high . . . Two pages are sufficient to specify the details and identification of the organization soliciting the funding, along with its mission, objectives and methodology of the proposal. . . ," confirmed Ronald Ulrich, OTI program manager, in statements made to the Venezuelan press.

A two-page proposal that included the organization's information was sufficient to receive up to $100,000 of U.S. taxpayer money? Such low standards are unheard of amongst expert grant writers in the United States. Moreover, the USAID-DAI contract required "immediate availability of liquid funds" since local grants would need to be issued "on an urgent basis."

It is hard to understand how a forum entitled Electoral Solutions to the Political Crisis in Venezuela at the ritzy Hotel J. W. Marriot in Caracas, attended by Venezuela's wealthiest and most influential members of the business community, and not a Chávez supporter in sight, was an "urgent" matter in need of immediate funding from the United States. Particularly considering that at that time, Venezuela's next constitutionally permitted elections were not for another four years.

USAID operations in general are highly secretive. No DAI or USAID Representatives or workers would respond to any questions about work in Venezuela. The USAID website does not mention its program in Venezuela though it contains information about its work in all other nations around the world. Venezuela is conspicuously left off the list, despite evidence proving USAID does maintain programs in Venezuela. The OTI website hides its work in Venezuela. A search has to be run for "Venezuela" on the site and little information is produced. There is no link to a program description of OTI's operations in Venezuela, though all 28 other OTI offices worldwide have links and program information on the website.[11]

11. See http://www.usaid.gov/our_work/cross-cutting_programs/Transition_initiatives/country/indet.html.

On the OTI website, the Venezuela program "exit" date has been changed from August 2004 to TBD (To Be Determined). Other OTI programs with a TBD end date include Sudan, Afghanistan, Iraq, Haiti and Bolivia—all nations with a heavy U.S. presence, and, with the exception of Bolivia, severe war-induced crises.

In August 2004, a reporter visited the DAI office in Caracas to inquire about grant programs in Venezuela. A DAI Representative told the reporter: "I can't give you any information on that. Because of our work with Súmate, we have to be careful."

The DAI had good reason to be careful. The NED-financed Súmate, led by Carmona coup-decree signor María Corina Machado, was also involved in creating fraudulent exit polls, amongst other violations of Venezuelan law, a point covered in detail in chapter Nine.

CHAPTER EIGHT

Paro Petrolero: An Oil Industry Sabotage

MILLION OF DOLLARS RESULT IN BILLIONS IN LOSSES

After the launch of its Venezuela: Construction of Confidence Initiative program, DAI chose to fund many of those very same groups that had openly participated in and even led the coup against President Chávez just a few months prior. One of the first few grants DAI distributed in Venezuela, under its VICC program, was for the purpose of "promoting social dialogue and citizen formation" using mass media. The project involved the creation of television and radio commercials to promote "democratic and modern values, rupturing with the patterns of paternalism and populism."[1] The project assured the collaboration of Fedecámaras President Carlos Fernández.

After the failed April coup, Carmona had escaped from his home arrest and fled the country, seeking and obtaining political asylum in neighboring Colombia. The Colombian Government had been quick to endorse Carmona as "interim president" during the coup. According to a heavily censored cable on April 12, 2002, from U.S. Ambassador to Colombia, Ann Patterson, Colombia's Foreign Minister at the time, Clemencia Forero (sic) "spoke warmly about Venezuelan interim President Pedro Carmona. Forero said she has known Carmona for many years, that Carmona is well known to the

---

1. DAI grant, G-3822-101-008. See http://www.venezuelafoia.info. Please note that USAID and DAI deleted the names of all recipients of the Venezuela project funds. Their stated reason was "fear of persecution" from the Venezuelan Government of the groups they were financing.

Colombian business community, is committed to regional integration, and is a great friend of Colombia."[2]

A few days later, after the coup crumbled, Foreign Minister Forero denied she had ever expressed public support for Carmona. But when Carmona came running for asylum in May 2002, Colombia received him with open arms. From Colombia, he was able to make frequent trips to Washington and Miami, until the U.S. could no longer defend itself against the protests from the Venezuelan Government and the media, and his visa was revoked in August of that year. From Bogotá, Carmona was still closely working with Fedecámaras and the opposition. Note the irony: the U.S. had previously prevented Chávez from entering the country when he was a candidate due to his involvement in the 1992 rebellion against Carlos Andrés Pérez. Yet its open door policy to Carmona made clear that its stand against Chávez was not a principled one against coups; in the U.S.'s eyes, Chávez had attempted the wrong kind of rebellion while Carmona's attempt was just fine.

In Venezuela, Carlos Fernández was left holding the reigns of the nation's most powerful business association, and he continued Carmona's efforts to seek premature removal of President Chávez from office.

Media War against the People

The particular timing of the DAI-USAID project focused on radio and television commercials was key. On December 2, 2002, Fedecámaras, the CTV and the opposition parties, now known as the Coordinadora Democrática (Democratic Coordinator) (CD) launched a national "general strike" intended to destabilize Venezuela's economy and force President Chávez to resign. In support of the opposition's objectives, the private media symbolically joined the strike by suspending all regular programming and commercials and donating one hundred percent of air space to the opposition.

2. See Appendix, p. 219.

Though the strike was not supported by the majority of Venezuelans, many were forced to stay home because business owners and "bosses" closed shops and companies, inhibiting workers from fulfilling their duties. For 64-days, many Venezuelans suffered from the effects of the forced "bosses" strike, particularly because of the high-level oil industry managers and employees that halted oil production to dangerously low levels, forcing an oil and gas drought that made transportation to anywhere nearly impossible.

The private media channels donated all air time to strike coverage and promotion, practically forcing Venezuelans to listen to negative, anti-Chávez messages all day long.

The Coordinadora Democrática, with the help of Venezuela's top public relations firms and USAID, produced some of the most highly crafted anti-Chávez commercials Venezuelans had ever seen. These commercials, broadcast often ten at a time in between coverage of opposition marches, speeches and interviews, contained varying messages on Chávez's failures, alleged human rights abuses and on the overall political crisis and poor state of the nation. Some of the commercials exploited images of children singing and stamping red colored handprints, symbolizing blood, on walls, with messages about the "future of the nation," the "safety of children" and the "need for a new Venezuela."

The following is a transcription of a television advertisement played on a Venezuelan private media channel during the December 2002 strike. The commercial that follows was interspersed amongst 10 back-to-back similar propagandas. The ads were played during breaks from 24-hour news coverage of opposition marches, speeches and interviews. During the 64-day stoppage, approximately 700 similar, yet varied, ads were broadcast daily.[3]

Advertisement: A big "NO" appears in red letters. Smaller letters state: "Don't be deceived" and a male

3. I provide my own testimony here, and the transcription is taken from my own footage of the private television channels in Venezuela during December 2002-January 2003, as I was witness to this historical and reprehensible period.

voice narrates the same. The same voice continues, as the written words appear: "In this country, our country, there is only one person responsible for so much abuse, impunity, anarchy and lack of governance." [A fast paced music builds in the background]; a women's voice narrates, as the written words appear over an image of thousands of opposition marchers in the streets, "Venezuela, don't be deceived." Return to male narrator, "The only one responsible for the violation of the Constitution" [words pasted over scenes of national guard repression and violence]; return to female voice, "of financing the circles of terror created in the shadow of his government" [scenes of violence amongst people in the streets, tear gas in the air, people running, members of Bolivarian Circles speaking and gesturing]; male narrator, "to give away our petroleum" [image of PDVSA, the State-owned oil company], woman's voice, "of the taking of our Marine Merchants by mercenaries" [scenes of armed individuals mounting oil tankers]; male voice, "of the torture of PDVSA" [image of violence in the streets, tear gas, people screaming, running]; cut to woman's voice, "for politicizing our Armed Forces" [image of Armed Forces in the streets, violence]; cut to male voice, "disrespecting our institutions" [image of Armed Forces firing tear gas on civilians, chaos in the streets]; cut to woman's voice, "for the stoppage in the nation" [scene of marches in the streets, armed with sticks and rocks, yelling, fighting one another]; cut to male voice, "for the division of Venezuela" [violent street protestors yelling, fighting]; cut to female voice, "for the hate amongst brothers" [continue fighting in the streets, violence chaos]; cut to male voice, "Venezuela, don't be deceived" [image of a giant Venezuelan flag held by opposition marchers]; cut to female voice, "in this country, our country, there is only one person responsible for so much

128

horror" [image of opposition marchers in the background yelling and signaling "get out"]; male voice "for so much sadness" [image of Venezuelans carrying a coffin through a crowd]; female voice "for so much terror" [image of individual captured for firing at opposition protestors, bloodied and half naked, carried by police]; male voice, "for so much violence" [image in background of man with a stick, swinging it violently in the street]; female voice, "for so much intransigence" [scene of armed guards and police in the streets, harassing civilians]; cut to male voice, "for so much insensibility" [same scene of Armed Forces in the streets]; cut to female voice, "you, who have been judged in five elections in two years, what is the fear of being judged again?" [background image of polling machines, voters voting, elections volunteers with ballots]; cut to image of animated map of Venezuela with a big "HERE" written on it; male voice, "Here, there is only one responsible. . .;" cut to yellow screen, the words appear as they are yelled by a chorus of angry people, "Not one step back, OUT, GET OUT NOW." Ends with the Democratic Coordinator logo.[4]

The DAI radio and television commercial project in collaboration with Carlos Fernández began on December 9, 2002, just seven days after the strike and the propaganda war commenced.

Disinformation, flashing negative imagery, fear and stress induction techniques, quasi-hypnotic suggestion, excessive repetition and falsification and forgery are just but a few of the mindshock techniques deliberately being used, not just in overtly political

4. The Democratic Coordinator is the opposition movement umbrella group, representing the various factions and political parties that comprise the Venezuelan opposition.

spots but also in regular programming . . . Numbing repetition, relentless slandering and demonizing of Chávez supporters. Exaggeration, negative spinning and saturation coverage of any minor fact or event that can remotely make the Chávez government look bad. Loud, rapid-fire, invariably negative interviews. Excessive use of panic-inducing words ("Castro-Communism" is a favorite of Venevisión, along with "mobs," routinely used to describe Chávez supporters). Deliberate use of loaded terms like "crimes against humanity" or "genocide" in the wrong contexts, to describe current events in Venezuela. Exploitation of children in interviews to stir up anti-Chávez sentiment . . . Venezuelans are being subject to a massive Chávez-aversion therapy program, 24 hours a day, seven days a week, month after month, *ad nauseam*. People wake up and go to sleep with it. . .[5]

In Nicaragua and Chile, the U.S. had to buy the press. *El Mercurio* in Chile and *La Prensa* in Nicaragua were heavily funded and controlled by the CIA. But in Venezuela, the U.S. lucked out. With little investment and encouragement from the U.S. Government, Venezuelan media owners voluntarily jumped aboard the anti-Chávez bandwagon.

The mere existence of these commercials is telling. A truly popular uprising, such as that which toppled Ferdinand Marcos in the Philippines, doesn't generally have the resources to buy air time on TV and radio. Such massive commercial campaigns cost money and resources, suggesting that their agenda serves those who financed them. In Venezuela's case, the donation of air time by those controlling media meant that the media owners were, along with the creators of the commercials, essentially financing—and intending to benefit from—these efforts.

5. Carlos Rensseler, "Venezuela's Media Mindshock," December 20, 2002. See http://www.thegully.com/essays/venezuela/021220-media-mindshock.html. Carlos Rensseler is the pseudonym of a Maracaibo businessman whose family immigrated to Venezuela when he was a child. He prefers not to use his real name to protect himself and his family.

In Venezuela, five major private television networks control at least 90% of the market and smaller private stations control another 5%. This 95% of the broadcast market began to express its opposition to President Chávez's Administration as early as 1999, soon after Chávez began his first term in office. After President Chávez came to power in 1998, the five main privately owned television channels—Venevisión, Radio Caracas Televisión, Globovisión, Televen and CMT—and nine out of the ten major national newspapers, including *El Universal, El Nacional, El Impulso, El Nuevo País* and *El Mundo,* took over the role of the losing traditional political parties, AD and COPEI. The investigations, interviews, reports and commentaries of these mass media have all pursued the same objective for the past five years: to undermine the legitimacy of the government and to severely damage the president's popular support.[6]

A small group of businessmen own fifteen television stations in Venezuela. Only six of these stations are national, and the rest are local channels. Three of the local stations, Televisora Andina de Mérida, Canal de los Niños Cantores del Zulia and Vale TV belong to the Catholic Church. There is only one public television station with a national broadcasting frequency, Venezolana de Televisión (or Channel 8), another with UHF frequency, VIVE TV, and growing community media stations, such as Catia TVe and Boconó have an extremely limited range.[7] During several decades, commercial television in Venezuela has belonged to an oligopoly of two families, the Cisneros, who own Venevisión, and the Bottome & Granier Group, which owns Radio Caracas Televisión and Radio Caracas Radio. Against the determined opposition of these two families, Televen, Globovisión, CMT and La Tele were

6. President Chávez won the elections in 1998 with more than 57% of the vote, beating out 6 other candidates from the tradicional political parties. See also "How Hate Media Incited the Coup Against the President: Venezuela's Press Power," *Le Monde Diplomatique,* August 2002.
7. Luis Britto García, *Venezuela golpeada. Mediocracia contra democracia* (País Vasco: Editorial Hiro. Colección Sediciones, 2003). See also http:// www.analitica.com/biblioteca/britto/investigación_medios-asp.

able to enter the private media market, although the latter two only have VHF frequency, with limited reach.

This same small group of media owners are not just the proprietors of broadcast circuits but also own advertising and public relations agencies that operate for the benefit of the stations, as well as record labels and other cultural industries that produce material to be promoted, released and broadcast on the stations. Cisneros also owns, in addition to Venevisión, the largest station in Venezuela, over 70 media outlets in 39 countries, including DirecTV Latin America, AOL Latin America, Caracol Television (Colombia), the Univisión Network in the U.S., Galavisión and Playboy Latin America, as well as beverage and food product distribution (Coca Cola bottling, Regional Beer, Pizza Hut in Venezuela, dairy distributors and other local food products) and cultural entities such as Los Leones baseball team of Caracas and the Miss Venezue-la Pageant. These are precisely the types of monopolies that some developed nations seek to prohibit. These media monopolies broadcast to more than four million television screens in Venezuela, reaching millions upon millions of ordinary Venezuelans.[8]

Print media are similarly concentrated in the hands of just a few wealthy families. For example, the six largest dailies are owned by specific family groups. There are two hundred magazines and fifty daily papers circulating in Venezuela. Owners of tabloids are also proprietors of magazines, dailies and public relations agencies.[9] One of the original opposition leaders against President Chávez, Teodoro Petkoff, later founded the daily *Tal Cual*, another print mechanism of opposition propaganda that has played a key role in the media war against Chávez.[10]

With the private media so willingly and adamantly on the side of the opposition, it was no wonder that the strike was able to last 64 days.

8. *Ibid.*
9. *Ibid.*
10. *Ibid.*

Media mogul Cisneros contributed more to the strike than mere television coverage. He ordered the closure of his beverage and food product distribution companies so that no commodities were available in markets. With food shortages abounding, Venezuelans would become desperate and be forced to join the call for Chávez's ouster. At Cisneros' milk farm in the State of Mérida, witnesses saw workers pouring milk into the rivers instead of bottling it for sale. Cisneros had decided that depriving Venezuelan children of milk was a just casualty in the war to get rid of Chávez.

Despite the fact that the strike was a lockout, originating and imposed by bosses, owners and managers, rather than workers, the private channels portrayed it as a massive general worker's strike. This news was picked up around the world, and perceived, although mistakenly, as an oil industry worker's strike, supported by laborers and business owners throughout the nation. In reality, high level managers and executives in the oil industry sabotaged equipment, changed access codes and locked workers out of computer information systems, halting production. Workers were forced off jobs, business closed. The sabotage in the oil industry led to the most severe gas shortage in Venezuelan history, crippling the economy and destabilizing the nation for more than three months.

As millions of Venezuelans were unable to work and had no gas to travel, they were forced to remain at home and engage in the one free-of-cost activity still available to them, watching television. The private media snatched up the opportunity to launch the most massive information war ever experienced in modern times. The four primary stations suspended all regular programming throughout the duration of the 64-day strike: no product commercials, no soap operas, no movies, no cartoons, no sitcoms. According to media expert Luis Britto García:

No less than four television channels (to not bring in radio and print media) joined together 24 hours a day in December 2002 and January 2003, and broadcast 17,600 propaganda announcements

against the government, dedicating all of their programming, without a second of rest, to denigrate the
government through yellow journalism, to cause all
classes of alarm and rumors to invoke terror, precisely.[11]

The situation was so severe during those 64 days that
Venezuelan citizens did not know which information source
to rely on; the private channels, or the government. On the
State-run Channel 8, the Minister of Education would state in
a press conference that all public universities and schools were
open and functioning normally, while the private media would
broadcast announcements claiming all public universities and
schools were on strike and closed down. In the end, Venezuelans were left with a government denied access to media and
a private media functioning as a *de facto* government.[12]
  Perhaps most damaging was the broadcast of violent images and opposition propaganda by all the private stations
during children's viewing hours, in explicit violation of Venezuelan law.[13] One Venezuelan testified how dramatically the
media war had affected his child:

> Last night I made the mistake of not checking if my
> six-year old was watching TV. He woke up in the

11. Roberto Hernández Montoya, "El terrorismo considerado como una de las
bellas artes," *Question,* March, 2003, p. 9.
12. This is all based on my own experience in Venezuela during the December 2002-
January 2003 strike. I watched and recorded the private and State-run channels
and interviewed numerous Venezuelans about the media war in Venezuela.
13. See La Ley Orgánica de Protección al Niño y al Adolescente, Artículos 38
(Derecho al Libre Desarrollo de la Personalidad), 32 (Derecho a la Integridad
Personal), 35 (Derecho a la Libertad de Pensamiento, Conciencia y Religión),
63 (Derecho al Descanso, Recreación, Esparcimiento, Deporte y Juego), 65
(Derecho al Honor, Reputación, Propia Imagen, Vida Privada e Intimidad
Familiar), 68 (Derecho a la Información), 71 ("Durante el horario reco-
mendado o destinado a público de niños y adolescentes o a todo público,
las emisoras de radio y televisión solo podrán presentar o exhibir programas,
publicidad y propagandas que hayan sido consideradas adecuadas para
niños y adolescentes, por el órgano competente"), 74 (Envoltura para los
Medios que Contengan Informaciones e Imágenes Inadecuadas para Niños
y Adolescentes), and Artículo 79 (Prohibiciones para la Protección de los
Derechos de Información y a un Entorno Sano).

middle of the night in a cold sweat, hyperventilating, unable to breathe. He pleaded to be allowed to sleep with his mother and me. He was afraid the "Chavistas" would come in the middle of the night and kill him.[14]

Another successful and effective use of U.S. taxpayer dollars.

"DEMOCRATIC" COORDINATOR

After the failure of the coup in April and the installation of the OTI in June, the Coordinadora Democrática emerged. Interesting timing, familiar name. Born in the likes of the Coordinadora Democrática Nicaragüense, the Venezuelan CD was composed of Fedecámaras, the CTV, numerous civil society organizations and about ten different political parties, many of which were ongoing NED recipients. Instead of reflecting on the incidents of April 11-14 that had paralyzed the nation and altered Venezuela's future, the CD immediately began working on the next phase. Although the Organization of America States had sent a delegation to help "negotiate" a solution, led by Secretary General César Gaviria, the opposition was set on just one way out of the crisis: Chávez's removal from the presidency.

In October 2002, dissident military officers, many of whom had played key roles in the coup, declared a state of rebellion and claimed a plaza in the wealthy eastern section of Caracas, declaring it a "liberated zone." The CD and the private media, which publicly supported the military rebellion, utilized the growing chaos as a platform to call for a "national strike" in early December.

On the second day of the strike, Secretary of State Colin Powell met with the former interim coup President Pedro Carmona in Bogotá, Colombia, who according to Colombian

14. Carlos Rensseler, "Venezuela's Media Mindshock," December 20, 2002. See http://www.thegully.com/essays/venezuela/021220-media-mindshock.html.

papers, had met frequently with the U.S. Ambassador in that nation, Ann Patterson.[15] Considering that Carmona was still in contact with his Fedecámaras counterpart and that the business association was the principal instigator and promoter of the strike, the meeting between the U.S. Secretary of State and an exiled coup leader playing an ongoing role in destabilizing a democratic nation seemed out of place. But, apparently, such behavior was the norm for the U.S. Government. In fact, Pedro Carmona had made frequent, uninhibited trips to the United States right after the coup in April and it wasn't until international pressure augmented that the State Department revoked his tourist visa.[16]

The CD-led strike lasted into February 2003. The economic damage exceeded US$10 billion. The strike, which in many areas was more of a lockout, since business owners shut down companies therefore forcing employees to not work, had focused on the oil industry, Venezuela's lifeline and principal source of income. A faction of workers in PDVSA, primarily high management employees led by Juan Fernández, formed an entity denominated Gente de Petróleo that became a part of the CD. Gente de Petróleo received indirect funding from both NED and USAID.

INTESA: A Shoddy Deal

The high level managers and other workers in PDVSA who joined the strike, not only violated their own contracts, but also made it impossible for supplemental workers to access codes and authorized areas in order to run the refineries and other industry operations. A little known but strategically important venture between a U.S. company with CIA ties, Science Applications International Corporation (SAIC), and PDVSA, called INTESA, played a key role in crippling Venezuela's oil industry.

15. Gina María Ramírez, "Powell en Bogotá con golpistas venezolanos," *Indymedia Colombia,* December 21, 2002. See http://www.colombia.indymedia.org/news/2004/05/12839.php.
16. Cable from the U.S. Embassy in Caracas, August 14, 2002. See http://www.venezuelafoia.info.

INTESA, the Information and Technology enterprise that was formed to run all electronic operations at PDVSA and to update many of the older, analog systems to high tech, not only promptly joined the strike, but also intentionally sabotaged essential equipment and networks necessary to run the industry. From remote locations, INTESA employees altered access codes and programming, making it impossible for remaining PDVSA workers to run computers, machines and refinery equipment. As a result, Venezuela's oil production was brought to a halt, and the losses were devastating. Not only were common Venezuelans denied gas and oil, but also Venezuela's contracts with international partners were severely threatened.

It's easy to see why the oil industry would benefit the opposition in the long term from shutting down. By doing so, it looks to outsiders like Chávez has lost control, and supports the idea that a new leader is needed to restore order. The fact is the shutdown was very ordered—the opposite of the chaos it was meant to imply. For the short term costs of losing revenue, the opposition, and Washington, believed the industry would get a new Head of State more sympathetic to its agenda.

Venezuela had to purchase petroleum from other nations in order to minimally cover its contractual obligations. Lines for gasoline in some parts of Venezuela were more than five miles long. As the strike continued through the end of December, many taxi drivers and car owners spent Christmas Eve staked out in their cars on line, waiting for a ration of gasoline. Millions of citizens with no electric appliances were forced to cook with wood fires, even in the middle of Caracas, throughout the 64-day strike.

INTESA's majority shareholder, SAIC, which owned 60% of the company to PDVSA's 40%, is the major contractor for the U.S. Government. With former chiefs of staff, ex-CIA agents, and high-level government employees comprising its Board of Directors, SAIC is closely linked to the U.S. Government, and not just through contracts. Cables sent from the U.S. Embassy during the negotiations between PDVSA and SAIC regarding the formation of INTESA stated that the joint venture was of "critical importance" to the United States.

Right before President Chávez took office in 1998, SAIC was negotiating a similar venture with Venezuela's Ministry of Defense. Such a contract would have given this company led by former CIA officers and high-level U.S. Government officials complete control over Venezuela's defense systems and national security. President Chávez nixed the deal before it could be solidified. But the PDVSA-SAIC venture INTESA was already in place, and the government could only wait for the contract to expire in late 2002.

PDVSA's then President, Alí Rodríguez, tried to amicably resolve the situation with INTESA during the strike by informing the company of its contractual obligations requiring it to continue its provision of services, despite exterior occurrences. Once INTESA's management refused to comply with PDVSA, Rodríguez requested they turn over access codes to equipment so that PDVSA employees could operate the machinery and get the industry off the ground. This exchange went on for several weeks. INTESA continued to refuse cooperation with PDVSA and eventually, PDVSA employees had to enter INTESA headquarters and seize operating equipment in order to return Venezuela's oil industry to a functional state.

SAIC later sued PDVSA for "expropriation" of its equipment and won. The case was heard at the Overseas Protection for International Companies (OPIC), a U.S. Government agency that provides insurance to U.S. companies investing abroad. It was hardly surprising that a U.S. Government agency would rule in favor of another U.S. Government-connected company. PDVSA was ordered to pay approximately $6 million in damages to SAIC.

"EARLY ELECTIONS"—CONSTITUTION, WHAT CONSTITUTION?

When the strike was at its peak, the White House called for "early elections" in Venezuela in order to end the political crisis. The U.S. Government, which had supported the coup just nine months prior, now again supported another unconstitutional solution in Venezuela. The Venezuelan Constitution has no provision for calling "early elections" when political crises arise, just as the U.S. Constitution has no provision for early presidential elections. Nevertheless, on December 13, 2002, the White House issued a statement declaring: "The United States is convinced that the only peaceful and politically viable path to moving out of the crisis is through the holding of early elections."[17]

On that same day, Richard Boucher, spokesman for the State Department made a revealing comment in a daily press briefing, stating: ". . . an early election, we think, is the kind of solution that's needed. And I guess you could say that's our objective. . ."[18] Clearly, the U.S. had an objective in mind: undermine the Venezuelan Constitution by calling for unconstitutional elections in order to push Chávez out of office under the guise of a democratic electoral process.

The public relations spin was neatly organized. Since elections are inherently essential to democracy, calling for early ones can be seen as an attempt to safeguard democracy. By ignoring both the unconstitutional nature of early elections and the U.S. role in attempting to force Chávez out, the call for elections appears as a move to strengthen democracy, when in fact it is designed to subvert the process.

During that same period, the Department of Defense was sending bogus intelligence reports to Washington in an attempt to paint a pariah image of President Chávez, once again justifying any actions taken against him. One December 2002 cable falsely claimed that Chávez had "ordered the destruction of television stations Globovisión, Televen, Canal Dos and possibly other media outlets. These attacks are scheduled to take place on the evening of 12 December." Such allegations were entirely false. President Chávez had never ordered such attacks, nor were these stations ever destroyed. In fact, those very same television outlets were broadcasting 24-hour a day, uncensored anti-Chávez messages that in many cases were

17. See http://www.whitehouse.gov/news/releases/2002/12/20021213.html.
18. See http://www.state.gov/r/pa/prs/dpb/2002/15976.html.

violent and aggressive and the State had taken no action to inhibit freedom of expression.

But those receiving the information up in Washington did not know that the report was false. The same report discussed: "Cuban troops and Revolutionary Armed Forces of Colombia guerrillas in Venezuela to support Chávez," clearly intending to link the Venezuelan leader to Colombian guerrilla groups, opening the door to international intervention.[19]

19. Cable from the Department of Defense. See http://www.venezuelafoia.info. See Appendix, p. 199.

CHAPTER NINE

Electoral Intervention: The U.S.'s Last Hope

THE RISE OF SÚMATE

In a strange coincidence of time, place and facts, a new entity was born in Venezuela. As SAIC was pushed out of PDVSA, losing its grip on the most important oil industry in the Western Hemisphere, Súmate, a technologically advanced, elections-focused non-profit run by opposition-aligned wealthy Venezuelans was established.[1] Súmate's premiere came at the tail end of the strike, which had failed in its objective of ousting Chávez, but had succeeded in making Venezuelans' lives miserable through economic devastation. The opposition was heeding the "early elections" calls of the U.S., but the government rightfully refused to permit such an unconstitutional gesture. Súmate offered an alternative to a desperate opposition movement and an eager U.S. Government: a referendum.

Venezuela's 1999 Constitution includes a provision in Article 72 to request a recall referendum on any public official's mandate after the halfway point of the term has been met. The referendum must be solicited by 20% of the electorate and then a greater number of voters than elected the official must vote to recall, and those recall votes must be a majority over those voting to keep the official in office. It is a complex process. Unfortunately, Súmate, riding high on its clever proposal, forgot to read the content of Article 72 and in early February 2003, and began a signature drive to petition for a referendum.

---

1. On an interesting note, SAIC had recently taken over the development of security systems and databases for electronic voting machines in the U.S. market.

141

In early 2003, more than 3000 laptop computers had been shipped to Súmate headquarters in Caracas from an unknown source in the United States. On the day of the petition drive, Venezuelan authorities discovered several hundred laptops with PDVSA tags in the possession of Súmate workers—they had been stolen from the oil industry offices during the strike.

Claiming they had collected 27 million signatures[2] in support of a recall referendum on President Chávez's mandate in just one day, Súmate demanded the government immediately convene an election. Súmate's demands fell short on the ears of the Venezuelan Government, since the halfway point of President Chávez's term had not yet been met.

Another government heard their cries loud and clear. The U.S. Government awarded Súmate for their brave and bold actions handsomely. Both the NED and USAID granted Súmate funds to continue their fight for the referendum.[3]

Súmate, in the likes of Vía Cívica in Nicaragua, was held out by the U.S. Government to be a neutral entity devoted to electoral education, but Súmate's own website clearly stated the organization's objective was to "promote a recall referendum against President Chávez."[4] Furthermore, Súmate's Vice-President and Treasurer, María Corina Machado, had signed the infamous "Carmona Decree"[5] during the coup, evidencing a clear anti-Chávez bias and undemocratic tendencies. And Súmate's President, Alejandro Plaz, was the Director of the Andean Office of McKinsey & Company, a consulting firm notoriously linked to the CIA.

THE REFERENDUM

For fiscal year 2003, USAID's OTI requested $5,074,000 for its Venezuela operations. NED gave out more than $1 million

2. Venezuela only has 24.5 million citizens total.
3. See http://www.venezuelafoia.info. See Appendix, p. 246.
4. See http://www.sumate.org.
5. See *Semanario Quinto Día*, November 7-December 31, 2003, p. 19.

to its Venezuela grantees and counterparts, which were the very same organizations that had just spearhead the illegal 64-day strike that devastated Venezuela's economy. DAI also continued to dish out grants to projects falling within its VICC program.

After the failure of the strike, it became clear that the opposition needed to consolidate and focus on a "real" solution, an electoral solution that would appear legitimate in the eyes of the world. The Constitution opened the doors to the possibility of the recall referendum and in May 2003, after more than nine months of brokering by the OAS, the opposition agreed to seek a "peaceful and constitutional" solution to the crisis. Since early elections were unconstitutional, the referendum would be the only possible way of prematurely removing President Chávez from office.

Súmate immediately spearheaded a campaign to force the government to accept the signatures it had gathered back in February 2003. The private media and international press, encouraged by the U.S. Government, supported this demand. Claims that the Chávez's Government was preventing a cons-titutional referendum from occurring were continuously repeated by U.S. Government spokesmen, despite the fact that the Article 72 requirements had not been met. Venezuela's National Electoral Council (CNE), an autonomous governmental body, pronounced that it would not accept signatures gathered in clear violation of referendum requirements. The CNE then released a clear set of rules and guidelines that would regulate the referendum process. A date was set in late November for a petition drive to be held in support of a recall referendum. If the required 20% of registered voters' signatures, approximately 2.4 million, were obtained, then a recall referendum on President Chávez's mandate would be held.

Súmate promptly launched a massive media and propaganda campaign in support of the petition drive, referred to as the "Reafirmazo." Utilizing NED and USAID funding, Súmate mass-produced anti-Chávez and pro-referendum materials which were distributed nationwide. The organization also produced little blue cards that affirmed a voter had signed the petition for a recall referendum. The cards were distributed at petition drive tables and voters were told to turn them in to employers, or else face termination. It was blackmail paid for by the United States Government.

In fall 2003, the OTI requested and was authorized an additional $6,345,000 for use in Venezuela during 2004.

USAID also gave $1.775 million to the Carter Center, run by former U.S. President Jimmy Carter, to observe and mediate the referendum, who would, despite this infusion of cash, later certify the referendum results in favor of Chávez.

Around that date, USAID awarded the International Republican Institute and the National Democratic Institute more than $2 million for "ensuring credible electoral processes" and "strengthening political parties" in Venezuela during 2003-2004.

In one grant totaling $769,000 to NDI, USAID required $300,000 to be distributed to local sub-grantees. Súmate was the primary local group referred to in the grant. The grant project called for local organizations to engage in electoral observation, voter registry monitoring and training of polling site officials—activities that when conducted at the behest and supervision of a foreign government are sure signs of intervention. Moreover, it is hard to believe a grant program aimed at "conducting pre-election, election day and post-election monitoring, including a quick count" for a recall referendum on President Chávez's mandate premised on the notion that Chávez is "populist," "authoritarian" and "controversial" would be fair and balanced.

With USAID money, NDI helped Súmate build its organization and volunteer-based structure. The $769,000 grant permitted NDI to "design observer manuals for the Venezuelan context, work with groups to establish an effective 'train-the-trainers' pyramid training structure" and "help groups build alliances with other institutions and sectors to strengthen their volunteer base." NDI helped Súmate develop training materials, "observer forms, software, public education information and other tools in Spanish." Basically everything Súmate needed to run the recall referendum campaign—paid for by the U.S.

While NDI was focusing on Súmate and the recall referendum campaign, IRI was making use of a $450,000 USAID grant to train opposition political parties for the anticipated upcoming elections that would take place once Chávez lost the recall referendum. Working with parties such as Primero Justicia, Proyecto Venezuela, AD, COPEI, MAS, Alianza Bravo Pueblo and others, IRI provided training in campaign organization and structure, message development, grassroots campaigning, membership and recruitment fundraising and other aspects of professional campaigning.

The U.S. Government sure was banking on Chávez's removal by the looks of its heavily financed preparations and trainings for a post-Chávez's Government. As Roger Noriega, Assistant Secretary of State for Western Hemisphere Affairs, affirmed shortly before the referendum: "We have invested a lot of money in this process. . ."[6]

THE VENEZUELA TERRORIST CONNECTION

Right around the time of the "Reafirmazo," in Fall 2003, the U.S. launched another attack against the Chávez's Government, this time claiming Venezuela was harboring "terrorist" training camps and was collaborating with the Colombian FARC and ELN, both groups on the U.S. list of international terrorist organizations. An October article in *U.S. News and World Reports* by Linda Robinson, entitled "Terror Close to Home," claimed that Al Qaeda, FARC and ELN terrorists had training camps scattered throughout Venezuela. The article included a big map of Venezuela with markings identifying the training camps.

> The oil-rich but politically unstable nation of Venezuela is emerging as a potential hub of terrorism in the Western Hemisphere, providing assistance to Islamic radicals from the Middle East and other terrorists, say senior U.S. military and intelligence officials . . . Middle Eastern terrorist groups are operating

6. See http://www.bogota.usembassy.gov.

support cells in Venezuela and other locations in the Andean region . . . Venezuela is supporting armed opposition groups from neighboring Colombia; these groups are on the official U.S. list of terrorist organizations and are also tied to drug trafficking. . . ."[7]

The allegations were based on comments by an "anonymous U.S. official" and an "exhaustive" investigation conducted by the magazine that was never substantiated.

In fact, Brigadier General Benjamin R. Mixon, Director of Operations at the Pentagon's Miami-based U.S. Southern Command, later confirmed to *The Miami Herald*, ". . . the Southern Command has no information about Venezuela supporting terrorists."[8]

A *United Press International* (UPI) article also claimed there was a connection between the Venezuelan Government and Islamic terrorist networks. The UPI article went so far as to claim that Chávez was harboring Al Qaeda suicide bombers that were involved in the September 11, 2001 attacks in the United States:

Investigators name two Venezuelan based al-Qaeda suspects: Hakim Mamad Al Diab Fatah who was deported from the U.S. on suspicion of involvement with the Sept. 11, 2001 attacks and Rahaman Hazil Mohammed Alan who is jailed in the U.K. for smuggling an explosive device onto a British Airways flight. American and British officials complain that their investigations are stymied because the government of President Hugo Chávez has dismantled U.S.-trained intelligence units which tracked terrorist connections among the half-million strong Venezuelan Arab community . . . Chávez has instead brought in

7. Linda Robinson, "Terror Close to Home," *U.S. News and World Reports,* October 6, 2003.
8. Juan O. Tamayo, "U.S. Split Grows over Chávez Links to Rebels," *The Miami Herald,* December 28, 2003, p. 21A.

Cuban and Libyan advisors to run his security services according to American, British and other European diplomatic officials in Caracas.[9]

The UPI article mentions no official sources by name nor provides any substantive evidence for its claims. Moreover, subsequent to this round of articles making outrageous claims about Venezuela's alleged connections to Al Qaeda and other terrorist groups, no further mention was made of the issue. But in the end, the claims were merely scare tactics and part of a strategy to isolate the Chávez's Government in the international community and provide a justification for intervention.

Yet again, the strategy failed.

"THE GUARIMBA"

Despite these international pressures, the signature collection process to institute the referendum went smoothly. The CNE later determined only 1.9 million signatures valid, while another nearly 1 million were set aside and questioned for fraud. More than 800,000 signature lines had been filled out with duplicate handwriting in violation of CNE regulations. The opposition reacted to the news with violence.

In February 2004, newly formed extremist factions in the Coordinadora Democrática launched "the Guarimba," a plan allegedly created by Cuban-Venezuelan Robert Alonso. "The Guarimba" called for right-wing groups to engage in widespread civil disobedience and violence in the streets of Caracas and other metropolitan areas, provoking repressive reactions from State forces that would then justify cries of human rights violations and lack of constitutional order.

---

9. Martín Aróstegui, "Analysis: Venezuela's Islamic Links," *United Press International*, September 1, 2003.

"The Guarimba" lasted from February 27 to March 1, 2004, and during that period, numerous Venezuelan citizens were injured and arrested for violations of law. "Guarimba" provocateurs burned garbage in the streets, blocked roadways and threw Molotov cocktails and other homemade bombs at security forces. The opposition-controlled media in Venezuela quickly broadcast to the world a prepared version of events that cited the government as the "repressor" and portrayed claims of those arrested during that period for breaking the law as "victims of torture and unlawful arrest." "The Guarimba" starkly resembled the "Chileanization" strategy applied in Chile and Nicaragua, using similar tactics and provoking identical results.

As a result of the violence and instability again caused by the opposition, the Venezuelan Government, agreed to allow those signatures that had appeared fraudulent to be "reaffirmed" by the signors over a four-day period regulated by the CNE. The opposition was provided with a second opportunity to legitimately obtain the necessary 2.4 million signatures needed to hold the recall referendum. The signature repair period, "reparo," as it was known, was held at the end of May 2004. The Carter Center and the OAS provided international observation, paid for by USAID. By about 100,000 signatures, the opposition obtained the necessary 2.4 million and the referendum date was set for August 15, 2004.

"PLAN CONSENSO PA' BUSH"
(PLAN CONSENSUS FOR BUSH)

About five days after the announcement confirming the referendum, the opposition released an alternative plan for a transitional post-Chávez's Government. Entitled Plan Country Consensus, the project appeared as the first attempt by the opposition to offer Venezuelans anything beyond a strict "get Chávez out of office" position. The opposition had been highly criticized internationally for having no concrete plans, no viable candidates to oppose Chávez and no platform on which to campaign. The Plan Country Consensus appeared as the magic solution. But Plan Consensus' polished offerings were not born independently from the opposition. They were in fact the result of a NED grant to CIPE-CEDICE in 2003, combined with USAID funding that had gone through DAI to several opposition groups, including Liderazgo y Visión and Queremos Eligir.

Additionally both IRI and NDI had played roles and had financed the crafting of this "alternative agenda." It was the goal of the U.S. to win the referendum and install a transitional government that would work best in its interests. As such, the referendum campaign, via Súmate and the CD, and the alternative agenda, via NED and USAID grantees, were financed and overseen by U.S. Government agents.[10]

The NED chose CEDICE as the principal drafter of an agenda for a "transitional government" despite the fact that CEDICE's President, Rocío Guijarro, was one of the initial signors of the Carmona Decree and was chosen by Carmona to represent NGOs at his "swearing in ceremony." CEDICE also happened to be one of the most fervently outspoken anti-Chávez groups in Venezuela, whose leaders attempted several times to convince NED program Director Christopher Sabatini that a coup d'état did not take place on April 11, 2002, but rather it was a popular uprising against a "dictator."[11]

But the Plan Consensus project represented nothing to Venezuelans that they hadn't heard before: shallow promises and a return to a neo-liberal agenda. The NED-funded project brought together representatives from almost every organization and political party connected to the opposition umbrella group, the Coordinadora Democrática, and even included members of the Catholic Church and former PDVSA executives. Many of these same individuals and their organizations had just participated in two illegal and destructive activities against democracy: the coup and the strike.

10. See http://www.venezuelafoia.info. See Appendix, pp. 193-194.
11. See http://venezuelafoia.info.

The CEDICE Plan Consensus project was based on the premise that:

> A national agenda that induces the adoption of free market reforms is particularly important at the present time . . . The one thing separating the country from full revolutionary control are (sic) the fact that the Chávez government was the result of free elections, as was the Nazi regime in its inception....[12]

The U.S. Government was funding an organization that nonchalantly compared the Chávez's Administration to the Nazi regime and was working to implement the type of free market reforms the Venezuelan Government had been elected to avoid. Furthermore, the list of organizations represented in the project read like a "who's who" of coupsters and organizations feverish to get rid of Chávez by any means.

Plan Consensus Committee members Maxim Ross of Asamblea de Ciudadanos and Domingo Alberto Rangel of Resistencia Civil were Carmona Decree signors along with Rocío Guijarro, Director of CEDICE and supervisor of the project; Cipriano Heredia, representing Visión Emergente and Tomás Páez of Red Universitaria and Elías Santana, Head of Alianza Cívica, signed onto a public Civil Society Document recognizing the legitimacy of Carmona's coup government; Project Advisory Committee members Hugo Fonseca Viso, Jorge Botti and Albis Muñoz were representatives of Fedecámaras, which had spearheaded both the coup and the strike; Advisory Committee members Jesús Ubieta[13] and Nelson Landaez represented the CTV, the labor union responsible for teaming up with Fedecámaras during the coup and the strike; and Committee member Nelson Benítez represented Gente de Petróleo, the PDVSA worker organization responsible for initiating the illegal oil industry strike. Representatives from the opposition parties COPEI, AD, Un Solo Pueblo, Alianza Bravo Pueblo and Primero Justicia were also paprticipants in the project.[14]

---

12. See http://www.venezuelafoia.info.
13. Urbieta is the way it appears in the document. See Appendix, pp. 193-194.
14. See Appendix, pp. 193-194 for full document and list of individuals and organizations involved.

Once it was revealed that Plan Consensus had been financed by the U.S. Government, Chávez went wild. "Plan Consenso Pa' Bush" (Plan Consensus for Bush) he called it —"Made en USA" (Made in USA). Diego Urbaneja, Representative of the Coordinadora Democrática and spokesman for the Plan Consensus project conceded defeat almost immediately. Though initially launched with great enthusiasm by the opposition as "the alternative to Chávez," within a week, there was no mention at all of the infamous Plan Consensus. The opposition's own misjudgment, and the U.S. Government's, had once again led to their failure.

THE PETARE EXPERIMENT

Meanwhile, DAI had distributed 67 grants totaling $2.3 million over the previous few months, more than half of which were focused on the referendum and a post-Chávez Venezuela.

When USAID responded to the FOIA request for information on its Venezuela projects, it purposely decided to withhold the names of all organizations and recipients of U.S. taxpayer dollars in Venezuela. In a few cases, administrative errors were made and beneficiaries such as Súmate, Carlos Fernández and Mirador Democrático were revealed. But as for the majority of the 67 grants, only project names were left uncensored along with the program descriptions. Some projects were easy to decipher, such as the Un Sueño Para Venezuela (A Dream for Venezuela), a proposal of the NED-funded organization Liderazgo y Visión for yet another alternative to Chávez, but most were identifiable by project name only.

Of the 67 grants for 2003-2004, one thing in particular stood out: six grants were focused on the community of Petare, one of Venezuela's most populated neighborhoods and a major pro Chávez support base.

Petare is the most populated sector of greater Caracas. Located in the municipality of Sucre in Miranda State, Petare is primarily a working class and poor barrio with a few middle and upper class zones. Although typically known as a Chávez stronghold, to the surprise of many, something happened in

Petare during the recall referendum against President Chávez on August 15, 2004: the opposition "SÍ" vote received higher numbers than expected in contrast to the "NO" vote to keep Chávez.

The six USAID-DAI grants in Petare were primarily focused on "citizen development and political formation" and improving community relations. One grant worth $22,081 titled Tendiendo Puentes Comunitarios para Fortalecer la Vida Democrática en Nuestras Comunidades (Building Community Bridges to Strengthen Democratic Life in Our Communities) was allegedly set on helping to mend relations between the upper and middle class communities in the Petare sector and the majority lower class. Another grant to the tune of $53,000, Mi Barrio: Un Espacio Democrático para el Consenso y el Desarrollo (My Neighborhood: A Democratic Space for Consensus and Development) was focused on helping poor community members develop democratic values.

Diálogo y Resolución de Conflictos (Dialogue and Conflict Resolution) was another Petare-based USAID-DAI effort to allegedly teach the working poor how to communicate in a democracy. And the flowery Acciones Vecinales para la Armonía y el Entendimiento (Neighborhood Actions for Harmony and Understanding) was a $34,215 project to try and help community members get along. The more obscure Experiencia Local de Negociación y Legitimación de Consensos. Los Derechos de la Infancia en Sucre (Local Experience in Negotiation and Consensus Legitimatizing. The Rights of Infants in Sucre) brought in another $6000 and the more general, Prevención de la Violencia Cotidiana (Prevention of Everyday Violence) brought a whopping $49,830 into the neighborhood.

There are two things striking about these Petare-based grants. One, the USAID-DAI grants in Petare were not only condescending and patronizing to community members, treating them all as poor, uneducated and valueless citizens, but they were also attempts to teach democratic values and development methodologies not native to Venezuela. The grants brought in U.S.-imposed values and notions to attempt a sway of public opinion. Precisely the idea behind these "formation" focused grants was to influence the ideology and political formation of Venezuela's base: its vast poor majority, which also just happens to be Chávez's largest support base. In Petare, the true "battle of the ideas" was taking place, and by the looks of the referendum results, the U.S. was winning.

The second striking aspect about the grants was the fact that the majority of Petare community members had never heard of a single one of them. More than $200,000 was invested in their community for democratic and political formation and conflict resolution and most Petare residents never even partook in the projects. But even more intriguing were the numerous eyewitness accounts to Miranda State Deputy Carlos Oscariz of the opposition party Primero Justicia, IRI's Venezuelan counterpart, going door-to-door, along with his aides, in Petare's poorest neighborhoods in the weeks before the referendum, offering 150,000 bolívares (about $75) and a bag of food for a "SÍ" vote. It is not hard to imagine that hunger would win over principles, even in a politically charged environment.

It would make sense then, that if USAID-DAI had invested more than $200,000 in Petare in the months proceeding the referendum and the majority of Petare residents had never even heard of the grant projects and programs allegedly taking place in their neighborhood, that somehow, some of that $200,000 showed up in Carlos Oscariz's offerings to poor Petare community members.

In the end, the desired result was the same, whether via legitimate grant programs or political bribes: win the recall referendum and get rid of Chávez. In Petare, they figured out an easy way to achieve that goal: prey on poverty.

Lucky for Chávez and his supporters, the State of Miranda, which houses Petare, won the "NO" vote by a mere few percentage points. So the Petare losses had no serious impact on the vote outcome, though they did affect the stability of a community more than one million strong. The Petare Experiment suffered a further defeat at the hands of pro-Chávez forces on October 31, 2004, during regional elections.

Then-Governor of Miranda State Enrique Mendoza lost to a pro-Chávez candidate, Diosdado Cabello, demonstrating Chávez's enduring popularity there.

Witnesses in Petare say that since Mendoza lost the governorship, Primero Justicia has been suspiciously absent from their neighborhoods.

PENN, SCHOEN & BERLAND—U.S. POLLING FIRM OF CHOICE

Despite the millions of dollars invested in the opposition to Chávez,[15] on August 15, 2004, more than 59% of voters ratified his mandate to keep him in office. Even though both the Carter Center and the OAS certified the official CNE referendum results, the opposition, led by the U.S.-financed Súmate, cried fraud.

Súmate claimed it had conducted an exit poll, together with the U.S. polling firm Penn, Schoen & Berland, a firm previously used in electoral interventions in Nicaragua, Panamá and Yugoslavia, which showed the exact opposite results indicating that the vote to recall Chávez had exceeded 59%.[16] Another exit Poll, conducted by IRI's counterpart, Primero Justicia, also showed the same result. All other exit polls conducted by international firms and independent observers were in line with the official CNE results. However, Súmate and the CD claimed the vote had been fraudulently calculated and they refused to recognize the results.

---

15. On Friday, August 4, 2004, Roger Noriega, Assistant Secretary for Western Hemisphere Affairs of the State Department, stated: "We have invested a lot of money in the democratic process because we have faith in civil society, which is a pillar of representative democracy. We have given money to similar types of NGOs in Venezuela by means of the State Department and USAID. Civic groups with the mission to defend their democratic institutions and demand basic rights for Venezuelans also represent a good investment." See http://usaembassy.state.gov/posts/co1/wwwsrno7.shtml.

16. "U.S. Firm Embroiled in Venezuela Referendum Controversy Defends Its Exit Poll," *Associated Press*, August 19, 2004. See http://www.sfgate.-com/cgi-bin/article.cgi?file=/news/archive/2004/08/19/inter-natio-nal2018EDT0734.DTL&type=printable.

A few strange things happened on August 15, 2004. The British newspaper *The Independent,* released an article on the night of August 15 prior to the end of voting with the headline "Venezuela's Chávez on Brink of Referendum Defeat." The article claimed that: "The Venezuelan President, Hugo Chávez, looked to be losing his grip on power last night as exit polls showed him to be trailing the opposition by almost a million votes . . . The mid-morning results showed that the opposition, already boasting an enormous 1,758,000 votes to Chávez's 798,000, is well on its way to reaching the target of 3.76 million votes it needs to oust the authoritarian, left-wing President..."

Mid-morning results? Exit polls? *The Independent* was reporting the opposition winning as of 10:49 A.M. EST, a mere three to four hours after polls had opened. Not even the worst, most biased Venezuelan journalists reported such a "victory" before noon. The polls on August 15 were open until midnight. Per CNE regulations, release of exit poll data was prohibited before the official tally had been announced in order to avoid any disturbances or violence due to the very polarized and delicate political situation the nation was living. But Súmate, along with its U.S. counterpart, Penn, Schoen & Berland, leaked the information on the Internet, in clear violation of CNE rules.

The exit poll leak was part of a ploy to generate belief that the opposition was going to win. All day long, the private media gave full coverage to referendum-related events, but the stations primarily broadcast images of anti-Chávez voters at the polls. Opposition politicians and leaders were interviewed on private media news shows attesting to their belief that Chávez would lose.

The private media was clearly creating an opinion matrix and they were once again censoring voices and information that disproved their claims.

At about 9:30 P.M., it became clear that the opposition had lost. The private channels switched from coverage of anti-Chávez voter lines and began broadcasting old movies and infomercials. Despite the ongoing miles long lines in pro-Chávez neighborhoods that continued well into midnight, the private media had decided the voting was over. They couldn't show what was really happening, that more "Chavista" voters were out there than the opposition had mustered up, or else the millions of Venezuelans watching television over the past few months and years would realize they had been deceived all along. No, it was best for opposition-aligned Venezuelans to go to bed watching old movies and believing that they had won the referendum. That way, they would buy the claims of fraud the opposition was prepared to present the next day once the official CNE results declared Chávez the winner.

After the polls closed around midnight, the results were fairly clear: the "NO" vote had maintained approximately a twenty-point lead over the "SÍ" vote throughout the day. Chávez had not been recalled. Before the official announcement could be made by the CNE Directorate, the Democratic Coordinator decided they would not accept the results. They informed the CNE of this decision, along with the Carter Center and the OAS. Though such a factor should not have altered the official determination of the CNE, the announcement was delayed. The Carter Center and the OAS had decided to hear out the Democratic Coordinator and their claims of fraud.

César Gaviria's Long Night

Around 1:00 A.M., there was a breakdown. César Gaviria, representing the OAS in Venezuela, had taken sides with the opposition: the OAS, per Gaviria's decision, was not going to certify the referendum results. The Carter Center, however, did not believe the claims of fraud, particularly considering the opposition had presented no evidence whatsoever of any fraud or wrongdoing during the referendum. Carter was going to certify.

In the days before the referendum, Jimmy Carter had requested a private meeting with President Chávez. In that meeting, Carter told Chávez he believed he would win the referendum. Carter felt sure that Chávez had the votes. He only

156

asked the Venezuelan President to take the win in stride and to be reconciliatory, not reproachful.

César Gaviria, on the other hand, had a history of tacitly supporting the opposition to Chávez. He considered Chávez an authoritarian and consistently pushed statements and measures against the Venezuelan Government on the rest of the OAS members. The representative Gaviria had chosen to lead the OAS mission in Venezuela, Fernando Jaramillo, had been expelled in May 2004 from Venezuela for allegedly showing bias towards the opposition.

Less than one month before the referendum, Walter Moreira, the Brazilian Ambassador to the OAS had been appointed as the Chief Envoy to Venezuela. Since Gaviria had spent the greater part of the previous two years working in Venezuela, he remained a part of the OAS referendum observation team.

In the early morning hours of August 16, Jimmy Carter and César Gaviria came head to head. Gaviria was not budging. He was not going along with Carter. Were Gaviria's decision based on solid evidence and fact, Carter probably would have joined him in rejecting the CNE's official results. But since Gaviria's last minute turnabout was due to his political alignment with the opposition, Carter was determined to convince him otherwise. Three hours of negotiations went by and at 4:00 A.M., Gaviria was still not going to certify the results.

Even when CNE President Francisco Carrasquero read the official results at 4:35 A.M., guaranteeing Chávez's victory, the uneasiness of Gaviria's decision echoed through Miraflores Palace. The general public, luckily, was not privy to this information, and those who supported Chávez were able to carelessly soak in their victory.

By noon on August 16, Gaviria had come around. Moreira was in Caracas and apparently had played a big part in Gaviria's change of heart. The OAS and Carter Center together gave a press conference around 1:00 P.M. that day, announcing their certification of the CNE official results. With Moreira at his side, Gaviria read the OAS statement endorsing the results. His attempts to interject comments supporting opposition claims of possible fraud were thwarted by Moreira's stern glances.

In the northern continent, the U.S. Government had not yet accepted the referendum results. Despite numerous assurances that the U.S. would accept the Carter Center and the OAS's decision on the referendum, no official announcements were made on August 16. It took the U.S. a day to soak it all in. On August 17, State Department spokesman Adam Ereli issued the U.S.'s conditional acceptance of the referendum results:

> We will join the group of friends of Venezuela in acknowledging the preliminary results of the referendum and noting that they show that President Chávez received the support of the majority of voters . . . We call on international observers to help conduct a transparent audit that will address those remaining concerns as part of a process of national reconciliation. . . .

The U.S. had qualified the official results as "preliminary" and called for an "audit" of votes. As Noriega declared right before the referendum: "The U.S. has invested a lot of money in this referendum." That's right, and they were not going to lose sitting down.

The audits were done with OAS and Carter Center supervision and certification and the result was the same: Chávez won, 59-41.

The results were a huge setback for the United States. For years it had worked to destabilize and replace Chávez. Then, in a final push, it backed the referendum. But the results, far from having a neutral impact on the status quo, were a huge validation of Chávez; he had in effect scored an unscheduled election victory years before his term was set to expire.

CHAPTER TEN

Up the Sleeve Strategies and Threats

THE SÚMATE CASE: NED ON THE OFFENSIVE

Súmate refused to accept the referendum results. The trips to Washington increased and efforts were made to convince the world that a "mega-fraud" had taken place during the recall referendum. "Hackers were brought in from Russia" to steal the votes, Súmate leaders cried. "The voting machines were rigged by the CNE to favor 'NO' votes" they swore. "Experts" were brought in from around the world, yet no real substantive or credible evidence was ever presented.

A few months before the referendum, in May 2004, the Venezuelan Attorney General had charged Súmate's Directors, María Corina Machado and Alejandro Plaz, with violation of Article 132 of the Penal Code, which makes it a crime to "conspire to destroy the government" and to "solicit international intervention in national politics" or to "incite civil war or defame the President or diplomatic representatives in the foreign press." The Attorney General alleged that Súmate committed a crime by soliciting financing from the NED, an arm of the U.S. Government, in order to campaign for and lead a recall referendum against President Chávez. Furthermore, the Chief Prosecutor alleged that Súmate violated the Constitution by usurping functions of the Electoral Power through its creation of a parallel electoral registry and database used to collect and count signatures during stages of the referendum process. Two other Súmate members, Luis Enrique Palacios and Ricardo Ludwig Estévez Mazza, had also been charged with aiding and abetting in the conspiracy. A preliminary hearing was scheduled in the Venezuelan courts for November 2, 2004.

When the charges were first announced against the Súmate Directors in May 2004, the National Prosecutor assigned to the case, Luisa Ortega Díaz, was kidnapped. Attorney Ortega Díaz was thrown into a car at gunpoint, along with a companion who was with her at the time. If it hadn't been for her companion, who put up a struggle and pushed her out of the moving car, Luisa would most likely not have survived the attack. After the kidnapping attempt, she was moved to a military base and was assigned twenty-four hour bodyguards. She continued to preside over the matter.

The case brought against NED-grantee Súmate caused uproar in the ranks of the U.S. State Department and the quasi-governmental NED, which is obligated to report to Congress annually on its activities and use of funds. In the weeks after the referendum, the U.S. State Department launched a massive campaign in defense of Súmate. State Department spokesmen made repeated declarations calling for the Venezuelan Government to drop the case and labeling the charges "political persecution." María Corina Machado became the "cover girl for democracy," jetting up to Miami, New York and Washington at a minute's notice to host conferences, forums and talks on the Súmate case and the political crisis in Venezuela. Her frequent visits to Washington began to raise eyebrows even within the ranks of the opposition.

The new U.S. Ambassador in Venezuela, William Brownfield, even visited Supreme Court Chief Justice Iván Rincón to request he intervene to prevent the case from proceeding. Although Rincón was clear in his respect for due process and the jurisdiction of the Attorney General, a separate power, one of the other justices in the Penal Chamber of the Supreme Court decided to heed Brownfield's call. He pulled the case to review it for "clarity" and "merit" before allowing it to continue. The November 2, 2004 hearing was postponed indefinitely.

On November 8, 2004, NED President Carl Gershman made a historical visit to Venezuela with a very peculiar purpose. Gershman traveled to the South American nation to request President Chávez influence the outcome of the case against Súmate, despite it residing in the hands of the independent Attorney General's Office. But much to Gershman's surprise, no meetings had been authorized with the Venezuelan President or cabinet members and he was unable to exert the weight of the United States-backed NED over the recently re-ratified Head of State. Gershman did meet with Attorney General Isaías Rodríguez and President of the Venezuelan Supreme Court, Iván Rincón.

In the meeting with Chief Justice Rincón, Gershman threatened to prevent the issuance of a credit from the World Bank for a judicial reform program the Supreme Court had been conducting over the past few years. In return, Gershman wanted Rincón to do everything in his power to get the case against Súmate dismissed. Rincón did not bow to Gershman's threats and sure enough, a few weeks later, the World Bank cut the credit for the Venezuelan Supreme Court.

With Attorney General Rodríguez, Gershman was more veiled. He urged the top legal authority to drop the case, hinting that its continuance could affect relations between the two nations.

Rodríguez, clear on the law backing his position, refused to heed Gershman's threatening request.

Gershman's visit, the first visit by the NED President to a foreign nation to defend the organization's interests, was an apparent "last chance" offer to the Venezuelan Government to stop the case or face the wrath of the U.S. Government. Even presidential candidate John Kerry got on the Súmate defense bandwagon in the days prior to the November 2, 2004 U.S. presidential elections, criticizing Chávez for "political persecution" and accusing him of heading towards a dictatorship. Other Súmate defenders included U.S. Congress members Christopher Cox and Gregory Meeks, both on the NED Board of Directors, and Senator John McCain and former Secretary of State Madeleine Albright, who chair the NED core grantee organizations, the International Republican Institute and the National Democratic Institute, respectively.

The aforementioned all authored letters defending NED's work in Venezuela and defending its grantees, despite their notorious unconstitutional behavior during the coup and the strike.

Though NED representatives and spokesmen have time and again claimed their work in Venezuela as "impartial" and only "promoting democracy," Gershman's declarations to the Venezuelan press showed otherwise. After being snubbed by the Executive, the Attorney General and the Chief Justice of the Supreme Court, Gershman angrily declared to the Venezuelan media that: "Venezuela is neither a democracy nor a dictatorship but rather something in between." In the same breath, Gershman claimed that in Venezuela, the NED "only finances democratic groups," which must imply that groups involved in coups d'état fit within the NED's view of democracy. He also tried to make a weak comparison between the Venezuelan Government and the Chilean dictator Augusto Pinochet by claiming: "In the eighties, we were attacked by the Pinochet Government, which didn't like the fact that we supported the groups that moved forward the democratic transition in Chile."

There is something deeply troubling when a representative of a group allegedly promoting democracy arrives in country to argue against upholding that country's laws. The U.S. has all sorts of regulations about money and elections—how much can be given, publication of the donor's name and address, and so on. For a foreign visitor to come and ask that the U.S. not uphold such laws would widely be seen as a violation of U.S. sovereignty.

Gershman followed through on his threats to the Venezuelan Government to increase international pressure in defense of the Súmate case and to attempt to convert Chávez into an international "pariah" and "human rights abuser." Just twenty-four hours after Gershman's departure from Venezuela, a letter was released from an alleged group of 70 "international democrats" demanding the Venezuelan President intervene in the Súmate action and prevent the Attorney General from proceeding with the case.

The letter was riddled with misinformation and errors about Venezuela's legal system and laws and strangely demanded respect for democracy while asking the Venezuelan President to violate the constitutional separation of powers by intervening in a case under the authority of the Attorney General. The letter called for an abandonment of the law and demanded the Súmate Directors be granted "above the law" status, just because they received support from the NED and its 70 prominent "international democrats."

Although the letter was intended to look like an independent statement by 70 renowned "democrats," its ties to the NED were all too obvious. The letter was released to the public by the NED Press Department and of the 70 signors, more than half were linked to either the NED Board of Directors or had received its financial support.

In the weeks that followed, U.S. Congressman Tom Lantos (D-CA) introduced a resolution on Capitol Hill, expressing support for the National Endowment for Democracy and its work in Venezuela. The resolution also called for the Venezuelan Government to drop the case against Súmate:

[Excerpts]

108th CONGRESS 2d Session H. RES. 867
RESOLUTION
The House of Representatives
(1) expresses its firm support for the efforts of the National Endowment for Democracy to promote democracy around the world;
(2) commends all Venezuelans who have peacefully exercised the political rights which are accorded to them under Venezuela's Constitution to resolve their differences by democratic means and abhors all acts of political violence;
(3) views charges filed against members of the Venezuelan civic organization known as Súmate of conspiring with the National Endowment for Democracy to overthrow Venezuela's Government as politically motivated; and

(4) would welcome a decision by the Government of the Bolivarian Republic of Venezuela not to prosecute Venezuelan citizens, including citizens associated with Súmate, for activities that were protected under the laws and Constitution of Venezuela when those activities were carried out.

The Resolution not only applauds NED's work in Venezuela, making no mention of the hundreds of thousands of dollars given to coup leaders and instigators, but it also tacitly requests the Venezuelan judiciary drop the legal case against members of Súmate. Following in the footsteps of Gershman and Brownfield, the Lantos Resolution attempts to undermine Venezuelan law. Unfortunately for Súmate and Rep. Lantos, Congress went on vacation before the resolution could be passed. But Congress did approve another piece of legislation relating to NED's activities in Venezuela. New York Congressman José Serrano (D-NY) introduced specific language into the FY2005 Omnibus Bill, a/k/a the "budget," that made clear NED's activities in Venezuela were questionable. The language, in the bill approving $51 million for all of NED's programs in 2005, stated:

The Committee reaffirms the role that NED plays in strengthening democratic institutions around the world. Any perception that funds are used to directly support a particular party or candidate, or to support the removal of elected leaders through unconstitutional means, undermines the credibility and effectiveness of NED programs. The Committee expects NED to take all necessary measures to ensure that all sponsored activities adhere to the core NED principles. The Committee directs NED to provide the Committee with a comprehensive report on its activities in Venezuela from fiscal year 2001 through the present, by December 15, 2004.[1]

1. House Report, 108-576 to bill H.R. 4754, *National Endowment for Democracy*. Note that the language included in this bill was directly the result of what my investigation has uncovered.

For the first time in history, language was inserted into legislation about NED that raised concerns about its programs and commitment to democracy.

MIAMI: A TERRORIST HUB

Miami has become a haven for self-exiled Venezuelans seeking new ways of ousting President Chávez from his democratically elected office. In early October 2004, "The Guarimba" author Robert Alonso surfaced in Miami, after a warrant had been issued for his arrest in Venezuela in connection with approximately 80 Colombian paramilitaries found on his farm outside of Caracas in May 2004, apparently implicated in a plot to assassinate Chávez. Former Venezuelan President Carlos Andrés Pérez has also taken root in Miami in recent months. From his home in Miami in July 2004, Carlos Andrés Pérez declared to *El Nacional* newspaper that Chávez deserved to "die like a dog" and that "violence is the only way to remove him."[2]

On October 25, 2004, Venezuelan actor Orlando Urdaneta, also fleeing from an arrest warrant, surfaced in Miami. He appeared on a local Miami television show, "María Elvira Confronta" (María Elvira Confronts) on October 25, 2004, ordering the assassination of Chávez and other influential members of his Government. Orlando stated:

> . . . of the 150,000 men in uniform in Venezuela, there must be a high percentage of honest people who, in the right moment, will rise up . . . But this will only happen with the psysical disappearance of the "top dog" and a significant part of his pack. There is no room for doubt: there is no other way out. Physical disappearance definitely."

2. "Violence Will allow us to remove him. That's the only way we have... [Chávez] must die like a dog, because he deserves it..." Ex-President Carlos Andrés Pérez interview with Venezuelan newspaper *El Nacional*, July 26, 2004. See also http://perso.wanadoo.es/camilofidel/2004/JULIO/26-07-04carlosandres-perez.html.

When prompted by the program host as to how this would happen, Urdaneta replied: "This happens with a few men with long guns that have telescopic views, that won't fail . . . It's an order that I am giving right at this moment, let's go, hurry up. . ."[3]

Weeks later, on November 18, 2004, National Prosecutor Danilo Anderson was assassinated in a car bombing in Caracas. Two charges of C4 explosive had been fixed to Anderson's car and the explosion was detonated by remote control. Anderson was the most high profile prosecutor at the time in Venezuela. He was handling politically charged cases involving powerful interests.

Danilo had just issued subpoenas to the almost 400 Carmona Decree signors as part of an ongoing investigation into the April 2002 coup. Though none had yet been indicted on criminal charges, several of those implicated fled to Miami.

He had also recently indicted Henry Vivas and Lázaro Forero, former Metropolitan Police Commissioners along with the ex-mayor of Greater Caracas, Alfredo Peña, for their involvement in the coup. Peña showed up in Miami right after the indictment was made public. Anderson had also been the prosecutor on the case against Baruta mayor Henrique Capriles Radonski, charged with facilitating the assault on the Cuban Embassy back during the 2002 coup.

Anderson's assassination was the first political murder in contemporary Venezuelan history. It was meticulously planned and carried out, and was strikingly similar to the 1976 assassination of Orlando Letelier and Ronni Moffitt, one of the worst terrorist acts ever carried out on U.S. soil before the World Trade Center attacks on September 11, 2001. Letelier had been the Defense Minister under Salvador Allende's democratic Government, before it was overthrown in the 1973 coup at the hands of Chilean dictator Augusto Pinochet and the Nixon's Administration. Letelier and Moffitt were killed in

3. "Orlando Urdaneta llama al magnicidio desde Miami," *Temas*, November 2, 2004. See http://www.temas.com.ve/modules. php?name=News-&new - topic=9.

a car bombing on Washington's Embassy Row, executed at the behest of Pinochet, coached by the CIA and sanctioned by Washington.

At the end of 2004, those who ordered Anderson's murder remained unknown.

TERRORIST CAMPS

Several ex-military officers known to have participated in the coup have also appeared in Miami, alongside Carlos Fernández, the former Fedecámaras President and Carlos Ortega, former CTV President, who had obtained political asylum in Costa Rica, but later lost it once he clandestinely returned to Venezuela and appeared on television in a pre-referendum rally. The Venezuelan Government issued arrest warrants for both Fernández and Ortega in 2003 for their leadership of the illegal 64-day strike that caused billions of dollars in losses to Venezuela's economy. The Venezuelan Government also has pending extradition requests with the U.S. Government for two military officers, Germán Rodolfo Varela and José Antonio Colina, alleged to be the masterminds behind the bombings of the Colombian and Spanish Embassies in Caracas in fall 2003. The officers' requests for political asylum in Miami were denied by the Deparment of Homeland Security, yet they were allowed to remain in the U.S., pending appeal.

The F-4 Comandos, an anti-Castro Cuban militia group operating in Miami joined forces with the Junta Patriótica Venezolana (Venezuelan Patriotic Junta), run by dissident Venezuelan military official Capitán Luis García Morales, in late 2002. The two organizations, led by professed "freedom fighters," run terrorist training camps in the greater Miami area for those seeking to overthrow both Chávez and Castro.[4]

An article in *The Wall Street Journal* entitled "Miami's Little Havana Finds New Foe in Venezuelan Leader" revealed the intentions of this Miami-based exile group: "Capt. García

4. See http://www.comandosf4.org.

says he is providing military training for some 50 members of the F-4 Commandos, 30 of them Cuban-Americans, the rest Venezuelans, in a shooting range close to the Everglades. "We are preparing for war," he says. Nevertheless, his movement opposes military coups. "Our struggle is to show the world how Chávez is the enemy of democracy."[5]

Despite requests from the Venezuelan Government for the U.S.Government to investigate these camps, no action has been taken.

FUTURE RELATIONS

Incoming Secretary of State Condoleeza Rice set the tone for future relations with the Venezuelan Government. In an October 2004 statement to the press, Rice declared that Chávez is a "real problem" for the region and that other nations in the hemisphere should "mobilize to both watch him and be vigilant about him."[6]

With more than $6 million allotted for its 2005 interventions, it is clear that the U.S. Government's job in Venezuela is not finished. But as Venezuela's Bolivarian Revolution gains strength and support around the world, one question arises: Just how far is the U.S. Government willing to go in its covert war against Chávez?

It would seem, with the re-election of Bush and appointment of Rice as Secretary of State, that the answer is almost certainly "as far as necessary." How far that would have to be is suggested by the extraordinary resilience of Chávez and Venezuela over the last few years.

In the words of President Hugo Rafael Chávez Frías: "We will not rest until we break all the chains that oppress our people, the chains of hunger, misery and colonialism. This country will be free or we will die trying to free it."[7]

5. José de Córdoba, "Miami's Little Havana Finds New Foe in Venezuelan Leader," *The Wall Street Journal,* January 29, 2003.
6. *Pittsburgh Post Gazette,* October 22, 2004.
7. Hugo Chávez Frías, *Speech to the Guarniciones Militares* in the Patio de Honor of the Academia Militar in Fort Tiuna, Caracas, December 27, 2004.

Epilogue

You may wonder why the CIA is not mentioned more in this book. When you think of U.S. intervention in a foreign nation, obviously the CIA must be involved. We know from the SEIB documents revealed through this investigation that the CIA had intimate, detailed knowledge of the coup plans. We also know that the CIA was issuing Spot Commentaries on the days of the coup, which implies the Agency was clearly operating in Venezuela.

Ex-CIA officials confirm that 75% of U.S. Embassy political office employees are CIA operatives. The majority work covertly, under the guise of Embassy officials, and even carry out Embassy duties as a cover. The embassy in Venezuela is no different.

Just have a look at the hundreds of cables from the U.S. Embassy in Caracas declassified under FOIA through this investigation. The Ambassadors, Maisto, Hrinak, Shapiro and Brownfield, and other Embassy employees, Cook, MacFarland and Ellis, to name a few, were all sending multiple daily informative reports up to Washington about every imaginable detail pertaining to Venezuela. These reports are then compiled and analyzed by the CIA and determinations are made based on the information received on just how the intervention should proceed.

NED and USAID function as outlets for the CIA to penetrate civil society, funneling in millions legitimately and therefore avoiding congressional scrutiny. As much as NED and USAID deny any connection to the CIA, no one can negate these agencies were born to overtly engage in activities practiced by the CIA at a time when Congress was clamping down hard on the Agency's budget and past clandestine operations. Both USAID and NED employees have at times been CIA operatives, carrying out the Agency's agenda under the guise of "promoting democracy."

And there is no doubt that the CIA maintains hundreds, perhaps thousands of paid agents in Venezuela, providing intelligence information, carrying out operations and attempting to invoke a political crisis. These individuals live freely and anonymously in Venezuelan society earning their salaries from the conflict they work to encourage.

The CIA also maintains non-official covert operations in Venezuela. DAI, IRI, NDI, SAIC and numerous U.S. corporations with offices throughout the country provide fronts for CIA activities. These entities also help the CIA launder funds for its Venezuela operations.

So, no need to think that the CIA is not active and alive in Venezuela. It most certainly is. Agency operatives in Venezuela were caught red-handed during the horrific bombing of a Cubana Airlines plane in flight from Barbados on October 6, 1976. CIA agent Luis Posada Carriles, an anti-Castro Cuban, had recruited two Venezuelans to carry out the terrorist act that killed all 73 people on board. Hernán Ricardo Lozano and Freddy Lugo were later caught by Venezuelan authorities for placing the fatal bombs aboard that flight and served 20 years in prison. Luis Posada Carriles was also caught. But with the help from the U.S. Government-funded Cuban American National Foundation, he escaped from a maximum-security prison in Venezuela on August 18, 1985. After carrying out numerous other terrorist acts against Cuba, he was jailed in Panama in 2000, when Cuban President Fidel Castro announced the discovery of a plot to assassinate him, headed by Posada Carriles. Out going Panamanian President Mireya Moscoso pardoned Posada Carriles in 2004 as a final act.

Posada Carriles worked hand in hand with Orlando Bosch, infamous anti-Castro Cuban terrorist responsible for more than 100 terrorist attacks against Venezuela, Spain,

England, Japan, Mexico, Poland, and other countries that traded with Cuba, even on U.S. soil. Bosch was also known to be part of a CIA assassination squad, Operation 40 along with the recently named Director of the CIA, Porter Goss, responsible for the political murders of Cubans and others associated with the Cuban Revolution.

Bosch was jailed for 11 years in a Venezuelan prison for his role in the Cubana airplane bombing in 1976, but he was released in 1987 with the help of old friend Otto Reich. At that time, Reagan had just rewarded Otto Reich with the Ambassadorship in Venezuela after his good work in Nicaragua, heading the State Department's Office of Public Diplomacy, responsible for creating a "black propaganda" campaign intended to smear the Sandinistas, and Reich sent numerous cables to the State Department requesting a visa for Bosch to enter the U.S.

Despite denial from the State Department, President George H. W. Bush pardoned Bosch after he was caught illegally entering the U.S. in 1988 and imprisoned.

Bosch resides freely in Miami today, along with a crew of self-exiled Venezuelans conspiring against Venezuela's democratic Government. Posada Carriles is currently a fugitive at large, thought to be hiding somewhere in Central America.

Clearly, the CIA maintains a presence in Venezuela. But apart from the traditional covert operations the CIA is known for, more important are the newer sophisticated forms of intervention that are applied today in Venezuela. Civil society penetration, indoctrination and financing opposition movements seeking regime change are the modern forms of covert/overt CIA operations. The Venezuela case, as *The Chávez Code* reveals, is the CIA's 21st century experiment.

These strategies and methodologies will surely be applied, and are being applied, in other nations around the world where regime change glitters in the eyes of the U.S. Government.

Hopefully, advance knowledge will allow for preparation, and the interventions can be foiled, as the Venezuelans have successfully done thus far.

Never overestimate or underestimate the power and intelligence of the U.S. Government.

And as the U.S. Government has learned in Venezuela: never underestimate the will and determination of a people in the struggle for justice.

POST NOTE

The Chávez Code: A Model for Investigators

by Saul Landau[*]

When about-to-be Secretary of State Condoleezza Rice declared at her January 2005 confirmation hearings in the Senate that Venezuela belonged in the Latin American equivalent of the axis of evil (with Cuba of course), every informed citizen should have heard warning bells. Rice's declarations added to the growing body of official and non-official clamor demanding "action" against President Hugo Chávez. But what terrible crime had he committed?

A *The Washington Post* editorial found Chávez guilty of an "assault on private property." They referred to Chávez's "war on idle landed estates," and labeled taking over idle land as another step toward establishing dictatorship. The editorial omitted the fact that Venezuelans had reached consensus on the subject. Indeed, even some of Chávez's business enemies agreed that all Venezuelans would all benefit from ridding themselves of large idle "latifundios." The editorial also failed to mention the huge landless throughout Latin America, the shocking disparity of income between rich and poor and the fact, emphasized by UN researchers that the U.S.-backed "free market" solution had contributed to the worsening conditions.

Rice also failed to mention any of Chávez's specific "crimes." But, backed by Castro-hating senator Mel Martínez

---

[*]. Saul Landau is an internationally renowned scholar, commentator and filmmaker. He has received several awards for his films, books and activism, including the Letelier-Moffit Human Rights Award.

(R-FL), she raised the definition of verbal chutzpah to new levels by accusing Chávez of interfering in the affairs of other nations. Can any serious person imagine a high U.S. official accusing others of interfering?

Did memory fail this Solonic body? Did Senators forget that in March 2003 President Bush invaded Iraq, without a trace of *casus belli*? Indeed, over the last century the United States has interfered in the affairs of almost every Third World country.

The Senators and the media also failed to confront Rice about her knowledge of U.S. support for a coup in Venezuela in April 2002 and about ongoing efforts to undermine a government that received solid electoral support on nine separate occasions.

Ignorance, denial or avoidance? It doesn't matter. Citizens need to know what U.S. operatives are doing around the world to alter the destiny of others. Venezuelans chose Chávez in democratic election on nine occasions. That's why Eva Golinger's book should hit the moral reader with a shock—of recognition, not surprise. She lays out a well-written, legal brief as current history to show that the U.S. Government has made a concerted effort to destabilize and overthrow the elected Government of Venezuela. She demonstrates that the threads of imperial history have far more strength than the republican principles that once served as foundation for U.S. laws and treaties.

She allows the documents she obtained through the Freedom of Information Act to guide her fastidious reasoning on the U.S. role in attempting to overthrow the Chávez's Government. All students of History know that the CIA overthrew the Government of Iran in 1953, Guatemala in 1954, tried to or did assassinate Patrice Lumumba in the Congo in 1960, orchestrated an invasion of Cuba at the Bay of Pigs in 1961, knocked off the Goulart Government in Brazil in 1964 and participated in the destabilization and coup in Chile, 1970-73. The CIA operated the murderous Phoenix Program in Vietnam after the United States illegally invaded and occupied that country for more than a decade. Are you starting to yawn over the very partial list of interventions?

174

In each case, the CIA always emerges as the black hat, the agency ready and willing to take the rap. But the blame goes higher. The CIA functions as one of the President's Praetorian guard units that become activated of every time people of a foreign nation elect a leader who pans to redistribute some wealth toward the poor. A veritable red alarm bell sounds in Washington's national security apparatus and like Pavlovian dogs the CIA and the other attack dogs respond automatically to the stimulus. Occasionally, presidents and secretaries of State repent—years later of course—for the damage caused by "aberrant" CIA operations. Colin Powell apologized for Chile —thirty years after the United States helped instigate a 9/11 (1973) massacre there. Bill Clinton said he was sorry for what the CIA did in Guatemala—almost forty years later. As many as one hundred thousand Guatemalans died as a result of the Agency's overthrow of their democratically elected government.

In the case of Venezuela, as *The Chávez Code* makes clear, the U.S. Government added yet another stain to the U.S. national honor. Golinger shows the incontrovertible facts of Washington's attempt to overthrow the Government of Chávez. She obtained the documents from National Security sources—a vestige of older freedoms—and turns them into prosecutorial swords that generate moral outrage instead of wounds to the plotters and liars. I visualize high officials placing hands on Bibles and swearing to uphold the laws while holding images in their minds of crossed fingers.

Golinger's prose radiates a fierce sense of the law's moral importance. This young Venezuelan-American attorney, uses her fact-filled pages, almost like a legal brief to show the jury, the reading public, that the defendant, the U.S. Government, acted in a premeditated conspiracy with the wealthy classes of Venezuela to undo a democratic process in that country: free and fair elections, a functioning legislative and legal system.

Worse, as the brief continues, we see that the U.S. Government worked with its Venezuelan (and Israeli) counterparts to involve the mass media in its efforts to mis and dis inform the world's public as to the nature of reality before, during and after the April 2002 coup. During the presidential debates

175

of 2004, John Kerry eagerly fed at the interventionist trough. He dutifully followed the Bush line—lie—that the democratically elected President of the Bolivarian Republic of Venezuela, Hugo Chávez, constitutes a threat to the United States. Kerry bought into the media portrayal of Chávez as an authoritarian villain who seeks to "Cubanize" his country.

When I met Eva Golinger in Caracas in December 2004, we both observed that contrary to the U.S. stereotype Chávez was trying to redistribute wealth and power to the majority —the poor.

Far from acting like the "terrorist threat," Chávez showed himself to be a well-educated, clear-thinking and responsible political leader.

Washington never complained when a Kleptocracy governed Venezuela for more than three decades, until the mid 1990s. We heard no complaints from Bush, Kerry, Rice and the major media when in 1989 Venezuelan soldiers and police killed as many as 2000 persons ("the Caracazo") who refused to tolerate more "structural adjustment" from the International Monetary Fund.

The federally funded National Endowment for Democracy Directors, did not see a threat to democracy when Venezuelan presidents routinely kissed U.S. butt in international fora. They saw nothing wrong with shooting poor people when they protested. The very misnamed National Endowment for Democracy understands "promoting democracy" to consist of financing a small and wealthy minority who reject the ballot when they lose elections. Indeed, as Golinger makes clear in her book, National Endowment for Democracy funded some of the very people who backed the 2002 military coup.

The Chávez Code not only reveals and analyzes the nefarious plots, but sets a model for researchers. Students and professors alike should imitate Golinger's care in presenting and interpreting documents and drawing conclusions based on the facts.

Appendix

Flow of U. S. $$ in Venezuela

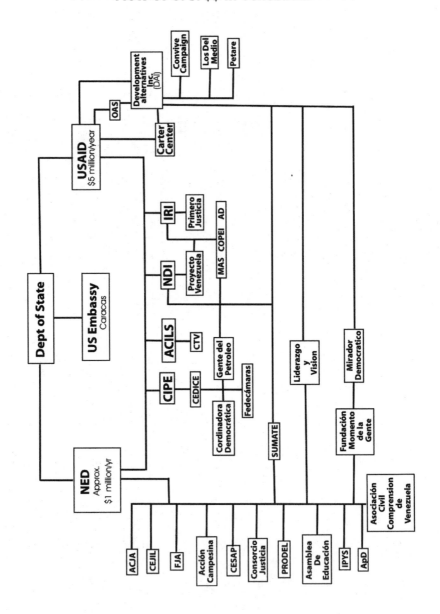

Overall Structure of Money Flow to Venezuela

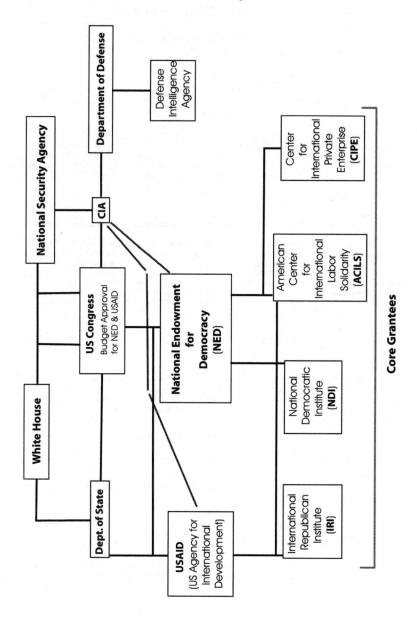

Summary of NED's Projects Approved
2000-2004: Venezuela

SUPPORT FOR DEMOCRATIC UNION ELECTIONS $60,084
Venezuela
The American Center for International Labor Solidarity / None

The American Center for International Labor Solidarity (ACILS) will support the efforts of the Confederation of Venezuelan Workers (CTV) to effect a process of reforms intended to reduce the influence of political parties and increase rank and file control over decision making. To this end, ACILS will conduct ten, two-day courses for regional federations of the CTV which will focus on the following topics: problems and challenges for unions in a changing world, restructuring of labor organizations, and the electoral process. 1/00

RECASTING LIBERTY: CONSTITUTIONAL REFORM
                                                            $56,000

Venezuela
Center for International Private Enterprise /Center for the Dissemination Economic Information (CEDICE)

The Center for International Private Enterprise (CIPE) will work with CEDICE to launch a program to move the economic reform discussions toward a more participatory and democratic process that includes concrete reforms encouraging individual initiative and private enterprise. CEDICE will sponsor, in conjunction with interested business organizations and nonprofit groups, four large-scale national forums and at least six regional forums on legislation that is constitutionally required to be enacted in the National Assembly's first year of operation. Specific focus will be placed on the Organic Labor Act and the new Organic Tax Codes. Members of legislation committees, as well as national and foreign experts, and representatives of the social and economic sectors will be involved. 6/00

SUPPORT TO LOCAL GROUPS FOR ELECTION OBSERVATION $16,747
Venezuela
Fundacion Momento de la Gente / None

Fundacion Momento de la Gente will conduct a pre-electoral monitoring campaign, which will monitor the use of public funds in the campaign, participate in the electoral audit committee (CNE), review election materials, and conduct training for some election-day observers in various regions of the country. These activities will help promote civilian oversight and transparency in the voting and vote counting process. 6/00

FOSTERING YOUTH PARTICIPATION IN THE POLITICAL PROCESS
Venezuela $50,000
International Republican Institute / *Fundación Participación Juvenil*

The International Republican Institute (IRI) will work with Fundación Participación Juvenil to instill democratic values in Venezuelan youth so they can play an integral role in maintaining society's interest in establishing effective democratic institutions. 9/00

REGIONAL FORUM FOR DECENTRALIZATION $50,000
Venezuela
PRODEL-Venezuela / None

PRODEL-Venezuela will conduct a series of activities to establish and train a network of national and state legislators and local mayors to monitor government activity concerning decentralization and advocate for the rights and responsibilities of state and local government in Venezuela. A series of seminars and courses will be held so participants can analyze and debate pending legislation and share information about laws and policies affecting local government and decentralization. 9/00

FY 2001

STRENGTHENING POLITICAL PARTIES $340,000
Venezuela
International Republican Institute / None

The International Republican Institute (IRI) will train national and/or local branches of existing and/or newly created political parties on such topics as party structure, management and organization; internal and external party communications; and coalition building. 1/01

CIVIL-MILITARY RELATIONS $57,820
Venezuela
Asociación Civil Comprensión de Venezuela / None

Asociación Civil Comprensión de Venezuela will organize a series of meetings, which will bring representatives of organizations from civil society together with active and retired members of the Venezuelan armed forces, to initiate a national debate on the newly changing role of the military in the country. The meetings will be held in both civilian and military institutions, under the consultation of instructors at military colleges, university professors and representatives of civil society. 1/01

STRENGTHENING CIVIL SOCIETY LINKS FOR FUNDAMENTAL POLITICAL RIGHTS
$19,740

Venezuela
Asociación Civil Consorcio Justicia / None

Asociación Civil Consorcio Justicia will help build the capacity of civil society organizations in Venezuela to become active in the struggle against authoritarianism. *Consorcio Justicia* will host an international conference to explore examples of how civil society in countries such as Serbia and Mexico worked together to protect themselves against and defeat authoritarian regimes, as well as build a network of Venezuelan civil society organizations committed to the defense of democratic freedoms in the country. 1/01

LEGISLATIVE MONITORING FOR PROTECTION OF POLITICAL RIGHTS $40,000
Venezuela
Momento de la Gente / None

    Momento de la Gente received continued Endowment funding to organize Venezuelan civil society groups to monitor the National Assembly on key pieces of legislation pertinent to civil liberties. *Momento* will organize a series of working meetings for representatives of civil society groups to establish monitoring mechanisms and developing proposals to be submitted to congressional committees responsible for drafting the final law, with the additional aim of creating link among organizations. NED funding will also be used to cover core institutional costs. 1/01

SUPPORT FOR DEMOCRATIC UNION ACTION $154,375
Venezuela
The American Center for International Labor Solidarity /None

    The American Center for International Labor Solidarity (ACILS) will support the Confederation of Venezuelan Workers' (CTV) efforts to organize disparate unions and federations into a unified national industrial unions and define a new mission and role for the union movement in the development of the nation. 9/01

RE-ENGAGING CITIZENS IN STATE-LEVEL POLITICS $210,500

Venezuela
National Democratic Institute for International Affairs / *Momento de la Gente*

    National Democratic Institute for International Affairs (NDI), in collaboration with Momento de la Gente, will assess and conduct pilot programs in up to three states to engage citizens in the policy-making process, specifically focused on government accountability and transparency. NDI will also work with state governments to include citizens' input into the decision-making process. 9/01

STRENGTHENING CIVIL SOCIETY TO PROMOTE DEMOCRATIC EDUCATION $55,000

Venezuela
Education Assembly Civil Association /None

    The Education Assembly Civil Association will organize grassroots groups to monitor education reform plans in Venezuela and formulate draft legislation for the Superior Education law, as well as create a network of parents, teachers and community leaders to pro-actively monitor the quality of education in the country. 9/01

ENHANCING DEMOCRACY THROUGH ALTERNATIVE DISPUTE RESOLUTION METHODS
Venezuela
Center for International Private Enterprise / None

The Center for International Private Enterprise (CIPE) will collaborate with CEDCA, a Venezuelan non-profit group, to launch a strategic public awareness campaign and to offer a series of rigorous alternative dispute resolution (ADR) training modules. For each type of training module, CEDCA will design a training guidebook and recruit experienced instructors. 1/02

STRENGTHENING CIVIL SOCIETY LINKS FOR FUNDAMENTAL POLITICAL RIGHTS
Venezuela $84,000
Asociación Civil Consorcio Justicia / None

Asociación Civil Consorcio Justicia (Consorcio Justicia) will use Endowment funding to host a broad range of civil society groups at a working conference in late January 2002 to evaluate the situation in Venezuela and develop a policy agenda, after which Consorcio Justicia will conduct a campaign within Venezuela to improve communication and coordination among Venezuelan NGOs and to raise public awareness of their work. Finally, Consorcio Justicia will conduct a program in ten states throughout the country to educate communities on local justice issues, help organize elections to select justices of the peace and train locally elected justices. 1/02

LEGISLATIVE MONITORING AND MUNICIPAL TRAINING $64,000
Venezuela
Momento de la Gente / None

Momento de la Gente (Momento) will organize Venezuelan civil society groups to monitor the National Assembly and provide policy input on key pieces of legislation pertinent to civil liberties. Momento will also work with and help organize local elected officials to improve their ability to oversee public budgets and advocate for decentralization. Finally, Momento will maintain and strengthen its links with different civil society organizations in Venezuela and continue to work with international organizations to improve coordination and information on the political situation in Venezuela. 1/02

CONSENSUS BUILDING TO REDUCE THE INFORMAL SECTOR IN VENEZUELA
                                                                                                     $66,266
Venezuela
Center for International Private Enterprise / Center for the Dissemination of Economic Information

The Center for the Dissemination of Economic Information (CEDICE) will work with several Venezuelan NGOs to develop a Pact to Rebuild Venezuela, which will include a policy paper and a series of workshops. CEDICE will also address the problem of the growing informal sector in Colombia through a series of workshops and forums that will be developed jointly with civil society groups throughout Venezuela. 3/02

STRENGTHENING POLITICAL PARTIES $300,000
Venezuela
International Republican Institute / None

The International Republican Institute (IRI) will train national and local branches of existing and newly created political parties, both on a one-to-one basis and through group sessions. Possible training topics include party structure, management, and organization; internal and external party communications; effective constituent relations; membership and volunteer recruitment; candidate/leadership development; and coalition building. 3/02

CONSENSUS BUILDING TO REDUCE THE INFORMAL SECTOR IN VENEZUELA

$116,525

Venezuela
Center for International Private Enterprise / Center for the Dissemination of Economic Information

Through a joint effort between the Venezuelan Labor Confederation and the Citizens Assembly, a policy paper will be developed and a series of four national and ten regional workshops will be held, led by the Center for the Dissemination of Economic Information (CEDICE). CEDICE will also carry out project activities to address the problem of the growing informal sector, such as a series of workshops and forums that will be developed jointly with business groups in Zulia and Aragua States and the National Council on Commerce and Services (CONSECOMERCIO) in Caracas, as well as with the participation of other civil society groups throughout Venezuela. 6/02

MONITORING SOCIAL PROGRAMS $63,000
Venezuela
Centro al Service de la Acción Popular (CESAP) / None

The Centro al Servicio de la Accion Popular (CESAP) will monitor social expenditures, the impact of poverty-alleviation programs, and social development and change in Venezuela. The project will monitor government budgets and programs, gather data through surveys, and monitor social development indicators to develop a national picture of the state of poverty and social programs in Venezuela. CESAP will develop a network of local community groups to monitor local social programs and their implementation, and will publish a report based on its findings, which will be distributed nationally and internationally. 6/02

PROFESSIONALIZATION OF THE MEDIA $25,000
Venezuela
Instituto Prensa y Sociedad / None

The Instituto de Prensa y Sociedad (IPYS) will carry out a forum in partnership with its Venezuela-based affiliate for media owners, editors, journalists, and leaders of international media advocacy groups to reflect on the current state of freedom of expression and journalism in Venezuela. The forums' discussion will focus on analyzing the events surrounding the coup which involved the media, in addition to examining larger issues of freedom of expression in the country. The forum participants will propose recommendations for resolving issues of self-censorship, journalistic protection, and professionalization of the media. 6/02

VENEZUELA

$116,001

Venezuela

The American Center for International Labor Solidarity / None

The American Center for International Labor Solidarity (ACILS) will support the Venezuelan trade movement, represented by the CTV, in developing a program to extend organization, training, and representation to the informal sector. ACILS will also aid CTV in developing and publicizing its positions and strategies on economic and social issues as part of the development of an anti-poverty program emphasizing leadership training to articulate CTV positions more effectively with the national and international news media (including journalists union and IFJ) and on more effective use of the CTV website. 9/02

POLITICAL PARTY STRENGTHENING

$50,000

Venezuela

National Democratic Institute for International Affairs / None

The National Democratic Institute for International Affairs (NDI) will conduct focus groups to detail popular perceptions of political parties and present the results to political party leaders. NDI will then use this information to encourage parties to fully embrace the need for reform and to use the results of the focus groups to shape renewal strategies. 9/02

MONITORING LAND REFORM

$35,000

Venezuela

Acción Campesina / None

Acción Campesina will train monitors who will work in ten states to collect information on the effects of Venezuela's land redistribution law. The information provided by these monitors will then serve as the basis for a public information campaign. *Acción Campesina* will work with representatives of the National Assembly to communicate objective information about local disputes and conflicts generated by the law. At the end of the project, *Acción Campesina* will convene a national forum to discuss the land redistribution law and attempt to propose ways to reduce rural conflict. 9/02

CONFLICT RESOLUTION AT THE LOCAL LEVEL

$11,000

Venezuela

Asociación Civil Consorcio Justicia-Occidente / None

The *Asociación Civil Consorcio Justicia-Occidente* will work with communities in the state of Táchira to promote the election of local justices of the peace and train communities and the candidates to the office of justice of the peace in conflict resolution and mediation techniques. In addition, *Consorcio Justicia-Occidente* will work with local governments and communities to improve communication and collaboration at the local level. 9/02

EDUCATION ASSEMBLY

$57,000

Venezuela

Asociación Civil Asamblea de Educación / None

The *Asociación Civil Asamblea de Educación* (Education Assembly) received renewed Endowment support to monitor and distribute information on education policy issues. The Education Assembly will convene regular policy forums and press conferences to discuss education policy and their proposals and will work with the National Assembly to discuss draft legislation and reforms. Last, the Education Assembly will train local community leaders in eight states and Caracas to strengthen its national parent-teachers' network dedicated to democratic education. 9/02

CONFLICT RESOLUTION AT THE LOCAL LEVEL

$10,000

Venezuela

Asociación Civil Justicia Alternativa / None

The *Asociacion Civil Justicia Alternativa* will conduct two workshops each in four locations in the Venezuelan state of Aragua. The workshops will train newly elected justices of the peace, local citizens and local government officials in conflict resolution, political leadership, democratic values, and the institutions and processes of the political system. Each workshop will train 15 people, with the second workshop to follow-up with participants trained in the first round. 9/02

CONFLICT RESOLUTION AT THE LOCAL LEVEL $11,000
Venezuela
Fundación Justicia de Paz del Estado Monagas / None

Fundación Justicia de Paz del Estado Monagas will work in 32 communities in the state of Monagas to create local roundtables to promote dialogue among local political actors. *Fundación Justicia de Paz* will engage in a broad public education campaign in which they will distribute information to the communities about the techniques of political dialogue and peaceful resolution of conflicts. 9/02

FY 2003

STRENGTHENING POLITICAL PARTIES AT THE LOCAL LEVEL $116,000
Venezuela
International Republican Institute / None

The International Republican Institute (IRI) will seek out local partners in the states of Zulia, Anzotegui and Carabobo to conduct party training, and will place particular emphasis on party grassroots strengthening, external communications, and inclusion of marginalized sectors in the parties. 1/03

STRENGTHENING POLITICAL PARTIES $116,000
Venezuela
National Democratic Institute for International Affairs / None

The National Democratic Institute for International Affairs (NDI) will work with municipal leaders and governments to rebuild citizen confidence and participation in the political system and the parties through anti-corruption initiatives. NDI will also work to help renew traditional political parties, as well as assist with the building of new political parties. 1/03

POLITICAL PARTY BUILDING AT THE NATIONAL LEVEL
                                                                                                    $299,999
Venezuela
International Republican Institute / None

The International Republican Institute (IRI) will use a combination of polling and political party training in critical areas of party reform to help Venezuela's parties establish a stronger role in the country and regain the trust of the electorate. IRI will work toward the development of detailed party platforms reflective of constituent concerns, effective two-way internal communication structures, and processes for transparent and democratic selection of party leaders. 3/03

LOCAL CIVIC EDUCATION $10,000
Venezuela
Acción para el Desarrollo / None

Acción para el Desarrollo will conduct informal civic education workshops for leaders of neighborhood associations in poor neighborhoods in and around Caracas. Acción para el Desarrollo will hold a total of 30 workshops on democratic values and conflict resolution to train presidents of neighborhood associations in seven "*barrios populares.*" At the end of the workshops, participants will develop a plan to promote development and democratic dialogue within their communities. 3/03

STRENGTHENING THE JUDICIAL SYSTEM $54,000
Venezuela
Asociación Civil Consorcio Justicia / None

Asociación Civil Consorcio Justicia will implement a program that will monitor the status of the judicial system and its operation and work with the Congress to improve legislation and laws. Consorcio Justicia will also work with municipal officials and community leaders in the poor neighborhood of Libertador in Caracas to train local communities in the peaceful resolution of conflict and establish local mediation committees in 60 neighborhoods. 3/03

LEGISLATIVE ASSISTANCE $64,000
Venezuela
Fundación Momento de la Gente / None

The Fundación Momento de la Gente will organize Venezuelan civic groups to collaborate with the National Assembly in developing legislative initiatives and debate around three separate bills on muncipal government, electoral procedures and citizen participation. Momento will provide technical advice to assembly members, organize public seminars for the discussion of the bills, and design and propose ways of increasing public awareness of and debate on the proposed legislation. 3/03

SUPPORTING PRESS FREEDOMS $44,500
Venezuela
Instituto Prensa y Sociedad-Venezuela / None

The Instituto de Prensa y Sociedad-Venezuela (IPYS-Venezuela) will construct an alert network in Venezuela to report attacks against journalists that occur in the provinces in and around Caracas. IPYS-Venezuela will support correspondents in the provinces to monitor press conditions and investigate cases of attacks or threats, as well as offer a series of training sessions for journalists' professionalization. Finally, IPYS-Venezuela will participate in regional press advocacy meetings in order to connect with international groups and build their organizational network. 3/03

MONITORING SOCIAL PROGRAMS $65,000
Venezuela
Centro al Servicio de la Acción Popular / None

Centro al Servicio de la Acción Popular (CESAP) will monitor social expenditures, the impact of poverty alleviation programs and social development and change in Venezuela. The project will monitor government budgets and programs, gather data through surveys, and monitor social development indicators to develop a national picture of the state of poverty and social programs in Venezuela. CESAP will develop a network of local community groups to monitor local social programs and their implementation, and will publish a report based on its findings which will be distributed nationally and internationally. 6/03

MONITORING LAND REFORM

$58,000

Venezuela

Acción Campesina / None

    Acción Campesina will create three local groups of promoters of farmers' rights located in highly conflict-ridden rural areas to monitor land disputes, track the needs of the rural communities, and draft proposals to reform current agrarian public policies at the state and municipal levels. *Acción Campesina* will also serve as a source of information to policymakers, political parties, and civil society on the implementation of national laws and its effects. 9/03

CONFLICT RESOLUTION AT THE LOCAL LEVEL

$14,412

Venezuela

' *Asociación Civil Consorcio Justicia – Occidente* / None

    The *Asociación Civil Consorcio Justicia – Occidente* will work with communities to promote the election of local justices of the peace and train the communities and the candidates in conflict resolution and mediation techniques. 9/03

CONFLICT RESOLUTION AT THE LOCAL LEVEL

$14,107

Venezuela

Asociación Civil Justicia Alternativa / None

    The *Asociación Civil Justicia Alternativa* will conduct training on conflict resolution, human rights, the role of police and the local justice systems in conflict resolution, and police-community relations for the police and local justice officials in Giradot, in the state of Aragua. 9/03

CIVIC EDUCATION FOR POLICE

$42,207

Venezuela

Asociación Civil Liderazgo y Visión / None

    The *Asociación Civil Liderazgo y Visión* will conduct a democracy and human rights training program for officers of the Caracas metropolitan police force. To ensure the sustainability of the program, *Liderazgo y Visión* will train four representatives in each of the branches of the metropolitan police to serve as coordinators for follow-up and to help organize and conduct courses and informal workshops in the future. 9/03

HUMAN RIGHTS DEFENSE

$83,000

Venezuela

Center for Justice and International Law / None

    The Center for Justice and International Law (CEJIL) received Endowment assistance to support a staff attorney in CEJIL and two trips to Venezuela to train local human rights groups and journalists on how to prepare cases for the Inter-American system to defend freedom of expression. The staff attorney will also request and monitor the implementation of precautionary and provisional measures from the commission and the court in cases when the life of human rights defenders or journalists is in imminent danger. 9/03

CONFLICT RESOLUTION AT THE LOCAL LEVEL $11,698
Venezuela
Fundación Justicia de Paz del Estado Monagas / None

The *Fundación Justicia de Paz del Estado Monagas* will work in 32 communities in the state of Monagas to continue to support its mediation and conflict resolution roundtables by expanding the membership of the roundtables to include representatives from local government and local, as well as state, judicial and law enforcement offices. The program will include the training of officials in mediation and conflict resolution and the establishment of a state-wide network of mediators. 9/03

ELECTIONS EDUCATION $53,400
Venezuela
Súmate / None

Súmate will develop links with other organizations in the region that work on elections, produce election-related, voter mobilization materials, and consolidate its national network of volunteers for the referendum on the president's mandate. *Súmate* will establish a coordinator in each state and train people from local organizations on the referendum process and how to conduct a get-out-the-vote campaign for the general community, in addition to developing a public information campaign on the referendum and to encourage citizens to participate in the electoral process. 9/03

Instituto de Prensa y Sociedad – Venezuela (Press and Society Institute – Venezuela)
$72,000

To promote and defend freedom of expression. Instituto de Prensa y Sociedad – Venezuela (Press and Society Institute – Venezuela) will support an alert network, which reports attacks against journalists that occur in the provinces and in Caracas. Training workshops to strengthen the investigative reporting skills of journalists will also be held.

Asociación Civil Consorcio Justicia (Justice Consortium)
$67,000

To monitor the judicial system and its operation and work with the Congress to improve legislation and laws. The Asociación Civil Consorcio Justicia (Justice Consortium) will work with local organizations outside Caracas and with Ecuadorian and Peruvian NGOs to share information and programs and establish a regional judicial observatory. In addition, the Justice Consortium will work with the Peruvian NGO, Institute for Legal Defense to establish a democratic leadership training program that will train local and community leaders in the interior of Venezuela.

Acción para el Desarrollo (Action for Development)
$12,420

To conduct civic education in conflict resolution and community leadership. Acción para el Desarrollo (Action for Development) will conduct workshops for leaders of local "neighborhood associations" in poor neighborhoods in and around Caracas. The workshops will focus on the themes of democratic values, the role of civil society and community organizations in democracy, how to negotiate and mediate local conflicts, the Bolivarian Constitution and the rights of Venezuelans, and how to address the violation of political and human rights.

International Republican Institute
$285,000

To promote the development of responsive, democratic political parties. IRI will focus its efforts on long-term party strengthening in the following areas: political platform development; internal and external communications; strengthening party structure; coalition building; and youth involvement in the parties. IRI will offer trainings to all of the major political parties across the ideological spectrum. IRI will work to expand party outreach to marginalized groups through trainings of local party officials.

Center for International Private Enterprise
$92,488

To promote democratic mechanisms of participation for entrepreneurs that are currently left out of the policymaking process and help forge solutions to structural problems underlying informal commerce. CIPE and its Venezuelan partner Center for the Dissemination of Economic Knowledge (CEDICE) will conduct a survey of the informal sector in Sucre and Baruta: conduct outreach initiatives including workshops, fora, and publication of an informational brochure; and promote debate and discussion on the informal sector among government leaders at the local and national levels.

Centro al Servicio de la Acción Popular (Center at the Service of Popular Action)
$60,000

To monitor social expenditures, the impact of poverty-alleviation programs and social development and change in Venezuela. CESAP will develop a network of local community groups to monitor local social programs and their implementation, and will publish a report based on its findings which will be distributed nationally and internationally. The report will serve as the basis for a public education campaign on social development in Venezuela and how to improve social programs to better address Venezuelan poverty.

Center for International Private Enterprise
$33,006

To promote a debate on the relationship between institutions and economic growth. CIPE and its local partner Center for the Dissemination of Economic Knowledge will conduct a two-day international conference to bring together in Caracas leading scholars, businessmen and women, political leaders, university student leaders and representatives of think tanks throughout the Americas to discuss how to promote institutional reform, economic growth and the role of a liberal society in that process.

Acción Campesina (Farmers in Action)
$65,000

To promote farmers' rights at the national and local levels through policy reform on agriculture and land redistribution. *Acción Campesina* will serve as a source of information to policy makers, political parties and civil society on the implementation of national laws and its effects on the rural sector and on small farmers.

Asociación Civil Consorcio Justicia – Occidente (Civil Association "Justice Consortium" – West)
$16,000

To strengthen community leadership and peaceful resolution of conflict. *Consorcio Justicia-Occidente* will work with local community organizations in four municipalities in the state of Táchira, on the border of Colombia, to train over 100 community leaders in democratic rights, community organization and techniques of conciliation and negotiation. *Consorcio Justicia-Occidente* will then work with these leaders in their communities to help them carry out projects to develop strategies for addressing local problems.

Asociación Civil Justicia Alternativa (Civil Association "Alternative Justice")
$13,980

To promote conflict resolution and participation at the local level. *Justicia Alternativa* will train community leaders and elected officials in the city of Girardot in Aragua state. Through the training and follow-up, *Justicia Alternativa* will bring together community representatives and locally elected officials to initiate a dialogue for the development of communities and neighborhoods.

Asociación Civil Liderazgo y Visión (Civil Association "Leadership and Vision")
$56,000

To conduct a human rights and democracy training program for officers of the Caracas metropolitan police force. *Liderazgo y Visión* will conduct 60 training courses in the Caracas police academy, training a total of 1,800 members of the metropolitan force. In addition,

Liderazgo y Visión will train a total of twelve representatives in each of the branches of the metropolitan police to serve as coordinators for follow-up and to help organize and conduct courses and informal workshops in the future.

Center for Justice and International Law
$90,000

To promote and defend human rights in Venezuela. CEJIL will continue to present and litigate cases before the Inter-American System (IAS), train human rights activists, journalists, and young leaders in international human rights standards and the use of the IAS, and support and encourage Venezuelan NGOs and civil society organizations in their efforts to defend human rights and promote reasoned discourse and dialogue over the future of human rights and democracy in their country.

Fundación Justicia de Paz del Estado Monagas (Justice of Peace of Monagas State Foundation)
$11,490

To promote women's leadership and conflict resolution at the local level. *Fundación Justicia de Paz* will work with community organizations throughout the state of Monagas to train local women leaders and female judicial officials in peaceful resolution of conflict, constitutional rights, and state judicial institutions.

NED's Grants to CIPE-CEDICE
2002-2003
"Plan Consensus"

PROJECT ACTIVITIES

Project Advisory Committee

The project advisory committee will consist of the following individuals and organizations:

Hugo Fonseca Viso	Fedecámaras
Jorge Botti	Fedecámaras
Jesus Urbieta	Confederación de Trabajadores Venezolanos
Nelson Landáez	Confederación de Trabajadores Venezolanos
Maxim Ross	Citizens Assembly
Marisol Fuentes	Sol Communications
William Echeverria	Radio Caracas
Jorge Reyes	Sinergia
Tiziana Polesel	CEDICE
Luis Eduardo Rodríguez	CEDICE
Aurelio Concheso	CEDICE
Mikel De Viana, SJ	Catholic Church

Meetings with Civil Society Groups

Four meetings will be organized with Fedecámaras, CTV, as well as civil society groups in Venezuela. The business and labor sectors, the media, the church, and other non-profit groups will gather to discuss and develop a broad consensus on a National Agenda—the specific economic policies that Venezuela should adopt in order to resolve the urgent crisis that the country currently faces in the economic as well as political and social arenas.

In addition, four members of CEDICE's academic group and two representatives of the Citizens Assembly will conduct a study to investigate the causes of the current economic crisis as well as to identify measures for both sustainable economic development as well as social improvement.

Development and Dissemination of a Policy Paper

Based on the collaborative analysis and consensus from the four meetings and the research study described above, the groups will develop a National Agenda document to describe their economic policy recommendations. To present and promote the results to the public at large, the groups will work with the media (*El Nacional*, *El Universal*, and Globo Visión) to design and implement a dissemination strategy.

Regional Workshops and National Forums

193

Organization	Representative
Asamblea de Ciudadanos (civil association)	Mr. Axel Capriles
Abriendo Caminos (political movement)	Mr. Pedro Penzini
Alianza Bravo Pueblo (political party)	Mr. Antonio Ledezma
Fundación Raúl Leoni/Acción Democrática (political party)	Mr. Ramón Rangel
Gente de Petróleo (civil association)	Mr. Nelson Benitez
Instituto Altos Estudios Sindicales/CTV (workers' union)	Mr. Alfredo Padilla
Alianza Cívica de la Sociedad Civil (civil association)	Mr. Elias Santana
Ifedec-Copei (political party)	Mr. Eduardo Fernández
Liderazgo y Visión (civil association)	Mr. Alonso E. Dominguez
Proyecto Venezuela (political party)	Mrs. Maria Isabel Canales
Red Democrática Universitaria (civil association)	Mr. Tomás Páez
Visión Emergente (political party)	Mr. Cipriano Heredia
Un Solo Pueblo (political party)	Mr. William Ojeda
Bandera Roja (left political party)	Mr. Carlos Hermoso
Resistencia Civil (civil association)	Mr. Domingo A. Rangel
Democratic Coordinator (opposition umbrella organization)	Mr. Diego B. Urbaneja
Fedecámaras (strategic committee) (business association)	Mrs. Albis Muñoz Mr. Fedor Saldivia

NED Project Report to Venezuela,
Heading by Christopher Sabatini
June 16-25, 2002

To: Carl, Barbara, Sandra, and Taryn
From: Chris Sabatini
RE: Trip Report Venezuela, June 16-25

    1.   General political situation

Complicated. It's the word you always hear when you ask people to explain what's happening in Venezuela. They say it with a sense of despair and defeat. The political agendas of different actors and alliances are complicated and obscure (What is the end-game of the ex-chavistas, such as Luis Miquilena, who are now backing a plan to remove Chavez? Does Chavez know about the political conspiracies that are swirling around him, according to some, within his own inner circle? Is he planning to use them to his own advantage?) The role of the military and their intentions are complicated. (The military has become factionalized, and it's unclear who backs whom and why.) And for these reasons, it's difficult, if not impossible, to predict what will happen in the future. (The lines are clearly drawn between Chavistas and anti-Chavistas, with the anti-Chavez groups—military and civilian—hatching numerous and conflicting plans to remove the president and Chavez publicly and aggressively proclaiming his intention to defend the revolution, in a phrase borrowed from Fidel Castro, "to the death.") In the midst of this polarized, political muddle two things become clear: first, the border that once divided military and civilian politics has been broken, perhaps irrevocably and second Venezuelan politics are locked in a confrontation for which it appears there is no consensus exit, and which admits very little room for outside mediation. Since April 11th, the government and the opposition have become locked in a zero-sum game, while much of the population waits to see its outcome. In the meantime, the economy continues to deteriorate, with some observers predicting a collapse of the financial and public sector within months.

Venezuelan politics have become a dizzying swirl of plots, counterplots and hidden agendas. Members of the traditional opposition (the CTV, the business community, and opposition parties) continue to mobilize protest marches to call for Chavez's resignation. Shortly before I arrived, the opposition had organized a march to the presidential palace. At the march, one opposition party, *Acción Democrática*, declared that it would remain in front of the palace until Chavez resigned. (They later decamped, unvictorious.) In the same march, several of the more political civil society groups (led by Elias Santana of *Queremos Elegir*) called for mass protest against the government by refusing to pay taxes--a plan which is actually unworkable since most Venezuelan taxes are based on sales tax which is automatically calculated in the charge when you make a purchase. For many of these groups, the goal is to mobilize sufficient public pressure and protest to force the resignation of the government. There are a number of politicized civil society groups (among them *Queremos Elegir* and *Red de Veedores*) that have joined in this call for immediate resignation. Many had hoped that the march planned for July 11th, the third anniversary of April 11th, would bring the full force of popular opposition against the government and force the president to step down. But even then, many people claimed—as they have been saying for years—that Chavez wouldn't last that long—that

195

the military will attempt to remove him before then. At the same time, Chavez has stepped up his political attacks against his opponents and has allegedly increased his distribution of arms to the Bolivarian Circles.

One of the more active groups that has been plotting Chavez's removal is a group of ex-Chavistas, named *Solidaridad*, led by ex-interior minister Luis Miquilena. In collaboration with a number of groups, *Solidaridad* has initiated several judicial cases against the president. In all, there have been 61 cases brought against the President, the most important of these include allegation of mis-appropriation of state funds (FIEM) derived from the oil windfall of the last three years, campaign finance violations in which the president allegedly did not declare $1.5 million in funds received from the *Banco de Vizcaya*, and charges stemming from the shooting on April 11th. The plan to prosecute Chavez for any of these charges was given a boost the week I was in Venezuela when the supreme court ruled that plaintiffs in cases against the government could bring the cases directly to the Supreme Court, rather than through the Prosecutor General. The Prosecutor General, Isais Rodriguez, is an avowed Chavista who has openly voiced his continued support for the president. (The Supreme Court's decision was actually a violation of the recently approved criminal procedures code, which removed justices from prosecution and established a more U.S.-style adversarial system.) Many people credit the supreme court's decision to the machinations of Miquilena, who, as interior minister under Chavez, had named a number of the justices to the court. The decision and the cases that will result represent the opposition's more "institutionalist" route for removing Chavez.

But while the more democratic path to changing the government signals a greater intent by some sectors of the opposition to use state channels to force a change of government, the opposition's enthusiasm for Miquilena's actions is curious. Only months before, when he was in government, many people deeply distrusted Miquilena, believing him to be the sinister, ideological pupeteer of the charismatic Chavez. The belief was that the 84 year-old Miquilena was using Chavez as the charismatic public face for his ideological master plan. Now he has become the architect and dealmaker in support of the opposition. There are also rumors that he maintains close contact with several people in the administration and some sectors of the military.

The military's role in all of this is unclear. It is clearly factionalized, among units and between officer classes. There are strong rumors of conspiracies being hatched by the military and dissident officer groups. But the extent to which these individuals and groups command loyalty among the ranks is unclear. First there is the COMACATE, a group of dissident junior officers (commanders, captains, majors and lieutenant colonels). A week before I arrived they issued a public declaration denouncing the government as illegitimate. Another faction includes retired military officers, which held a march to protest the Chavez government. There are also rumors that different civilian leaders are maintaining regular contact with various elements in military, and that the opposition to Chavez within the military extends to the inner circle of military hierarchy around the President. The big event was to have come July 5th when the president announced a new round of military promotions. While the much-anticipated uprising never occurred, many believe that this leapfrogging of promotion (in a military that has always prided itself—though not always followed it—on its merit-based system) and the government's alleged support for the FARC in Colombia will ultimately provoke a coup by disaffected officers.

In all of this, military officers are assuming a greater political role. They now have an audience and pockets of support for their opposition to the government, and there is a sense that some military officers are enjoying this public role. There is a notable increase in their pronouncements and their general presence in the public debate. The military has now become a part and a victim of the political polarization within Venezuela. After the events of April 11th and the public reaction to them, however, there is a notable reluctance of civil society and civilian politicians (at least publicly) to embrace the military too closely. In contrast to the situation before April 11th, civil society leaders are less enthusiastic about military officers now declaring their opposition to the government, which they do with increasing frequency. The events of April 11th demonstrated the deep divisions within the military. Many fear that the next military coup would result in bloodshed. A coup d'etat now would likely provoke a confrontation between units and officers still loyal to the President and the rebellious officers. The Chavez government would also certainly unleash its *Circulos Bolivarianos*--which Chavez has continued to arm and incite to support the revolution. There are also claims that should the sectors of the military move against the government, its strategy would be one of "take no prisoners" and one which may also seek to exclude some of the more moderate and/or leftist civilian politicians from any future government.

For his part, Chavez has done little to demonstrate his good faith or desire for a mediated solution and has continued to inflame popular passions and class tensions. The events of April 11th appear to have only hardened its position. There are rumors—fairly common, if that's any indication of their veracity, but in this situation who knows?—that the government has distributed Uzi's to the Bolivarian circles. The person in charge of organizing the Bolivarian Circles has an office in the presidential palace and the arms are apparently financed by the state. The government has also installed anti-aircraft missiles on the roofs of several buildings around the city, allegedly in anticipation of the July 11th march. Statements by the President have inflamed the situation and appear to be preparing the country for a conflict. In a speech, delivered in a shantytown on the same day of the march of the retired-military officers, the President, encircled by mid-level officers and dressed in an orange jumpsuit, asked his followers "not to be unaware" of what was going on and to be ready to "defend the revolution" against those who are trying to undermine it. The verbal assaults against his opponents continue daily, on the radio, on t.v, in press conferences, and in public speeches. The intention obviously is to prepare his followers (he has supposedly at least 20% core support in the population) to back him—violently if necessary—against any attempts to remove him. As a result, middle and upper classes feel extremely insecure and fear for their lives and property. Contingency plans have been developed in middle and upper class neighborhoods for residents to defend themselves in the event that private groups armed by the government attack.

Unclassified Documents

1. Secret Document from the Department of Defense
2. Cable from the Department of State, September, 2001, pp. 1-2
3. Cable from the Department of State, December, 2001
4. Cable from the Department of State, March, 2002, pp. 1-4
5. CIA SEIB's Report, March 11, 2002, pp. 1-2
6. CIA SEIB's Report, April 6, 2002, pp.1-2
7. Cable from the Department of State, April 9, 2002, pp. 1-2
8. Cable from the Department of State, April 11, 2002, pp. 1-7
9. Cable from the Department of State, April 13, 2002, pp. 1-4
10. Cable from the Department of State, April 14, 2002, pp. 1-2
11. Cable from the Department of State, April 14, 2002 (Otto Reich), pp. 1-4
12. Department of State Press Guidance, April 16, 2002, pp. 1-3
13. Department of State Press Guidance, April 17, 2002, p. 1
14. Department of State Press Guidance, April 19, 2002, pp. 1-2
15. Department of State Press Guidance, April 22, 2002, p.1
16. Department of State Press Guidance, August 12, 13, 2002, pp. 1-2

1. Document from the Deparment of Defense

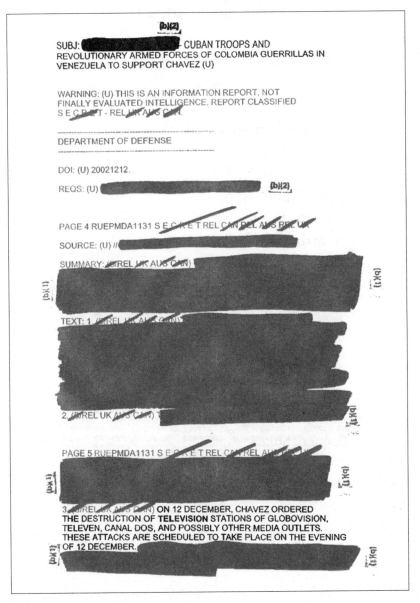

(b)(2)

SUBJ: ████████████ - CUBAN TROOPS AND REVOLUTIONARY ARMED FORCES OF COLOMBIA GUERRILLAS IN VENEZUELA TO SUPPORT CHAVEZ (U)

WARNING: (U) THIS IS AN INFORMATION REPORT, NOT FINALLY EVALUATED INTELLIGENCE. REPORT CLASSIFIED S E C R E T - REL UK AUS CAN.

DEPARTMENT OF DEFENSE

DOI: (U) 20021212.

REQS: (U) ████████████████ (b)(2)

PAGE 4 RUEPMDA1131 S E C R E T REL CAN REL UK

SOURCE: (U) //█████████████

SUMMARY: (S//REL UK AUS CAN)

(b)(1)   (b)(1)

TEXT: 1. (S//REL UK AUS CAN)

2. (S//REL UK AUS CAN)   (b)(1)

PAGE 5 RUEPMDA1131 S E C R E T REL CAN REL AUS

(b)(1)   (b)(1)

3. (S//REL UK AUS CAN) ON 12 DECEMBER, CHAVEZ ORDERED THE DESTRUCTION OF **TELEVISION** STATIONS OF GLOBOVISION, TELEVEN, CANAL DOS, AND POSSIBLY OTHER MEDIA OUTLETS. THESE ATTACKS ARE SCHEDULED TO TAKE PLACE ON THE EVENING OF 12 DECEMBER.

(b)(1)   (b)(1)

```
   Current Class: UNCLASSIFIED          UNCLASSIFIED
Current Handling: n/a

                         UNCLASSIFIED      PTO9054

PAGE 01          CARACA   02839   272141Z        RELEASED IN FULL
ACTION EB-00

INFO   LOG-00   AIT-03   CEA-01   CIAE-00  CTME-00  DODE-00  ITCE-00
       WHA-00   SRPP-00  EXME-00  E-00     UTED-00  VC-00    FRB-00
       H-01     TEDE-00  INR-00   ITC-01   L-00     VCE-00   AC-01
       NSAE-00  NSCE-00  OES-01   OMB-01   OPIC-01  ACE-00   SP-00
       SSO-00   SS-00    STR-00   TEST-00  TRSE-00  USIE-00  PMP-00
       EPAE-00  DRL-02   G-00     NFAT-00  SAS-00   /012W
                -----------------265FBA  272141Z /38
R 272125Z SEP 01
FM AMEMBASSY CARACAS
TO SECSTATE WASHDC 3380
USDOC WASHDC
INFO DEPT OF COMMERCE WASHDC
DEPT OF ENERGY WASHDC

UNCLAS CARACAS 002839

STATE FOR EB, H, WHA/AND
USDOC FOR 4331/MAC/TWELCH; 3134/USFCS/OIO/WH/DLUTTER

E.O. 12958: N/A
TAGS: EFIN, ETRD, WTO, VE
SUBJECT: VENEZUELA-U.S. BUSINESS COUNCIL REQUESTS WASHINGTON
MEETINGS

1.   ACTION REQUEST; SEE PARAGRAPH 5.

2.   SENIOR OFFICERS OF THE VENEZUELA-U.S. BUSINESS COUNCIL (CEVEU)
                     UNCLASSIFIED

PAGE 02          CARACA   02839   272141Z
PLAN TO VISIT WASHINGTON D.C. FROM NOVEMBER 1-2, 2001 AND WISH TO
MEET WITH SENIOR GOVERNMENT OFFICIALS IN THE DEPARTMENT, OFFICE OF
U.S. TRADE REPRESENTATIVE, DEPARTMENT OF COMMERCE, DEPARTMENT OF
ENERGY, AND SELECTED MEMBERS OF CONGRESS. CEVEU (CONSEJO DE
EMPRESARIOS VENEZUELA-ESTADOS UNIDOS) IS A HIGHLY RESPECTED
BUSINESS AND TRADE ASSOCIATION THAT HAS TAKEN THE LEAD IN
PROMOTING INITIATIVES THAT CLOSELY MIRROR U.S. POSITIONS.  THIS
VISIT IS AN EXCELLENT OPPORTUNITY FOR SENIOR U.S. OFFICIALS TO
HEAR ABOUT PENDING U.S.-VENEZUELAN TRADE ISSUES FROM THE
VENEZUELAN PRIVATE SECTOR PERSPECTIVE.  CEVEU PARTICULARLY LOOKS
FORWARD TO AN EXCHANGE OF VIEWS ON FTAA, THE PROPOSED BILATERAL
INVESTMENT TREATY, THE PROPOSED NEW ROUND OF WTO NEGOTIATIONS, AND
THE POSSIBLE INCLUSION OF VENEZUELA IN THE ANDEAN TRADE
PREFERENCES ACT (ATPA).

Current Class: UNCLASSIFIED
```

UNCLASSIFIED

2. Cable from the Department of State
September 2001, p. 2

Current Class: UNCLASSIFIED
Current Handling: n/a

3.   THE CEVEU DELEGATION WILL CONSIST OF GUSTAVO MARTURET,
PRESIDENT OF CEVEU AND CHIEF EXECUTIVE OFFICER OF BANCO MERCANTIL;
LOPE MENDOZA, PRESIDENT OF CONINDUSTRIA (COUNCIL OF INDUSTRIES);
DR. PEDRO CARMONA, PRESIDENT OF FEDECAMERAS (NATIONAL COUNCIL OF
CHAMBERS OF BUSINESS); ALEJANDRO REYES, VICE PRESIDENT OF CEVEU;
ANA TERESA WALLIS, EXECUTIVE DIRECTOR OF CEVEU; LUIS ENRIQUE BALL,
CEVEU DIRECTOR AND CEO OF THE PRIVATE FIRM EUROCIENCIA; AND
TENTATIVELY, DR. GUSTAVO JULIO VOLLMER, CEVEU DIRECTOR AND
PRESIDENT OF THE PRIVATE FIRM CORPALMAR.

4.   THE CEVEU REPRESENTATIVES HAVE REQUESTED MEETINGS WITH GRANT
D. ALDONAS, UNDER SECRETARY OF COMMERCE FOR INTERNATIONAL TRADE;
VICKY BAILEY, ASSISTANT SECRETARY FOR POLICY AND INTERNATIONAL
AFFAIRS, DEPARTMENT OF ENERGY; ANTHONY WAYNE, ASSISTANT SECRETARY
OF STATE FOR ECONOMIC AND BUSINESS AFFAIRS; AND REGINA VARGO, U.S.
TRADE REPRESENTATIVE FOR LATIN AMERICA.   THEY HAVE ALSO REQUESTED
                          UNCLASSIFIED

PAGE 03   CARACA 02839 272141Z
APPOINTMENTS WITH U.S. REPRESENTATIVE CASS BALLENGER, U.S.
REPRESENTATIVE GREGORY MEEKS, U.S. REPRESENTATIVE MARK SOUDER, ALL
OF WHO HAVE RECENTLY VISITED VENEZUELA AND SHARE AN ACTIVE
INTEREST IN IMPROVED BILATERAL RELATIONS.   LASTLY, THEY WISH TO
MEET WITH U.S. SENATOR BOB GRAHAM AND U.S. REPRESENTATIVE PHILIP
CRANE, WHO ARE SPONSORING RECENTLY INTRODUCED ATPA LEGISLATION IN
THE SENATE AND HOUSE OF REPRESENTATIVES, RESPECTIVELY.

5.   EMBASSY CARACAS STRONGLY SUPPORTS THIS REQUEST FROM CEVEU.
THE MEMBERS OF THE CEVEU DELEGATION ARE HIGHLY REGARDED AND
INFLUENTIAL BUSINESS LEADERS WHO HAVE CONSISTENTLY PLAYED A
CRITICAL ROLE IN ADVANCING U.S. COMMERCIAL INTERESTS IN VENEZUELA.
EMBASSY REQUESTS THE DEPARTMENT AND OTHER AGENCIES ASSISTANCE IN
ARRANGING THESE MEETINGS.

HRINAK

                     UNCLASSIFIED

<< END OF DOCUMENT >>

Current Class: UNCLASSIFIED

UNCLASSIFIED

3. Cable from the Department of State
December 2001

CONFRONTATION OF IDEAS, NOT A CONFRONTATION IN THE STREETS.
END SUMMARY.

STATESMAN-LIKE CARMONA STRESSES NON-VIOLENCE
----

2. CARMONA ADDRESSED THE VENEZUELAN-AMERICAN CHAMBER OF
COMMERCE (VENAMCHAM) DECEMBER 6, AND GAVE A WIDELY COVERED
PRESS CONFERENCE ON DECEMBER 7. IN BOTH APPEARANCES,
CARMONA DELIVERED CALM AND STATESMAN-LIKE SPEECHES
EXPLAINING THE WORK STOPPAGE WILL NOT BE VIOLENT, BUT WILL
BE ONLY A QCONFRONTATION OF IDEAS.Q FEDECAMARAS HAS NOT
PLANNED ANY PUBLIC DEMONSTRATION FOR DECEMBER 10, BUT SAID
IT SHOULD BE A DAY TO QSTAY HOME FROM WORK.Q

3. AT THE VENAMCHAM EVENT, CARMONA RECEIVED AN EXTENDED
                    UNCLASSIFIED

PAGE 03   CARACA 03606 01 OF 02 080156Z
STANDING OVATION, AND WAS INTRODUCED AS QTHE RIGHT MAN FOR
THE RIGHT TIME IN VENEZUELA.Q AS WITH ALL OF HIS RECENT
PUBLIC APPEARANCES, THE PRESS SWARMED CARMONA, GIVING HIM AT
LEAST THE AURA OF A POLITICAL FIGURE AND PROVIDING SOME
FOCUS TO WHAT WERE DISPARATE OPPOSITION VOICES.

SUPPORT FOR THE SHUTDOWN
----

4. THE CONFEDERATION OF VENEZUELAN WORKERS (CTV) ANNOUNCED
THAT THEY SUPPORT THE DECEMBER 10 SHUTDOWN, BUT WOULD NOT
HOLD ANY PUBLIC MARCH OR DEMONSTRATION ON DECEMBER 10.
HOWEVER, CTV SAID IF THE GOV DOES NOT LISTEN TO THEIR
CONCERNS THEY WILL CONSIDER FURTHER NATIONAL STRIKES.

5. THE TRANSPORTATION WORKERS, BANK EMPLOYEES, AND HEALTH
WORKERS ALSO ANNOUNCED SUPPORT FOR THE SHUTDOWN. LOCAL
GASOLINE SERVICE STATIONS HAVE NOT DECIDED IF THEY WILL
CLOSE. ALTHOUGH THE GOV ANNOUNCED THE CARACAS METRO WILL
REMAIN OPEN, SUPPORT FROM THE TRANSPORTATION SECTOR
(REPRESENTING TAXIS AND BUSES) COULD GUARANTEE A TRUE
SHUTDOWN OF CARACAS AND OTHER METROPOLITAN AREAS.

6. U.S. CORPORATIONS CONTACTED BY POST REPORTED A MIX OF
PLANNED ACTIONS. SOME WILL CLOSE AND OTHERS WILL OPEN BUT
MONITOR THE SITUATION. THE U.S. CORPORATIONS POINTED TO
SECURITY CONCERNS AND TRANSPORTATION DIFFICULTIES FOR
WORKERS AS REASONS FOR CLOSING. CITING CONCERN FOR
INVOLVEMENT IN DOMESTIC POLITICS, THOSE THAT EXPECT TO BE

```
      Current Class: UNCLASSIFIED        UNCLASSIFIED
   Current Handling: n/a

                          UNCLASSIFIED      PTQ6780
                                                              E15
   PAGE 01        CARACA  00546  01 OF 02  052201Z    RELEASED IN FULL
   ACTION INR-00

   INFO   LOG-00    NP-00    ACQ-00    DODE-00   WHA-00   DS-00    UTED-00
          VC-00     TEDE-00  VCE-00    AC-01     NSAE-00  ACE-00   IRM-00
          TEST-00   DSCC-00  DRL-02    NFAT-00   SAS-00      /003W
                    -----------------6FF49F  052202Z /38

   R 052151Z MAR 02
   FM AMEMBASSY CARACAS
   TO SECSTATE WASHDC 4949
   INFO CIA WASHDC
   DIA WASHDC
   NSC WASHDC
   USCINCSO MIAMI FL
   AMEMBASSY BOGOTA
   AMEMBASSY BRASILIA
   AMEMBASSY GEORGETOWN
   AMEMBASSY LIMA
   AMEMBASSY LA PAZ
   AMEMBASSY QUITO
   USINT HAVANA

   UNCLAS SECTION 01 OF 02 CARACAS 000546

   INR FOR COZART
   NSC FOR AMBASSADOR MAISTO
   USCINCSO FOR POLAD

   SENSITIVE

                         UNCLASSIFIED

   PAGE 02        CARACA  00546  01 OF 02  052201Z
   E.O. 12958: NA
   TAGS: PREL, PGOV, VE
   SUBJ: LABOR, BUSINESS AND CHURCH ANNOUNCE TRANSITION
   PACT

   1. (SBU) SUMMARY: WITH MUCH FANFARE, THE VENEZUELAN GREAT
   AND GOOD ASSEMBLED ON MARCH 5 TO HEAR REPRESENTATIVES OF
   THE CONFEDERATION OF VENEZUELAN WORKERS, THE FEDERATION OF
   BUSINESS CHAMBERS, AND THE CATHOLIC CHURCH PRESENT THEIR
   "BASES FOR A DEMOCRATIC ACCORD," TEN PRINCIPLES ON WHICH TO
   GUIDE A TRANSITIONAL GOVERNMENT. INITIALLY INTERPRETED IN
   THE PRESS AND SOME CIRCLES AS PERHAPS A BASIS OF DIALOGUE
   WITH THE CHAVEZ GOVERNMENT--THE DOCUMENT WAS ANNOUNCED, BUT
   NOT RELEASED, LAST WEEK--THIS ACCORD WAS CLEARLY INTENDED
   FOR THE OPPOSITION FORCES' EXCLUSIVE USE.  IT WAS

      Current Class: UNCLASSIFIED
```

UNCLASSIFIED

UNCLASSIFIED

Current Class: UNCLASSIFIED
Current Handling: n/a

ENTHUSIASTICALLY RECEIVED BY THE ASSEMBLED "ESCUALIDOS,"
WHO INTERRUPTED THE SPEAKERS OFTEN WITH ANTI-CHAVEZ CHANTS.
THIS ACCORD REPRESENTS AN IMPORTANT STEP FOR THE
OPPOSITION, WHICH HAS BEEN QUICK TO CONDEMN CHAVEZ BUT HAD
SO FAR OFFERED NO VISION OF ITS OWN. END SUMMARY.

TEN POINTS FOR A DEMOCRATIC ACCORD
----

2. (U) WITH MUCH FANFARE, THE VENEZUELAN GREAT AND GOOD
ASSEMBLED ON MARCH 5 IN CARACAS'S ESMERALDA AUDITORIUM TO
HEAR REPRESENTATIVES OF THE CONFEDERATION OF VENEZUELAN
WORKERS (CTV), THE FEDERATION OF BUSINESS CHAMBERS
(FEDECAMARAS), AND THE CATHOLIC CHURCH PRESENT THEIR "BASES
FOR A DEMOCRATIC ACCORD"--TEN PRINCIPLES ON WHICH TO GUIDE
UNCLASSIFIED

PAGE 03   CARACA 00546 01 OF 02 052201Z
A TRANSITIONAL GOVERNMENT. THE EXISTENCE OF THIS ACCORD
WAS ANNOUNCED LAST WEEK AND HAS SINCE DRAWN MUCH
SPECULATION ABOUT WHETHER IT WAS INTENDED AS THE BASIS FOR
A POST-CHAVEZ GOVERNMENT OR AS A LAST-DITCH EFFORT TO
PROMOTE A DIALOGUE WITH THE GOVERNMENT. IN HIS COMBATIVE
CENTERPIECE ADDRESS, CTV PRESIDENT CARLOS ORTEGA DISPELLED
ANY REMAINING DOUBTS; THIS ACCORD IS "A PACT FOR US," HE
EMPHASIZED, TO GUIDE US THROUGH THE TRANSITION AND TO
ESTABLISH A "GOVERNMENT OF DEMOCRATIC UNITY." THE CROWD
GREETED THESE REMARKS WITH ROUSING ANTI-CHAVEZ CHANTS.

3. (U) BESIDES ATTRACTING EXTENSIVE MEDIA COVERAGE, THE
SPEECHES ON THE ACCORD WERE BEING BROADCAST, WE WERE TOLD,
BY ALL NON-GOVERNMENTAL TV STATIONS. FR. LUIS UGALDE,
S.J., RECTOR OF THE CATHOLIC UNIVERSITY OF ANDRES BELLO,
EXPLAINED HOW THIS ACCORD BEGAN WITH CONFERENCES BETWEEN
BUSINESS AND LABOR HOSTED BY THE CATHOLIC EPISCOPAL
CONFERENCE LAST DECEMBER. JESUS URBIETA, FORMER CTV
INTERIM PRESIDENT AND HEAD OF THE CONFEDERATION'S THINK
TANK, READ THE MAIN POINTS, WHICH CAN BE SUMMARIZED
BRIEFLY:

--OVERCOMING POVERTY BY PROVIDING MORE ECONOMIC
OPPORTUNITIES. THIS INCLUDES "FIGHTING POPULIST VISIONS
THAT FOOL THE POPULAR SECTORS WITH MESSIANIC OR ERRONEOUS
VISIONS OF THE REALITY OF THE COUNTRY."

--FORGING NATIONAL UNITY THAT INCLUDES EVERYONE IN THE
DEMOCRATIC PROCESS AND INFORMAL SECTORS IN THE NATIONAL
ECONOMY.

Current Class: UNCLASSIFIED

UNCLASSIFIED

UNCLASSIFIED

Current Class: UNCLASSIFIED
Current Handling: n/a

UNCLAS SECTION 02 OF 02 CARACAS 000546

INR FOR COZART
NSC FOR AMBASSADOR MAISTO
USCINCSO FOR POLAD

SENSITIVE

UNCLASSIFIED

PAGE 02   CARACA 00546 02 OF 02 052201Z

E.O. 12958: NA
TAGS: PREL, PGOV, VE
SUBJ: LABOR, BUSINESS AND CHURCH ANNOUNCE TRANSITION
PACT

FUNCTION.

--PROMOTING COOPERATION BETWEEN LABOR AND CAPITAL, AND THE
RIGHT OF CONSUMERS, TOO.

--RECUPERATING THE INTERNATIONAL IMAGE OF VENEZUELA.

--STRIVING AGAINST CORRUPTION--"WE NEED MORAL LEADERSHIP
THAT PREACHES BY EXAMPLE AND WITH ITS ACTIONS"--AND
PROMOTING "PUBLIC AUSTERITY" TO PREVENT THE SQUANDERING OF
RESOURCES.

4. (U) FOR THE MOST PART, THE SPEAKERS AVOIDED DISCUSSING
THE POLITICS OF THE MOMENT, AND THEY HAD NO NEED TO POINT
OUT HOW THEIR POINTS CONTRAST WITH THE ACTUAL
CHARACTERISTICS OF THE CHAVEZ GOVERNMENT. FEDECAMARAS
PRESIDENT PEDRO CARMONA DID CALL FOR THE RESIGNATION OF THE
PDVSA'S BOARD OF DIRECTORS, AND AT ONE POINT ORTEGA
DENOUNCED CHAVEZ BY NAME. OTHERWISE, THE SPEAKERS
EMPHASIZED THEIR ACCORD AS "A SHARED VISION" AND "A SIGNAL
OF HOPE" FOR VENEZUELANS PREOCCUPIED WITH WHAT WAS DEEMED
"A TRUE NATIONAL EMERGENCY."

COMMENT: ANOTHER PIECE FALLS INTO PLACE
                 UNCLASSIFIED

PAGE 03   CARACA 00546 02 OF 02 052201Z
----

5. (SBU) THIS ACCORD REPRESENTS AN IMPORTANT STEP FOR THE
OPPOSITION, WHICH HAS BEEN ALWAYS QUICK TO CONDEMN CHAVEZ
BUT HAD SO FAR OFFERED NO COMPREHENSIVE VISION OF ITS OWN.
BUT ONCE AGAIN, IN THE ABSENCE OF A SINGLE OPPOSITION PARTY

Current Class: UNCLASSIFIED

UNCLASSIFIED

OR FIGURE THAT CAN RALLY PUBLIC SENTIMENT, BUSINESS AND
LABOR LEADERS, WITH THE SUPPORT OF THE CATHOLIC CHURCH,
HAVE STEPPED INTO THE BREACH. THE OPPOSITION PARTIES NOW
WILL CERTAINLY HASTEN TO ENDORSE THIS ACCORD, WHICH, THOUGH
SOMEWHAT VAGUE AND FEEL-GOODY, MAY WELL FORM THE FRAME OF
REFERENCE AND CODE OF CONDUCT FOR A TRANSITIONAL
GOVERNMENT. THEY MAY FIND IT DIFFICULT, HOWEVER, TO
RECAPTURE THE SPOTLIGHT FROM ORTEGA AND CARMONA, THE TWO
UNLIKELY ALLIES BUT INDISPENSABLE LEADERS OF THE ANTI-
CHAVISTA OPPOSITION.

COOK

<< END OF DOCUMENT >>

MORI DocID: 1136215

TOP SECRET

Senior Executive Intelligence Brief

(b) (1)
(b) (3)

The SEIB must be returned to CIA within 5 working days

Monday, 11 March 2002

National Security Information

Unauthorized Disclosure Subject to Criminal Sanctions
Reproduction of this Document Prohibited

APPROVED FOR RELEASE
DATE: OCT 2004

CIA PASS SEIB 02-457CHX

TOP SECRET

MORI DocID: 1136215

~~TOP SECRET/~~

Key Current Warning Issues

The DCI Strategic Warning Committee considers the following the most critical warning issues during the next few weeks.

Venezuela. There are increased signs that Venezuelan business leaders and military officers are becoming dissatisfied with President Chavez, and he clearly is concerned and is trying to tone down his rhetoric. The opposition has yet to organize itself into a united front. If the situation further deteriorates and demonstrations become even more violent or if Chavez attempts an unconstitutional move to add to his powers, the military may move to overthrow him.

The DCI Strategic Warning Committee, chaired by the National Intelligence Officer for Warning, comprises representatives from the Directors of the National Security Agency, the Defense Intelligence Agency, and the National Imagery and Mapping Agency; the Assistant Secretary of State for Intelligence and Research; and the Deputy Director for Intelligence, Central Intelligence Agency.

TOP SECRET/

11 March 2002

MORI DocID: 1136214

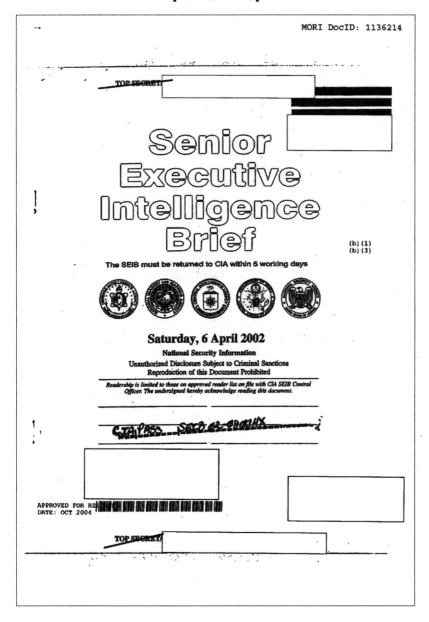

TOP SECRET

Senior Executive Intelligence Brief

(b)(1)
(b)(3)

The SEIB must be returned to CIA within 5 working days

Saturday, 6 April 2002

National Security Information

Unauthorized Disclosure Subject to Criminal Sanctions
Reproduction of this Document Prohibited

Readership is limited to those on approved reader list on file with CIA SEIB Control Officer. The undersigned hereby acknowledge reading this document.

APPROVED FOR RE
DATE: OCT 2004

TOP SECRET

MORI DocID: 1136214

TOP SECRET

Venezuela: **Conditions Ripening for Coup Attempt**

Dissident military factions, including some disgruntled senior officers and a group of radical junior officers, are stepping up efforts to organize a coup against President Chavez, possibly as early as this month, The level of detail in the reported plans— targets Chavez and 10 other senior officials for arrest—lends credence to the information, but military and civilian contacts note that neither group appears ready to lead a successful coup and may bungle the attempt by moving too quickly.

     — Civilian groups opposed to Chavez's policies, including the Catholic Church, business groups, and labor, are backing away from efforts to involve them in the plotting, probably to avoid being tainted by an extraconstitutional move and fear that a failed attempt could strengthen Chavez's hand.

Prospects for a successful coup at this point are limited. The plotters still lack the political cover to stage a coup, Chavez's core support base among poor Venezuelans remains intact, and repeated warnings that the US will not support any extraconstitutional moves to oust Chavez probably have given pause to the plotters.

     — Chavez is monitoring opponents inside and outside the military,

To provoke military action, the plotters may try to exploit unrest stemming from opposition demonstrations slated for later this month or ongoing strikes at the state-owned oil company PDVSA. White-collar oil workers began striking on Thursday at facilities in 11 of 23 states as part of an escalating protest against Chavez's efforts to politicize PDVSA.

     — Protracted strikes, particularly if they have the support of the blue-collar oil workers' union, could trigger a confrontation.

TOP SECRET

5

6 April 2002

210

7. Cable from the Department of State
April 9, 2002, p. 1

LAST NIGHT - BIG PARTY AT PDVSA AND LOUD CACEROLAZOS

----

8. (SBU) A JUBILANT CROWD, ESTIMATED BY ECONOFF TO BE FIVE
TO SEVEN THOUSAND STRONG, GATHERED AT PDVSA HEADQUARTERS
UNTIL LATE LAST NIGHT LISTENING TO A MYRIAD OF OPPOSITION
SPEAKERS AND GENERALLY CELEBRATING WHAT THEY PERCEIVED TO BE
THEIR GATHERING MOMENTUM.   VIRTUALLY ALL PROMINENT
OPPOSITION FIGURES INCLUDING PEDRO CARMONA, ALFREDO PENA,
AND CARLOS ORTEGA GAVE IMPROMPTU SPEECHES.   CARMONA SEEMED
PARTICULARLY ENERGIZED BY THE SIZE AND MOOD OF THE CROWD
                     CONFIDENTIAL

PAGE 05   CARACA   00966   01 OF 03   111109Z

                   CONFIDENTIAL

                       CONFIDENTIAL   PTQ8421

PAGE 01   CARACA   00966   02 OF 03   111110Z
ACTION WHA-00

INFO   LOG-00   NP-00   AID-00   ACQ-00   CEA-01   CIAE-00   COME-00
      CTME-00   DINT-00   DODE-00   DOEE-00   DOTE-00   PERC-00   SRPP-00
      DS-00   EB-00   EXIM-01   E-00   FAAE-00   VC-00   FRB-00
      H-01   TEDE-00   INR-00   ITC-01   LAB-01   L-00   VCE-00
      AC-01   NSAE-00   NSCE-00   OES-01   OMB-01   OPIC-01   PA-00
      PM-00   PRS-00   ACE-00   P-00   SP-00   IRM-00   SSO-00
      STR-00   TRSE-00   USIE-00   PMB-00   DSCC-00   DRL-02   G-00
      NFAT-00   SAS-00   /011W
                  -----------------8279D0   111145Z /38
O 111048Z APR 02
FM AMEMBASSY CARACAS

UNCLASSIFIED

Current Class: CONFIDENTIAL
Current Handling: n/a

TO SECSTATE WASHDC IMMEDIATE 5429
INFO OPEC COLLECTIVE IMMEDIATE
AMEMBASSY BOGOTA
AMEMBASSY QUITO
AMEMBASSY LA PAZ
AMEMBASSY LIMA
USCINCSO MIAMI FL

C O N F I D E N T I A L SECTION 02 OF 03 CARACAS 000966

NSC FOR AMB MAISTO
USCINSCO FOR POLAD

E.O. 12958: DECL: 1.6X1
                    CONFIDENTIAL

PAGE 02   CARACA 00966 02 OF 03 111110Z
TAGS: ECON, PGOV, PREL, EPET, ETRD, VE
SUBJECT: "PARO" UPDATE/GENERAL STRIKE ANNOUNCED

AFTER APPEARING LESS THAN ENTHUSIASTIC ABOUT CONTINUING
OPPOSITION ACTIONS DURING THE DAY.

9. (SBU) THROUGHOUT CARACAS, "CACEROLAZOS" WERE CONSTANT AND
LOUD. MANY PARTS OF CARACAS WERE FILLED WITH PEOPLE
GATHERED ON STREET CORNERS, CARS DRIVING WITH LIGHTS
BLINKING AND HORNS SOUNDING. IT WAS A CELEBRATORY
ATMOSPHERE NOT UNLIKE AFTER VENEZUELA DEFEATED PARAGUAY IN
WORLD CUP QUALIFYING. TELEVISION REPORTED SIMILAR EVENTS IN
MANY OTHER PARTS OF VENEZUELA.

CADENA BATTLE
----
10. (SBU) THE BATTLE OVER THE GOV ORDERED CADENAS CONTINUED
LAST NIGHT WITH ALL STATIONS USING A SPLIT-SCREEN WITH THE
OFFICIAL CADENA ON ONE SIDE AND COVERAGE OF OPPOSITION
EVENTS ON THE OTHER. (NON-NEWS CHANNELS ALSO TOOK ADVANTAGE
OF THE SPLIT-SCREEN AS A SPORTS ONLY CHANNEL CONTINUED
SPORTS COVERAGE ON ONE HALF OF THE SCREEN).

11. (SBU) THROUGHOUT THE DAY TODAY, THE GOV HAD NO CADENAS.
MVR SOURCES SAID THAT CHAVEZ HAD MADE A DECISION TO BACK
DOWN. HE WAS DESCRIBED AS A "BOXER WHO MADE A TACTICAL
RETREAT." INSTEAD, THE GOV LEADERS SPOKE THROUGH TELEVISION
INTERVIEWS THROUGHOUT THE DAY WHICH WERE COVERED AS ORDINARY
NEWS EVENTS BY THE TELEVISION STATIONS.

                    CONFIDENTIAL

Current Class: CONFIDENTIAL

UNCLASSIFIED

```
        Current Class: UNCLASSIFIED        UNCLASSIFIED
Current Handling: SBU

                       UNCLASSIFIED      PTQ0954              E23

PAGE 01        CARACA  00985  01 OF 02  120403Z
ACTION DS-00

INFO  LOG-00   MFA-00   NP-00    AMAD-00  ACQ-00   CIAE-00  COME-00
      DODE-00  DOTE-00  WHA-00   EB-00    FAAE-00  UTED-00  VC-00
      TEDE-00  INR-00   VCE-00   AC-01    NSAE-00  NSCE-00  PER-00
      ACE-00   IRM-00   SSO-00   SS-00    TEST-00  EPAE-00  DSCC-00
      DRL-02   NFAT-00  SAS-00   /003W
                       ---------------8512E6  120403Z /38
O 120341Z APR 02
FM AMEMBASSY CARACAS                      RELEASED IN PART
TO SECSTATE WASHDC IMMEDIATE 5455         B6, B1, 1.4(D)
INFO DEPT OF TREASURY WASHDC//OASIA//
AMEMBASSY BOGOTA
AMEMBASSY LA PAZ
AMEMBASSY LIMA
AMEMBASSY QUITO
USCINCSO MIAMI FL//POLAD//

UNCLAS SECTION 01 OF 02 CARACAS 000985

NSC FOR AMB MAISTO
STATE FOR DS/OP/WHA, S/ES-O_DS/OP/CC

SENSITIVE

E.O. 12958: N/A
TAGS: ASEC, ECON, PGOV, PREL, VE
SUBJECT: TALE OF TWO CITIES - THE MARCH ON MIRAFLORES PALACE

                       UNCLASSIFIED

PAGE 02        CARACA  00985  01 OF 02  120403Z
SENSITIVE BUT UNCLASSIFIED, PLEASE HANDLE ACCORDINGLY.

REF: CARACAS 000965

-------
SUMMARY
-------

1. (SBU) MEETING ON THE MORNING OF APRIL 11TH, THE OPPOSITION'S
"COORDINATING COMMITTEE FOR DEMOCRACY AND LIBERTY" DECIDED TO GO
FOR BROKE - TO SEEK THE IMMEDIATE DEPARTURE OF PRESIDENT CHAVEZ BY
POPULAR ACCLAMATION.  SEVERAL PARTICIPANTS VOICED UNEASE OVER THE
GROWING PRESSURE TO MARCH ON THE MIRAFLORES PRESIDENTIAL PALACE.
THE FOLLOWING OPPOSITION RALLY HELD IN FRONT OF PDVSA HEADQUARTERS
IN CHACAO WAS AN OVERWHELMING SUCCESS.  THE CTV AND FEDECAMARAS
```

UNCLASSIFIED

Current Class: UNCLASSIFIED
Current Handling: SBU

LEADERS WERE SWEPT INTO THE SPONTANEOUS MARCH ON MIRAFLORES. WHEN
THE PEACEFUL MARCHERS CAME TO WITHIN ONE BLOCK OF THE PALACE,
TROOPS FROM THE PRESIDENTIAL GUARD SHOT DOZENS OF TEAR GAS
CANISTERS TO KEEP THEM AT BAY. TENS OF THOUSANDS OF DEMONSTRATORS
REMAINED IN THE AREA THROUGHOUT THE AFTERNOON. END SUMMARY.

OPPOSITION'S STRONG DISPLAY OF RESOLVE AND UNITY
----

2. (SBU) THE OPPOSITION'S "COORDINATING COMMITTEE" MET AT
FEDECAMARAS FOR TWO HOURS TO DISCUSS AND REACH AGREEMENT ON
STRATEGY FOR THE MORNING'S UPCOMING MARCH FROM PARQUE DEL ESTE TO
PDVSA HEADQUARTERS IN CHACAO. IT WAS CLEAR THAT THERE WAS GROWING
SUPPORT TO CONTINUE THE MARCH FROM PDVSA ON TO MIRAFLORES.
SEVERAL ATTENDEES URGED CAUTION AND EXPRESSED THE BELIEF THE
                              UNCLASSIFIED

PAGE 03   CARACA 00985 01 OF 02 120403Z
OPPOSITION WAS NOT YET READY FOR THAT STEP. OTHERS STRONGLY
MAINTAINED THAT IT WAS TIME TO DIRECTLY CONFRONT THE EXECUTIVE AND
DEMAND THAT THE PRESIDENT AND HIS MINISTERS RESIGN. BY UNANIMOUS
VOICE VOTE, THE COMMITTEE DECIDED TO LET FEDECAMARAS PRESIDENT
PEDRO CARMONA AND CTV PRESIDENT CARLOS ORTEGA MAKE THE DECISION
REGARDING THE MARCH AT THE PDVSA RALLY -- TO ALLOW THEM TO GAUGE
THE TEMPERAMENT OF THE CROWD. THE 80 PLUS PARTICIPANTS BROKE UP
THE MEETING IN HIGH SPIRITS AND HEADED OUT TO CHACAO.

THE ROAR OF THE CROWD...
----

3. (SBU) BY 11:00AM, THE AREA SURROUNDING PDVSA HEADQUARTERS WAS A
SEA OF HUMANITY -- MEN, WOMEN, CHILDREN. FROM THE PRESS GALLERY
LOCATED ON A PEDESTRIAN BRIDGE OVER THE MAIN PLAZA, ECONOFFS
LOOKED OUT OVER A TIGHTLY PACKED CROWD STRETCHING FOR SEVERAL
BLOCKS IN ALL DIRECTIONS. WHEN THE FIRST SPEAKER WAS INTRODUCED,
THE ROAR OF APPROVAL WAS REMARKABLE - AND IT BUILT FROM THERE. BY
THE TIME PEDRO CARMONA SPOKE, IT HAD BECOME A FOREGONE CONCLUSION:
ON TO MIRAFLORES. WITH CARMONA, ORTEGA, AND FORMER PDVSA
PRESIDENT GUAICAIPURO LAMEDA IN THE VANGUARD, THE MULTITUDE SURGED
ONTO THE AUTOPISTA FOR THE FOUR-MILE MARCH DOWNTOWN.

4. (SBU) [   ]
[   ] THE COMMITTEE WAS HURRIEDLY PUTTING THE
FINAL TOUCHES ON A DOCUMENT DEMANDING THE RESIGNATION OF PRESIDENT
CHAVEZ -- BY POPULAR ACCLAMATION. [   ] THE DOCUMENT
WOULD BE DELIVERED TO CHAVEZ BY THE COMMITTEE'S LEADERSHIP WHEN
THE MARCH REACHED MIRAFLORES.

Current Class: UNCLASSIFIED

UNCLASSIFIED

UNCLASSIFIED

Current Class: UNCLASSIFIED
Current Handling: SBU

UNCLASSIFIED

PAGE 04   CARACA 00985 01 OF 02 120403Z
5. (U) **ALONG THE MARCH ROUTE, THE PARTICIPANTS -- NUMBERING EASILY
IN THE TENS OF THOUSANDS -- WERE IN A FESTIVE AND EXPECTANT MOOD,
SINGING THE NATIONAL ANTHEM AND CHANTING "NOT ONE STEP BACK!"
"CHAVEZ - JUST LEAVE!"** THERE WERE NO WEAPONS, ONLY MEN AND WOMEN
OF ALL AGES AND SOCIAL CLASSES. THE OVERRIDING SENTIMENT
EXPRESSED BY MANY PARTICIPANTS WAS ONE OF DISBELIEF - OVER THE
OBJECTIVE AND THE SIZE OF THE CROWD. A PHALANX OF METROPOLITAN
POLICE MOTORCYCLES RODE ALONG AT THE HEAD OF THE MARCH, CLEARING
THE STREETS OF TRAFFIC.

PRESIDENTIAL GUARD OVERREACTS
----

5. (U) AS THE MARCHERS TURNED THE FINAL CORNER AT ROUGHLY 2:00PM
AND APPROACHED THE LONG DRIVE LEADING UP TO THE PRESIDENTIAL
PALACE, IT APPEARED THEY WOULD REACH THEIR OBJECTIVE AND THE NOISE
FROM HORNS, WHISTLES, CLAXONS, AND SHOUTS REACHED A CRESCENDO.
LESS THAN A BLOCK FROM THE PALACE GATES, APPROXIMATELY A DOZEN
TEAR GAS CANISTERS WERE LAUNCHED FROM BEHIND THE PALACE WALLS AND
FELL AMONG THE LEAD ELEMENTS. AMID CRIES OF SURPRISE AND SOME
FEAR, THE CROWD TURNED AND FLED BACK TO THE CROSSROADS AT THE

UNCLASSIFIED

UNCLASSIFIED   PTQ0955

PAGE 01   CARACA 00985 02 OF 02 120403Z
ACTION DS-00

INFO LOG-00   MFA-00   NP-00   AMAD-00 ACQ-00   CIAE-00 COME-00
      DODE-00 DOTE-00 WHA-00   EB-00   FAAE-00 UTED-00 VC-00
      TEDE-00 INR-00   VCE-00   AC-01   NSAE-00 NSCE-00 ACE-00
      IRM-00   SSO-00   SS-00   TEST-00 ASDS-01 EPAE-00 DSCC-00
      DRL-02   NFAT-00 SAS-00   /004W
              ------------------8512EA 120403Z /38
O 120341Z APR 02
FM AMEMBASSY CARACAS
TO SECSTATE WASHDC IMMEDIATE 5456
INFO DEPT OF TREASURY WASHDC//OASIA//
AMEMBASSY BOGOTA
AMEMBASSY LA PAZ
AMEMBASSY LIMA
AMEMBASSY QUITO
USCINCSO MIAMI FL//POLAD//

UNCLAS SECTION 02 OF 02 CARACAS 000985

Current Class: UNCLASSIFIED

UNCLASSIFIED

    Current Class: UNCLASSIFIED
Current Handling: SBU

NSC FOR AMB MAISTO
STATE FOR DS/OP/WHA, S/ES-O_DS/OP/CC

SENSITIVE

E.O. 12958: N/A
TAGS: ASEC, ECON, PGOV, PREL, VE
SUBJECT: TALE OF TWO CITIES - THE MARCH ON MIRAFLORES PALACE

                    UNCLASSIFIED

PAGE 02   CARACA 00985 02 OF 02 120403Z
BOTTOM OF THE DRIVE.

6. (U) WITH THE CONTINUOUS ARRIVAL OF MORE MARCHERS, THE LEAD
SECTIONS TRIED ONCE AGAIN TO APPROACH THE PALACE APPROXIMATELY 20
MINUTES LATER. **THIS TIME THEY ADVANCED EVEN CLOSER, BUT BY NOW
THE PRESIDENTIAL GUARD HAD FORMED UP IN SOLID RANKS JUST BELOW THE
PALACE GATES. THIS TIME A BARRAGE OF ROUGHLY 20 GAS CANISTERS
RAINED DOWN ON THE MARCHERS -- THE CROWD RAN AND STARTED TO PANIC.
THEY REGROUPED AT THE CROSSROADS AND A NEARBY PLAZA, BUT NEVER
AGAIN ATTEMPTED TO APPROACH MIRAFLORES.**

7. (SBU) FOR THE NEXT TWO HOURS (3-5PM) THE CROWD MILLED AROUND A
LATE-ARRIVING SOUND TRUCK AND CHEERED A PROGRESSION OF SECONDARY
SPEAKERS. FEW FEDECAMARAS OR CTV LEADERS ARRIVED AND THE CROWD
GREW INCREASINGLY UNCERTAIN OF WHAT WOULD NEXT TRANSPIRE. TOWARD
5:00PM, ECONOFF OBSERVED INCREASING VIOLENCE IN THE NEARBY
STREETS. PARTICULARLY ON THE NEXT THOROUGHFARE, AVENIDA BARALT, A
SMALL CONTINGENT OF THE MARCH BECAME THE TARGET OF STEADY ROCK AND
BOTTLE THROWING BY CHAVISTAS AND REPEATED BARRAGES OF TEAR GAS
CANISTERS FIRED BY THE NATIONAL GUARD. THE DISTINCT SOUNDS OF
GUNFIRE ERUPTED AROUND 5:30PM IN THE SURROUNDING STREETS AND THE
REMAINING CROWD QUICKLY BROKE UP AND RETREATED TOWARD EASTERN
CARACAS ALONG AVENIDA BOLIVAR.

Current Class: UNCLASSIFIED

UNCLASSIFIED

Current Class: CONFIDENTIAL
Current Handling: n/a

CONFIDENTIAL   PTQ4212

E24

PAGE 01   CARACA 00995 01 OF 02 122049Z
ACTION WHA-00

INFO LOG-00   NP-00   AID-00   CEA-01   CIAE-00   CTME-00   DINT-00
      DODE-00 DOTE-00 PERC-00 SRPP-00 EB-00   EXIM-01   E-00
      FAAE-00 VC-00   FRB-00   H-01   TEDE-00   INR-00   ITC-01
      L-00   VCE-00   AC-01   NSAE-00 NSCE-00   OES-01   OMB-01
      OPIC-01 PM-00   PRS-00   ACE-00   SP-00   IRM-00   SSO-00
      SS-00   STR-00   TRSE-00 USIE-00 EPAE-00   PMB-00   DRL-02
      G-00   NFAT-00 SAS-00   /010W
      ------------------859814 122049Z /38

O 122027Z APR 02
FM AMEMBASSY CARACAS
TO SECSTATE WASHDC IMMEDIATE 5466
INFO USDOC WASHDC
DOE WASHDC
USINT HAVANA
AMEMBASSY MEXICO
AMEMBASSY PORT OF SPAIN
AMEMBASSY BRASILIA
AMEMBASSY QUITO
AMEMBASSY LIMA
AMEMBASSY BOGOTA
OPEC COLLECTIVE

RELEASED IN PART
B1, 1.4(D)

C O N F I D E N T I A L SECTION 01 OF 02 CARACAS 000995

E.O. 12958: DECL: 4/11/12
TAGS: ECON, EPET, ENRG, VE
SUBJECT: PDVSA: BACK TO NORMAL
                    CONFIDENTIAL

PAGE 02   CARACA 00995 01 OF 02 122049Z

1. CLASSIFIED BY AMBASSADOR CHARLES S. SHAPIRO FOR REASONS
1.5 (B) AND (D).

2. (C) SUMMARY: TELEVISED SCENES OF JOY HAVE MARKED THE
RETURN OF PETROLEOS DE VENEZUELA (PDVSA) EMPLOYEES TO THEIR
LA CAMPINA HEADQUARTERS BUILDING. FIRED EMPLOYEES HAVE
BEEN REINSTATED. FORMER VICE PRESIDENTS KARL MAZEIKA,
EDUARDO PRASELJ AND VICENZO PAGLIONE WILL ACT AS
COORDINATORS IN THE SELECTION OF A NEW BOARD. PDVSA
EXECUTIVES UNDERLINE THAT THE COMPANY SHOULD RETURN TO
NORMAL OPERATIONS BY EARLY NEXT WEEK. SHIPMENTS ARE
EXPECTED TO RESUME TODAY. PDVSA SPOKESPERSON STATED
PUBLICLY THAT NO OIL WILL BE SENT TO CUBA

UNCLASSIFIED

Current Class: CONFIDENTIAL   UNCLASSIFIED
Current Handling: n/a

END SUMMARY.

PDVSA GOVERNABILITY
- - - - - - - - - - - - - - - - - -

3. (U) THE PARRA BOARD RESIGNED ON APRIL 11 IN WHAT MANY
HERE DESCRIBE AS EX-PRESIDENT CHAVEZ'S LAST DITCH SCHEME TO
DEFUSE THE CRISIS BY TRYING FINALLY TO NEGOTIATE WITH THE
PDVSA DISSIDENTS. IN VIRTUALLY HIS FIRST ACT AS INTERIM
PRESIDENT, PEDRO CARMONA ESTANGA REINSTATED THE
FIRED/RETIRED/REMOVED EXECUTIVES TO THEIR POSITIONS. KARL
MAZEIKA, EDUARDO PRASELJ AND VICENZO PAGLIONE, THREE OF THE
FOUR VICE PRESIDENTS ON THE LAMEDA BOARD, WERE TAPPED TO
FORM A HIGH LEVEL COORDINATING COMMITTEE UNTIL THE
DESIGNATION OF A NEW PDVSA PRESIDENT AND BOARD. SOME HAVE
SUGGESTED THAT GENERAL LAMEDA MIGHT BE RE-APPOINTED AS
                              CONFIDENTIAL

PAGE 03   CARACA 00995 01 OF 02 122049Z
PRESIDENT BUT HE IS ALSO BEING MENTIONED AS A POSSIBLE
"MILITARY" PERSON ON THE TRANSITION TEAM. LUIS GIUSTI, NOW
ON HIS WAY TO CARACAS, IS ALSO SURE TO HAVE A ROLE IN
DECIDING VENEZUELA'S FUTURE ENERGY POLICIES.

4. (U) EDGAR PAREDES, EXECUTIVE DIRECTOR, REFINING SUPPLY
AND TRADING, (SUSPENDED ON APRIL 5) RESUMED THE ROLE HE HAS
PLAYED AS SPOKESPERSON FOR THE PAST SIX WEEKS, AND
ADDRESSED A NOON PRESS CONFERENCE. PAREDES UNDERLINED THAT
PDVSA EMPLOYEES HAVE BEEN WORKING SINCE THE NIGHT OF APRIL
11 TO RESTORE NORMAL OPERATIONS. HE NOTED THAT THE
DOMESTIC MARKET IS NOW GUARANTEED WHILE VENEZUELA'S EXPORT
PARTNERS ARE ON THEIR WAY TO BEING FULLY SUPPLIED AS WELL.
FULL OPERABILITY IS EXPECTED BY EARLY NEXT WEEK. PAREDES
ALSO CALLED FOR TOLERANCE IN DEALING WITH PDVSA EMPLOYEES
WHO DID NOT STRIKE.

CUBA CONNECTION TO END?
- -

5. (C) PAREDES ALSO SAID, "WE NOT GOING TO SEND EVEN ONE
BARREL OF OIL TO CUBA," WHICH DREW THUNDEROUS APPLAUSE.

Current Class: CONFIDENTIAL

UNCLASSIFIED

Current Class: CONFIDENTIAL
Current Handling: n/a

END SUMMARY.

COLOMBIAN GOVERNMENT SUPPORTS
NEW HEAD OF VENEZUELAN GOVERNMENT
----

2. (U) IN A TELEVISED INTERVIEW, ACTING COLOMBIAN
FOREIGN MINISTER CLEMENCIA FERERO SPOKE WARMLY ABOUT
VENEZUELAN INTERIM PRESIDENT PEDRO CARMONA. **FERERO SAID**
                    CONFIDENTIAL

PAGE 03   BOGOTA   03355   01 OF 02   122307Z
**SHE HAS KNOWN CARMONA FOR MANY YEARS, THAT CARMONA IS
WELL KNOWN TO THE COLOMBIAN BUSINESS COMMUNITY, IS
COMMITTED TO REGIONAL INTEGRATION, AND IS A GREAT
FRIEND OF COLOMBIA. TRADE MINISTER OROSCO TOLD THE
AMBASSADOR THE SAME: CARMONA IS WELL-KNOWN TO THE GOC
AND HAS WORKED CLOSELY WITH THEM ON A NUMBER OF ISSUES.**

Current Class: CONFIDENTIAL

UNCLASSIFIED

Current Class: UNCLASSIFIED
Current Handling: SBU

SENSITIVE BUT UNCLASSIFIED, PLEASE HANDLE ACCORDINGLY.

NEW GOVERNMENT SWORN IN

1.(SBU) ON THE EVENING FRIDAY, APRIL 12, PEDRO CARMONA
ESTANGA WAS SWORN IN AS INTERIM PRESIDENT OF
VENEZUELA. THOSE WHO SIGNED THE TEXT OF THE SWEARING
IN INCLUDED REPRESENTATIVES FROM VARIOUS SECTORS OF
CIVIL SOCIETY. THESE INCLUDED: THE CATHOLIC CHURCH
(CARDINAL JOSE IGNACIO VELASCO); THE BUSINESS
COMMUNITY (LUIS ENRIQUE PONS ZULOAGA); THE POLITICAL
PARTIES (JOSE CURIEL); NGOS (ROCIO GUIJARRO); MEDIA
(MIGUEL ANGEL MARTINEZ); REGIONAL GOVERNORS (MANUEL
ROSALES, GOVERNOR OF ZULIA STATE); INDUSTRY AND

UNCLASSIFIED

PAGE 03   CARACA 00996 01 OF 02 031745Z
COMMERCE (CARLOS FERNANDEZ, VICE PRESIDENT OF
FEDECAMARAS AND JULIO BRAZON, OF CONSECOMERCIO); AND
BANKING (IGNACIO SALVATIERRA).

NATIONAL ASSEMBLY DISSOLVED
----

2. (SBU) AFTER HIS SWEARING IN, CARMONA ANNOUNCED BY DECREE
THAT THE NATIONAL ASSEMBLY WOULD BE DISSOLVED, AND
THAT NEW NATIONAL ASSEMBLY ELECTIONS WOULD TAKE PLACE
NO LATER THAN DECEMBER OF THIS YEAR. PRESIDENTIAL
ELECTIONS WOULD TAKE PLACE IN NO LATER THAN 365 DAYS.
HE ALSO ANNOUNCED THAT "BOLIVARIAN" WOULD BE REMOVED
FROM THE OFFICIAL NAME OF THE COUNTRY, RETURNING IT TO
THE REPUBLIC OF VENEZUELA.

3. (SBU) THE DECREE ALSO ANNOUNCED THAT A CONSULTATIVE
COUNCIL WOULD BE FORMED, MADE UP OF 35 INDIVIDUALS
REPRESENTING VARIOUS SECTORS OF DEMOCRATIC SOCIETY.
IT IS UNCLEAR WHO THESE PEOPLE WILL BE, OR HOW THEY
WILL BE CHOSEN TO PARTICIPATE.

4. (SBU) ADDITIONALLY, CARMONA ANNOUNCED THAT THE 48
DECREES ANNOUNCED BY PRESIDENT CHAVEZ IN NOVEMBER OF
2001 WOULD BE SUSPENDED, AND THAT A COMMISSION
REPRESENTING DIFFERENT SECTORS OF SOCIETY WOULD BE
FORMED TO REVIEW AND REVISE THEM.

5. (SBU) CARMONA ALSO ANNOUNCED THAT PDVSA WORKERS WHO WERE
FIRED, SUSPENDED, OR FORCED INTO RETIREMENT WOULD BE

Current Class: UNCLASSIFIED

UNCLASSIFIED

UNCLASSIFIED

Current Class: UNCLASSIFIED
Current Handling: SBU

UNCLASSIFIED

PAGE 04   CARACA 00996 01 OF 02   031745Z
REINSTATED.

6. (SBU) FINALLY, CARMONA ASKED THE INTERNATIONAL COMMUNITY
TO HAVE PATIENCE WITH HIS NEW GOVERNMENT, AND
EXPLAINED THAT IN THE FIRST FEW HOURS, UNDESIREABLE
EVENTS COULD OCCUR, BUT THAT HE AND HIS GOVERNMENT
WERE AGAINST HATE AND RETALIATION. HE SAID THAT ALL
VENEZUELANS HAVE THE OBLIGATION TO CONTROL THEIR
PASSIONS AND KEEP EVENTS UNDER CONTROL.

NEW CABINET

7.(SBU) CARMONA'S NEW CABINET APPOINTMENTS INCLUDE:

MINISTER OF THE INTERIOR: RAFAEL DAMIAN BUSTILLOS
MINISTER OF THE EXTERIOR: JOSE RODRIGUEZ ITURBE
MINISTER OF FINANCE: LEOPOLDO MARTINEZ
MINISTER OF AGRICULTURE: RAUL DE ARMAS
MINSTER OF LABOR: CESAR AUGUSTO CARBALLO
MINISTER OF PLANNING AND DEVELOPMENT: LEON ARISMENDI
MINISTER OF DEFENSE: HECTOR RAMIREZ PEREZ
MINISTER OF HEALTH: RAFAEL ARREAZA
MINISTER OF THE SECRETARY: JESUS ENRIQUE BRICENO
PROSECUTOR GENERAL: DANIEL ROMERO
PRESIDENT OF PDVSA: GUAICAIPURO LAMEDA

ARRESTS AND DETENTIONS

UNCLASSIFIED

PAGE 05   CARACA 00996 01 OF 02   031745Z

UNCLASSIFIED

UNCLASSIFIED   PTQ8948

PAGE 01   CARACA 00996 02 OF 02   031748Z
ACTION DS-00

INFO	LOG-00	COR-01	MPA-00	NP-00	AID-00	AMAD-00	A-00
	ACQ-00	CA-01	CCO-00	CEA-01	CIAE-00	COME-00	CTME-00
	INL-00	DINT-00	DODE-00	DOEE-00	ITCE-00	DOTE-00	WHA-00
	SRPP-00	EB-00	EXME-00	E-00	FAAE-00	UTED-00	VC-00
	FRB-00	OBO-00	H-01	TEDE-00	INR-00	IO-00	ITC-01

Current Class: UNCLASSIFIED

UNCLASSIFIED

9. Cable from the Department of State
April 13, 2002, p. 3

```
Current Class: UNCLASSIFIED
Current Handling: SBU

        LAB-01    L-00      VCE-00    M-00      AC-01     NSAE-00   NSCE-00
        OCS-03    OES-01    OMB-01    OPIC-01   OPR-01    PA-00     PM-00
        PRS-00    ACE-00    P-00      SCT-00    SP-00     IRM-00    SSO-00
        SS-00     STR-00    TEST-00   TRSE-00   USIE-00   USSS-00   ASDS-01
        EPAE-00   ECA-00    IIP-00    PMB-00    DSCC-00   DRL-02    G-00
        NFAT-00   SAS-00     /017W
                      -----------------A9CB03  031753Z /38
O 131803Z APR 02
FM AMEMBASSY CARACAS
TO SECSTATE WASHDC IMMEDIATE 5469
INFO OPEC COLLECTIVE PRIORITY
AMEMBASSY BOGOTA PRIORITY
AMEMBASSY QUITO
AMEMBASSY LA PAZ
AMEMBASSY LIMA
AMEMBASSY PANAMA
USCINCSO MIAMI FL

UNCLAS SECTION 02 OF 02 CARACAS 000996

SENSITIVE

                      UNCLASSIFIED

PAGE 02        CARACA  00996  02 OF 02  031748Z
C O R R E C T E D   C O P Y - CAPTION AND PARA MARKINGS ADDED

NSC FOR AMB MAISTO
USCINSCO FOR POLAD
DEPT CA FOR MARY A. RYAN AND DS/OP/WHA AND S/ES-
ODS/OP/CC

E.O. 12958: N/A
TAGS: ECON, PGOV, PREL, EPET, ASEC, CASC, VE
SUBJECT: SITREP:  SATURDAY APRIL 13

8. (SBU) TO DATE, SEVERAL MEMBERS OF CHAVEZ'S MVR PARTY
HAVE BEEN DETAINED BY POLICE FORCES.  THESE INCLUDE
MVR DEPUTY WILLIAM TAREK SAAB AND FORMER INTERIOR
MINISTER RODRIGUEZ CHACIN.  WE HAVE ALSO HEARD REPORTS
THAT TACHIRA GOVERNOR RONALD BLANCO LA CRUZ AND MERIDA
GOVERNOR FLORENCIO PORRAS, BOTH OF MVR, WERE BEING
HELD.  WE DO NOT KNOW WHAT CHARGES, IF ANY, HAVE BEEN
FILED AGAINST THEM.  TAREK WILLIAM SAAB HAS REPORTEDLY
BEEN RELEASED AS OF APRIL 13.

-------------------
CONCERN EXPRESSED
-------------------

Current Class: UNCLASSIFIED
```

9. Cable from the Department of State
April 13, 2002, p. 4

Current Class: UNCLASSIFIED
Current Handling: SBU

9. (SBU) POLOFF HAS RECEIVED SEVERAL PHONE CALLS FROM PARTY
MEMBERS WHO ARE CONCERNED ABOUT THE NEW GOVERNMENT'S
COURSE OF ACTION, ESPECIALLY THE DISSOLUTION OF
CONGRESS. THEY RESENT NOT BEING INCLUDED IN THE NEW
GOVERNMENT, AND FEAR THAT THE CARMONA GOVERNMENT IS
PROCEEDING UNDEMOCRATICALLY. **ALTHOUGH MANY PARTY**

PAGE 03   CARACA 00996 02 OF 02 031748Z
**REPRESENTATIVES WERE INVOLVED IN THE DECISION TO NAME
CARMONA INTERIM PRESIDENT, THE PARTY REPRESENTATIVES
WHO ARE NOW EXPRESSING CONCERN SAY THAT THE PARTY
LEADERS THEMSELVES WERE NOT CONSULTED.**

10. (SBU) THE NGO COMMUNITY HAS ALSO EXPRESSED CONCERN
ABOUT THE NEW CARMONA GOVERNMENT. THEY ARE ESPECIALLY
CONCERNED THAT THE INDEPENDENT BRANCHES OF THE
GOVERNMENT THAT MAKE UP THE "PODER CIUDADANO," THE
FISCALIA GENERAL (ATTORNEY GENERAL'S OFFICE), THE
DEFENSORIA DEL PUEBLO (HUMAN RIGHTS OMBUDSMAN), AND
THE CONTROLARIA GENERAL (CONTROLLER GENERAL), ARE NO
LONGER FUNCTIONING.

DISTURBANCES NOT REPORTED
----

11. (SBU) THERE HAVE BEEN REPORTS THAT SPORADIC VIOLENCE
HAS TAKEN PLACE IN VARIOUS AREAS OF CARACAS. THE
NIGHT OF APRIL 12, WE RECEIVED WORD THAT THERE WERE
DISTURBANCES IN NEIGHBORHOOD OF PETARE, GUARENAS, 23
DE ENERO, EL VALLE, AND CATIA LA MAR. THE ROAD FROM
CARACAS TO MAIQUETIA AIRPORT WAS CLOSED BY THE
NATIONAL GUARD AFTER REPORTS OF SHOOTING. THESE
EVENTS HAVE NOT/NOT BEEN REPORTED BY LOCAL MEDIA.
ACCORDING TO PAS CONTACTS, THE MEDIA BELIEVED THAT THE
DISTURBANCES WERE PLANNED TO INCITE PANIC, AND FELT
THAT COVERAGE WOULD ADD TO THAT PANIC.

12. (SBU) THIS AFTERNOON, WE HAVE RECEIVED WORD THAT AT

PAGE 04   CARACA 00996 02 OF 02 031748Z
LEAST TWO SHOPPING CENTERS HAVE BEEN CLOSED BY GUARDS
AND EVACUATED, PERHAPS TO PREVENT LOOTING. AS OF
MIDDAY, AN EMBASSY CONTACT REPORTED THAT METRO HAS
BEEN CLOSED, AND THAT GUNFIRE COULD BE HEARD DOWNTOWN.
TEAR GAS IS ALSO REPORTEDLY BEING USED. NO LOCAL NEWS
CHANNELS ARE REPORTING THESE EVENTS.

Current Class: UNCLASSIFIED

```
        Current Class: CONFIDENTIAL       UNCLASSIFIED
      Current Handling: n/a                                      RELEASED IN PART
                                 CONFIDENTIAL    PTO4159 B1, 1.4(D)

      PAGE 01        CARACA  01009  141012Z
      ACTION DS-00

      INFO   LOG-00   MFA-00   NP-00    AID-00   ACQ-00   CA-01    CEA-01
             CIAE-00  COME-00  CTME-00  INL-00   DINT-00  DODE-00  DOEE-00
             DOTE-00  WHA-00   PERC-00  SRPP-00  EB-00    EXIM-01  E-00
             FAAE-00  VC-00    FRB-00   H-01     TEDE-00  INR-00   ITC-01
             LAB-01   L-00     VCE-00   AC-01    NSAE-00  NSCE-00  OCS-03
             OES-01   OMB-01   OPIC-01  PA-00    PM-00    PRS-00   ACE-00
             P-00     SCT-00   SP-00    IRM-00   SSO-00   SS-00    STR-00
             TRSE-00  USIE-00  ASDS-01  IIP-00   PMB-00   DSCC-00  DRL-02
             G-00     NFAT-00  SAS-00   /016W
                      ------------------85EC05  141015Z /38
```

```
      O 140950Z APR 02
      FM AMEMBASSY CARACAS
      TO SECSTATE WASHDC IMMEDIATE 5484
      INFO OPEC COLLECTIVE PRIORITY
      AMEMBASSY BOGOTA PRIORITY
      AMEMBASSY QUITO
      AMEMBASSY LA PAZ
      AMEMBASSY LIMA
      USCINCSO MIAMI FL

      C O N F I D E N T I A L CARACAS 001009

      NSC FOR AMB MAISTO
      USCINSCO FOR POLAD

      DEPT CA FOR MARY A. RYAN
                          CONFIDENTIAL

      PAGE 02        CARACA  01009  141012Z
      DEPT ALSO FOR DS/OP/WHA AND S/ES-ODS/OP/CC

      E.O. 12958: DECL: 04/14/12
      TAGS: ECON, PGOV, PREL, EPET, ASEC, CASC VE
      SUBJECT: VENEZUELA SITREP AS OF 4:00AM APRIL 14 - CHAVEZ RETURNS

      REF: A.CARACAS 1002 B.1001 C.1000 D.00998 E.00996 F.00984 G.00980
      H.00974 I.00973 J.00966  K.00948

      CLASSIFIED BY AMBASSADOR CHARLES S. SHAPIRO.  REASON
      1.5 (B) AND (D).

      TRIUMPHANT RETURN OF CHAVEZ
      ----------------------------
      1. (SBU) AT 2:50AM APRIL 14, HUGO CHAVEZ ARRIVED AT MIRAFLORES
      PALACE AND WAS GREETED BY A LARGE CROWD OF CELEBRATING SUPPORTERS.

      Current Class: CONFIDENTIAL
```

UNCLASSIFIED

UNCLASSIFIED

Current Class: CONFIDENTIAL
Current Handling: n/a

OFFICIAL TELEVISION REPORTED THAT CHAVEZ FLEW BY HELICOPTER FROM
ORCHILA ISLAND TO A MILITARY FACILITY IN MARACAY, AND THEN ON TO
MIRAFLORES IN CARACAS. THEREAFTER, OFFICIAL TELEVISION SHOWED
CHAVEZ GOVERNMENT MINISTERS AND MILITARY SUPPORTERS ARRIVING
INSIDE MIRAFLORES GATES.

2. (SBU) CHAVEZ APPEARED INSIDE OF MIRAFLORES, FLANKED BY WILLIAM
LARA, ISAIS RODRIGUEZ, DIASDADO CABELLO AND JOSE VICENTE RANGEL,
AND DELIVERED AN HOUR LONG ADDRESS WHICH STARTED AT 4:30AM APRIL
14. CHAVEZ IMMEDIATELY CALLED FOR CALM AND SAID EVERYONE SHOULD
GO HOME "TO YOUR HOUSE, TO YOUR FAMILY." HE PROMISED THAT THERE
WILL BE NO REVENGE OR PERSECUTION OF HIS OPPONENTS, BUT OBLIQUELY
NOTED THAT CHANGES HAVE TO BE MADE. HE REFERENCED THAT HE HAD
ACCEPTED THE RESIGNATION OF THE PDVSA BOARD OF DIRECTORS
(APPARENTLY TENDERED BY PRESIDENT GASTON PARRA ON APRIL 11), AND
CONFIDENTIAL

PAGE 03   CARACA .01009 141012Z
WILL WORK TO CONSTITUTE A NEW BOARD. HE ALSO ISSUED A CALL TO
FORM ROUNDTABLES FOR NATIONAL DIALOGUE. CHAVEZ EXPLAINED THAT HE
WAS NOT MISTREATED WHILE IN CUSTODY, AND FIRMLY DECLARED THAT HE
DID NOT RESIGN AT ANY TIME.

LOCAL TV COVERAGE
----
4. (SBU) ALL LOCAL TELEVISION CHANNELS (AND AT LEAST TWO
INTERNATIONAL CHANNELS) COVERED CHAVEZ'S ADDRESS LIVE, APPARENTLY
THROUGH A FEED FROM VENEZOLANA DE TELEVISION, THE STATE CONTROLLED
CHANNEL. EARLIER, LOCAL TELEVISION CHANNELS CARRIED FEEDS FROM
THE STATE-CONTROLLED CHANNEL IN WHICH CHAVEZ SUPPORTERS TALKED
FROM INSIDE THE STUDIO, OR CARRIED REGULAR ENTERTAINMENT. THERE
HAS BEEN NO INDEPENDENT LOCAL TELEVISION REPORTING THROUGHOUT THE
NIGHT.

CARMONA'S ILL-FATED DECLARATION

CONFIDENTIAL

Current Class: CONFIDENTIAL

UNCLASSIFIED

11. Cable from the Department of State
April 14, 2002 (Otto Reich), p. 1

CONFIDENTIAL   PTO5001   E33

RELEASED IN PART
B1, 1.4(D)

PAGE 01   STATE   070877   150111Z
ORIGIN WHA-00

INFO   LOG-00   NP-00   AMAD-00   ACQ-00   CIAE-00   INL-00   DS-00
        EUR-00   VC-00   TEDE-00   INR-00   IO-00   JUSE-00   LAB-01
        L-00   VCE-00   NSAE-00   OIC-02   P-00   SP-00   SS-00
        R-00   DSCC-00   DRL-02   NFAT-00   SAS-00   /005R

070877
SOURCE: DISKETTE.020728
DRAFTED BY: WHA/AND:BRNARANJO:BRN -- 04/14/02 X74216ANDVE02/CABLES/RAL
APPROVED BY: WHA:OJREICH
WHA:JCSTRUBLE   WHA/AND:JDFARRAR   D:KBUE   P:TLENDERKING
WHA/USOAS:RNORIEGA
                  ----------------8612CD 150112Z /38

O 150107Z APR 02
FM SECSTATE WASHDC
TO WESTERN HEMISPHERIC AFFAIRS DIPL POSTS IMMEDIATE
INFO NSC WASHDC IMMEDIATE 0000
JOINT STAFF WASHDC IMMEDIATE 0000
SECDEF WASHDC IMMEDIATE 0000
USSOUTHCOM MIAMI FL IMMEDIATE
USMISSION USUN NEW YORK IMMEDIATE
AMEMBASSY VATICAN IMMEDIATE
AMEMBASSY MADRID IMMEDIATE
AMEMBASSY LONDON IMMEDIATE
USMISSION GENEVA IMMEDIATE

C O N F I D E N T I A L STATE 070877

E.O. 12958: DECL: 04/14/12
                    CONFIDENTIAL

PAGE 02   STATE   070877   150111Z
TAGS: PREL, PGOV, PHUM, KDEM, VE
SUBJECT: RALLYING INTERNATIONAL SUPPORT FOR VENEZUELAN
DEMOCRACY

1.   (U)   CLASSIFIED BY ASSISTANT SECRETARY FOR WESTERN
HEMISPHERE AFFAIRS OTTO J. REICH.   REASONS: 1.5(B) AND
(D).

Current Class: CONFIDENTIAL
Current Handling: n/a

- - - - - - - - - -
BACKGROUND
- - - - - - - - - -

3. (U) ON APRIL 11, HUNDREDS OF THOUSANDS OF VENEZUELANS
GATHERED TO SEEK REDRESS OF THEIR GRIEVANCES. CHAVEZ
SUPPORTERS FIRED ON ANTI-GOVERNMENT PROTESTORS RESULTING
IN MORE THAN 100 WOUNDED OR KILLED. VENEZUELAN MILITARY
AND POLICE REFUSED GOVERNMENT ORDERS TO FIRE ON
DEMONSTRATORS. THE GOVERNMENT PREVENTED FIVE INDEPENDENT
TELEVISION STATIONS FROM REPORTING ON EVENTS. AFTER
MEETING WITH SENIOR MILITARY OFFICERS, CHAVEZ ALLEGEDLY
RESIGNED THE PRESIDENCY. A PROVISIONAL CIVILIAN
GOVERNMENT, LED BY PEDRO CARMONA, ASSUMED POWER AND
PROMISED EARLY ELECTIONS.

4. (U) ON APRIL 12, PEDRO CARMONA WAS SWORN IN AS
PROVISIONAL PRESIDENT. THE PROVISIONAL GOVERNMENT
ANNOUNCED THE DISSOLUTION OF VENEZUELA'S NATIONAL ASSEMBLY
AND SUPREME TRIBUNAL OF JUSTICE. SUBSEQUENTLY, ON APRIL

Current Class: CONFIDENTIAL

Current Class: CONFIDENTIAL UNCLASSIFIED
Current Handling: n/a

13, CARMONA, WHO HAD BEEN UNDER INTENSE U.S.,
CONFIDENTIAL

PAGE 04   STATE   070877 150111Z
INTERNATIONAL, AND DOMESTIC PRESSURE TO MAINTAIN
CONSTITUTIONAL CONTINUITY, REVERSED COURSE AND REINSTATED
THE NATIONAL ASSEMBLY AND CHARGED IT WITH SELECTING A
PROVISIONAL PRESIDENT.

5. (U) THROUGHOUT APRIL 13, HOWEVER, PRO-CHAVEZ FORCES
MADE A CONCERTED EFFORT TO RESTORE CHAVEZ TO THE
PRESIDENCY. PRO-CHAVEZ FORCES SEIZED THE MIRAFLORES
PRESIDENTIAL PALACE, SWORE IN CHAVEZ VICE PRESIDENT
DIOSDADO CABELLO AS ACTING PRESIDENT, AND SEIZED OR FORCED
THE EVACUATION OF ALL MEDIA OUTLETS. FINALLY, TROOPS
LOYAL TO CHAVEZ SEIZED CONTROL OF FUERTE TIUNA, HOME OF
VENEZUELA'S MINISTRY OF DEFENSE, AND ARRESTED CARMONA AND
HIS MILITARY HIGH COMMAND. CHAVEZ RETURNED TO CARACAS AND
RESUMED HIS PRESIDENCY.

6. (U) PRESIDENT CHAVEZ ADDRESSED THE NATION EARLY IN
THE MORNING ON APRIL 14. IN HIS ADDRESS, CHAVEZ:
PROMISED HE WOULD NOT RETALIATE AGAINST OR PERSECUTE HIS
OPPONENTS, SAID HE WOULD REFLECT ON HIS ACTIONS AND URGED
OTHERS TO DO SO AS WELL, ISSUED A CALL FOR NATIONAL
ROUNTABLES OF DIALOGUE TO BEGIN ON APRIL 18, SAID HE HAD
NOT BEEN MISTREATED, AND STATED THAT HE HAD NEVER
RESIGNED.

U.S. POSITION ON EVENTS IN VENEZUELA
----

7. (U) BEGIN TEXT OF WHITE HOUSE STATEMENT:

CONFIDENTIAL

PAGE 05   STATE   070877 150111Z
THE WHITE HOUSE
OFFICE OF THE PRESS SECRETARY

FOR IMMEDIATE RELEASE   APRIL 14, 2002

STATEMENT BY THE PRESS SECRETARY

THE UNITED STATES IS MONITORING THE SITUATION IN VENEZUELA
WITH GREAT CONCERN. WE DEEPLY REGRET THE VIOLENCE AND
LOSS OF LIFE, AND CALL ON ALL VENEZUELANS TO WORK
PEACEFULLY TO RESOLVE THIS CRISIS.

Current Class: CONFIDENTIAL

UNCLASSIFIED

UNCLASSIFIED

Current Class: CONFIDENTIAL
Current Handling: n/a

WE WELCOME AND SUPPORT THE DECISION BY THE ORGANIZATION OF AMERICAN STATES TO SEND IMMEDIATELY A FACT-FINDING MISSION HEADED BY SECRETARY GENERAL CESAR GAVIRIA TO VENEZUELA TO SUPPORT THE RE-ESTABLISHMENT OF FULL DEMOCRACY, WITH GUARANTEES FOR CITIZENS AND RESPECT FOR FUNDAMENTAL FREEDOMS, WITHIN THE FRAMEWORK OF THE INTER-AMERICAN DEMOCRATIC CHARTER.

THE PEOPLE OF VENEZUELA HAVE SENT A CLEAR MESSAGE TO PRESIDENT CHAVEZ THAT THEY WANT BOTH DEMOCRACY AND REFORM. THE CHAVEZ ADMINISTRATION HAS AN OPPORTUNITY TO RESPOND TO THIS MESSAGE BY CORRECTING ITS COURSE AND GOVERNING IN A FULLY DEMOCRATIC MANNER.

PRESIDENT CHAVEZ HAS NOW CALLED FOR NATIONAL REFLECTION AND DIALOGUE. HE NEEDS TO SEIZE THIS OPPORTUNITY TO ENSURE LEGITIMACY BY REACHING OUT TO THE POLITICAL OPPOSITION, CIVIL SOCIETY, AND TO ALL DEMOCRATIC FORCES IN VENEZUELA.

CONFIDENTIAL

PAGE 06   STATE   070877   150111Z

THE UNITED STATES AND THE WORLD COMMUNITY OF DEMOCRACIES WILL BE CLOSELY FOLLOWING EVENTS IN VENEZUELA. PRESIDENT CHAVEZ BEARS PARTICULAR RESPONSIBILITY TO PRESERVE THE PEACE, TO PROTECT HUMAN RIGHTS AND DEMOCRATIC FREEDOMS, AND TO CREATE THE CONDITIONS NECESSARY FOR A NATIONAL DIALOGUE. WE CALL ON HIM TO WORK WITH ALL VENEZUELANS AND WITH THE ORGANIZATION OF AMERICAN STATES TOWARD THIS END.

END TEXT OF WHITE HOUSE STATEMENT.
POWELL

CONFIDENTIAL

<< END OF DOCUMENT >>

Current Class: CONFIDENTIAL

UNCLASSIFIED

Current Class: UNCLASSIFIED UNCLASSIFIED
Current Handling: n/a

ALL POSTS FOR PAO, USSOCOM FOR POLAD

E.O. 12958: N/A
TAGS: OPRC, KPAO
SUBJECT: WHA GUIDANCE, APRIL 16, 2002

SUMMARY OF CONTENTS:
WHA PRESS GUIDANCE, APRIL 16 (VENEZUELA)
END SUMMARY.

WHA PRESS GUIDANCE, APRIL 16, 2002:

-- VENEZUELA: MEETINGS, U.S. INVOLVEMENT, LEGITIMACY,
REACTION TO CHAVEZ SPEECH, ARRESTS OF CARMONA ET AL --

Q: DID U.S. OFFICIALS MEET WITH VENEZUELAN OPPOSITION
OFFICIALS PRIOR TO THE APRIL 11 REMOVAL OF PRESIDENT CHAVEZ
UNCLASSIFIED

PAGE 03   STATE   072430 162107Z
FROM POWER?

A: U.S. OFFICIALS HAVE MET WITH A BROAD SPECTRUM OF
VENEZUELANS OVER THE PAST SEVERAL MONTHS BOTH IN CARACAS AND
IN WASHINGTON. U.S. OFFICIALS MET WITH BUSINESS COMMUNITY
REPRESENTATIVES, LABOR UNION OFFICIALS, CATHOLIC CHURCH
LEADERS, OPPOSITION POLITICAL LEADERS, AND A WIDE ARRAY OF
VENEZUELAN GOVERNMENT OFFICIALS.

IF ASKED:

IN THE COURSE OF NORMAL DIPLOMATIC CONTACTS, U.S. OFFICIALS
MET WITH PEDRO CARMONA, THE PRESIDENT OF THE VENEZUELAN
FEDERATION OF CHAMBERS OF COMMERCE (FEDECAMARAS).

OUR MESSAGE TO ALL VENEZUELAN CONTACTS HAS BEEN CONSISTENT.
THE POLITICAL SITUATION IN VENEZUELA IS ONE FOR VENEZUELANS
TO RESOLVE PEACEFULLY, DEMOCRATICALLY AND CONSTITUTIONALLY.
WE EXPLICITLY TOLD ALL OF OUR VENEZUELAN INTERLOCUTORS ON
NUMEROUS OCCASIONS AND AT MANY LEVELS THAT UNDER NO
CIRCUMSTANCES WOULD THE UNITED STATES SUPPORT ANY
UNCONSTITUTIONAL, UNDEMOCRATIC EFFORT, SUCH AS COUP, TO
REMOVE PRESIDENT CHAVEZ FROM POWER.

Q: WAS THE UNITED STATES INVOLVED IN THE EFFORT TO REMOVE
VENEZUELAN PRESIDENT CHAVEZ FROM POWER?

A: ABSOLUTELY NOT.

Current Class: UNCLASSIFIED

UNCLASSIFIED

Q: WHY THEN DID THE U.S. NOT CONDEMN THE REMOVAL OF
PRESIDENT CHAVEZ FROM POWER ON FRIDAY, APRIL 12 AND CALL FOR

PAGE 04   STATE   072430   162107Z
HIS IMMEDIATE REINSTATEMENT?

A: OUR RESPONSE TO THE SITUATION IN VENEZUELA ON APRIL 12
LAID OUT THE FACTS AS WE KNEW THEM TO BE DURING A VERY
CONFUSING TIME. THOSE FACTS WERE THAT HUNDREDS OF THOUSANDS
OF VENEZUELANS DEMONSTRATED PEACEFULLY AGAINST THE CHAVEZ
GOVERNMENT, THAT THE CHAVEZ GOVERNMENT RESPONDED WITH A
CRACK-DOWN AGAINST PROTESTORS AND THE INDEPENDENT MEDIA, THAT
PRESIDENT CHAVEZ WAS REPORTED TO HAVE DISMISSED HIS VICE
PRESIDENT AND CABINET AND RESIGNED, AND THAT A TRANSITIONAL
GOVERNMENT HAD ASSUMED POWERS AND CALLED FOR NEW ELECTIONS.

OUR POSITION WAS THAT THIS SITUATION SHOULD BE RESOLVED
PEACEFULLY AND DEMOCRATICALLY, AND IN ACCORDANCE WITH THE
INTER-AMERICAN DEMOCRATIC CHARTER.

WE FOLLOWED THIS STATEMENT BY HELPING TO DRAFT A RESOLUTION
AT THE ORGANIZATION OF AMERICAN STATES (OAS) INVOKING ARTICLE
20 OF THE INTER-AMERICAN DEMOCRATIC CHARTER. ARTICLE 20
ALLOWS FOR ANY OAS MEMBER STATE (OR THE SECRETARY GENERAL) TO
CONVOKE THE OAS PERMANENT COUNCIL TO UNDERTAKE A "COLLECTIVE
ASSESSMENT OF THE SITUATION" WHEN THERE HAS BEEN "AN
UNCONSTITUTIONAL ALTERATION OF THE CONSTITUTIONAL REGIME THAT
SERIOUSLY IMPAIRS THE DEMOCRATIC ORDER IN A MEMBER STATE."
WITH THAT OBJECTIVE, OUR REPRESENTATIVE TO THE OAS CLEARLY
STATED THAT THE SO-CALLED "PROVISIONAL GOVERNMENT" HAD YET TO
DEMONSTRATE THAT THEY ARE THE "LEGALLY CONSTITUTED CIVILIAN
AUTHORITY." OUR DELEGATION ALSO SAID THAT THE OAS MUST
RIGOROUSLY INSIST THAT VENEZUELAN AUTHORITIES RESPECT THE
ESSENTIAL ELEMENTS OF DEMOCRACY.

PAGE 05   STATE   072430   162107Z
WE JOINED THE CONSENSUS TO SUPPORT THE OAS RESOLUTION OF
APRIL 13 THAT CONDEMNED THE "ALTERATION OF CONSTITUTIONAL
ORDER," CALLED FOR THE "NORMALIZATION OF THE DEMOCRATIC
INSTITUTIONAL FRAMEWORK IN VENEZUELA, WITHIN THE CONTEXT OF
THE INTER-AMERICAN DEMOCRATIC CHARTER," AND CALLED FOR THE
OAS SECRETARY GENERAL TO CONDUCT A FACT-FINDING MISSION TO
VENEZUELA.

WE ARE PLEASED THAT THE HEMISPHERE IS ENGAGED IN SUPPORTING
DEMOCRACY IN VENEZUELA. WE TRUST THAT OUR HEMISPHERIC
PARTNERS WILL CONTINUE THIS ENGAGEMENT TO ENSURE THAT

Current Class: UNCLASSIFIED
Current Handling: n/a

VENEZUELA RESPECTS DEMOCRATIC INSTITUTIONS AND PROCESSES AND
FOLLOWS THROUGH ON ITS COMMITMENTS FOR NATIONAL DIALOGUE AND
RECONCILIATION.

Q: IS THE GOVERNMENT OF VENEZUELAN PRESIDENT HUGO CHAVEZ
LEGITIMATE?

A: YES. THE VENEZUELAN PEOPLE FREELY AND FAIRLY ELECTED
HUGO CHAVEZ TO BE PRESIDENT OF VENEZUELA IN DEMOCRATIC
ELECTIONS IN DECEMBER 1998 AND JULY 2000. LEGITIMACY EARNED
THROUGH ELECTIONS MUST BE MAINTAINED AND NURTURED THROUGH
DEMOCRATIC GOVERNANCE THAT RESPECTS THE ESSENTIAL ELEMENTS OF
DEMOCRACY. PRESIDENT CHAVEZ'S CALL FOR NATIONAL DIALOGUE AND
RECONCILIATION IS A WELCOME INITIAL INITIATIVE TOWARD FULLY
RESTORING THE ESSENTIAL ELEMENTS OF DEMOCRACY.

Q: DO YOU HAVE ANY REACTION TO PRESIDENT CHAVEZ'S APRIL 15
SPEECH?

A: WE WELCOME PRESIDENT CHAVEZ'S CALLS FOR ROUNDTABLES OF
UNCLASSIFIED

PAGE 06   STATE   072430   162107Z
NATIONAL DIALOGUE AND RECONCILIATION. THIS IS AN IMPORTANT
FIRST STEP IN RECLAIMING VENEZUELA'S DEMOCRACY. WE URGE THE
VENEZUELAN GOVERNMENT TO SUPPORT FULLY THE ORGANIZATION OF
AMERICAN STATES (OAS) SECRETARY GENERAL'S FACT-FINDING
MISSION TO VENEZUELA. THROUGH ITS GOOD OFFICES, THE OAS CAN
PLAY AN IMPORTANT ROLE BY SUPPORTING A BROAD AND INCLUSIVE
NATIONAL DIALOGUE THAT PROMOTES RECONCILIATION AND
STRENGTHENING THE ESSENTIAL ELEMENTS OF DEMOCRACY IN
VENEZUELA.

Q: DO YOU HAVE ANY COMMENT REGARDING THE DETENTION OF
PROVISIONAL PRESIDENT PEDRO CARMONA AND THE MILITARY OFFICERS
THAT SUPPORTED HIS GOVERNMENT?

A: IT IS OUR UNDERSTANDING THAT PEDRO CARMONA, INDIVIDUALS
WHO WORKED WITH CARMONA, AND MILITARY LEADERS THAT SUPPORTED
CARMONA HAVE BEEN DETAINED. AS WE WOULD WITH ANY VENEZUELAN
CITIZEN, WE URGE THE VENEZUELAN GOVERNMENT TO RESPECT THE
HUMAN RIGHTS OF THESE INDIVIDUALS AND TO HANDLE THEIR CASES
IN ACCORDANCE WITH THE FUNDAMENTAL PRINCIPLES OF JUSTICE.
PRESIDENT CHAVEZ HAS PROMISED TO RESPECT THE HUMAN RIGHTS OF
THOSE PERSONS WHO WERE DETAINED. WE WELCOME THIS PROMISE,
AND TRUST THAT PRESIDENT CHAVEZ WILL FOLLOW THROUGH ON IT.
POWELL

UNCLASSIFIED

Current Class: UNCLASSIFIED

13. Department of State Press Guidance
April 17, 2002, p. 1

```
      Current Class: UNCLASSIFIED
Current Handling: n/a

TAGS: OPRC, KPAO
SUBJECT: WHA GUIDANCE, APRIL 17, 2002

SUMMARY OF CONTENTS:
WHA PRESS GUIDANCE, APRIL 17 (VENEZUELA)
END SUMMARY.


-------------------------------------
WHA PRESS GUIDANCE, APRIL 17, 2002
-------------------------------------

-- VENEZUELA:   REICH CALL TO PEDRO CARMONA --

QUESTION:  DID ASSISTANT SECRETARY OF STATE REICH SPEAK WITH
VENEZUELA'S THEN INTERIM PRESIDENT ON FRIDAY APRIL 12 TO
ADVISE HIM TO NOT DISSOLVE THE NATIONAL ASSEMBLY?

                    UNCLASSIFIED

PAGE 03        STATE   073182   172107Z
A:   CONTRARY TO A REPORT IN THE NEW YORK TIMES, ASSISTANT
SECRETARY REICH DID NOT SPEAK WITH THEN-INTERIM PRESIDENT
PEDRO CARMONA ON FRIDAY APRIL 12 OR AT ANY OTHER TIME DURING
VENEZUELA'S CRISIS LAST WEEK.

THROUGH OUR EMBASSY IN CARACAS, AMBASSADOR REICH DID CONVEY
THE EXPECTATIONS OF THE U.S. GOVERNMENT THAT THE INTERIM
GOVERNMENT WOULD RESPECT THE INSTITUTIONS AND PRACTICES OF
DEMOCRACY IN VENEZUELA, INCLUDING THE CONTINUED FUNCTIONING
OF ALL BRANCHES OF GOVERNMENT.

IF PRESSED: OVER THE COURSE OF FRIDAY AND SATURDAY,
AMBASSADOR SHAPIRO SPOKE WITH A NUMBER OF VENEZUELANS
INVOLVED IN THE EVENTS THERE, INCLUDING THEN INTERIM
PRESIDENT CARMONA.

THE ASSERTION THAT THE UNITED STATES SOUGHT TO "STAGE MANAGE"
THE SITUATION IN VENEZUELA, IS FLATLY INCORRECT.  OUR
DIPLOMATIC EFFORTS, LIKE THOSE OF OUR DEMOCRATIC ALLIES, WERE
FOCUSED ON HELPING VENEZUELANS RESOLVE THEIR CRISIS
PEACEFULLY AND DEMOCRATICALLY.

THROUGH REGULAR DIPLOMATIC CONTACTS BOTH IN WASHINGTON AND IN
CARACAS, WE MADE CLEAR OUR REJECTION OF ANY UNCONSTITUTIONAL,
UNDEMOCRATIC EFFORT BY ANY PARTY IN VENEZUELA.
POWELL

                    UNCLASSIFIED

<< END OF DOCUMENT >>

Current Class: UNCLASSIFIED
```

UNCLASSIFIED

Current Class: UNCLASSIFIED
Current Handling: n/a

Q: WHAT ABOUT ASSERTIONS THAT U.S. OFFICIALS HAVE BEEN TOO
CLOSE TO THOSE VENEZUELANS WHO WERE INVOLVED IN THE EVENTS OF
UNCLASSIFIED

PAGE 04   STATE   075817 222122Z
APRIL 11-13?

A: U.S. OFFICIALS HAVE MET WITH A BROAD SPECTRUM OF
VENEZUELANS OVER THE PAST SEVERAL MONTHS BOTH IN CARACAS AND
IN WASHINGTON. U.S. OFFICIALS MET WITH BUSINESS COMMUNITY
REPRESENTATIVES, LABOR UNION OFFICIALS, CATHOLIC CHURCH
LEADERS, OPPOSITION POLITICAL LEADERS, PRO-CHAVEZ
LEGISLATORS, AND A WIDE ARRAY OF VENEZUELAN GOVERNMENT
OFFICIALS. IN THE COURSE OF NORMAL DIPLOMATIC CONTACTS, U.S.
OFFICIALS MET WITH PEDRO CARMONA, THE PRESIDENT OF THE
VENEZUELAN FEDERATION OF CHAMBERS OF COMMERCE (FEDECAMARAS).

OUR MESSAGE TO ALL VENEZUELAN CONTACTS HAS BEEN CONSISTENT.
THE POLITICAL SITUATION IN VENEZUELA IS ONE FOR VENEZUELANS
TO RESOLVE PEACEFULLY, DEMOCRATICALLY AND CONSTITUTIONALLY.
WE EXPLICITLY TOLD ALL OF OUR VENEZUELAN INTERLOCUTORS ON
NUMEROUS OCCASIONS AND AT MANY LEVELS THAT UNDER NO
CIRCUMSTANCES WOULD THE UNITED STATES SUPPORT ANY
UNCONSTITUTIONAL, UNDEMOCRATIC EFFORT, SUCH AS A COUP.

Q: WHAT ABOUT THE STATEMENT OF A DIPLOMAT PRESENT AT A
FEBRUARY 12 MEETING AT THE DEPARTMENT OF STATE THAT
DEPARTMENT OFFICIALS WERE QUICK TO POINT OUT THAT CHAVEZ HAD
RESIGNED?

A: OUR RESPONSE TO THE SITUATION IN VENEZUELA ON APRIL 12
LAID OUT THE FACTS AS WE KNEW THEM TO BE DURING A VERY
CONFUSING TIME. THOSE FACTS WERE THAT: (1) HUNDREDS OF
THOUSANDS OF VENEZUELANS DEMONSTRATED PEACEFULLY AGAINST THE
CHAVEZ GOVERNMENT, (2) THE CHAVEZ GOVERNMENT RESPONDED WITH A
BLOODY CRACK-DOWN AGAINST PROTESTORS AND THE INDEPENDENT
UNCLASSIFIED

PAGE 05   STATE   075817 222122Z
MEDIA, (3) PRESIDENT CHAVEZ HAD DISMISSED HIS VICE PRESIDENT
AND CABINET AND RESIGNED, AND (4) A TRANSITIONAL GOVERNMENT
WOULD ASSUME POWER AND CALL FOR NEW ELECTIONS.

IN ALL OF OUR STATEMENTS, WE EMPHASIZED THAT VENEZUELANS
NEEDED TO RESOLVE THIS SITUATION PEACEFULLY, DEMOCRATICALLY,
AND CONSTITUTIONALLY IN ACCORDANCE WITH THE INTER-AMERICAN
DEMOCRATIC CHARTER. AS STATED BEFORE, IT WAS OUR
UNDERSTANDING THAT PRESIDENT CHAVEZ HAD RESIGNED AND THAT
THERE WAS NO SUCCESSOR. IT WAS UP TO VENEZUELANS TO DECIDE
HOW TO RESOLVE THIS SUCCESSION CRISIS. ONCE VENEZUELANS HAD

Current Class: UNCLASSIFIED

UNCLASSIFIED

14. Department of State Press Guidance
April 19, 2002, p. 2

```
Current Class: UNCLASSIFIED
Current Handling: n/a
```

DETERMINED THEIR PATH FORWARD, THE INTER-AMERICAN COMMUNITY
WOULD EXAMINE THIS VENEZUELAN SOLUTION TO DETERMINE IF IT WAS
IN KEEPING WITH THE INTER-AMERICAN DEMOCRATIC CHARTER.

----
2.   WHA PRESS GUIDANCE, APRIL 19, 2002

-- CUBA: VOTE ON UNCHR HUMAN RIGHTS RESOLUTION --

Q: THE UN COMMISSION ON HUMAN RIGHTS (CHR) HAS AGAIN VOTED
TO ADMONISH CUBA OVER REPRESSING ITS CITIZENS' HUMAN RIGHTS.
ANY COMMENT?

A: TODAY'S 23-21-09 VOTE WAS A VICTORY FOR THE CUBAN PEOPLE.
IT DEMONSTRATES THAT THE WORLD IS AWARE OF THEIR PLIGHT AND
SUPPORTS THEIR BRAVE EFFORTS TO PRESS FOR BETTER HUMAN RIGHTS
OBSERVANCE AND FOR DEMOCRACY IN CUBA.
IT ALSO SENDS AN UNAMBIGUOUS MESSAGE TO THE CUBAN GOVERNMENT:
                     UNCLASSIFIED

PAGE 06   STATE   075817 222122Z
FOR THE FOURTH STRAIGHT YEAR , THE INTERNATIONAL COMMUNITY
HAS FOUND THE HUMAN RIGHTS SITUATION IN CUBA WANTING.

THERE'S SOMETHING NEW HERE: FOR THE FIRST TIME EVER, CUBA'S
NEIGHBORS IN LATIN AMERICA DRAFTED, INTRODUCED, AND BROADLY
SUPPORTED WITH THEIR CO-SPONSORSHIPS AND VOTES A RESOLUTION
ON HUMAN RIGHTS IN CUBA. PARTICULAR CREDIT MUST GO TO
URUGUAY, FOR TABLING THIS REMARKABLE AND GROUNDBREAKING
EFFORT, AND TO ALL THE LATIN AMERICAN COUNTRIES WHICH LENT
THEIR SUPPORT TO THE RESOLUTION.

IMPORTANTLY, THE RESOLUTION CALLS ON THE CUBAN REGIME TO MAKE
PROGRESS IN THE FIELDS OF CIVIL AND POLITICAL HUMAN RIGHTS,
AND REQUESTS THE UN HIGH COMMISSIONER FOR HUMAN RIGHTS TO
SEND A REPRESENTATIVE TO CUBA AND REPORT BACK TO THE
COMMISSION.

WE CALL ON CUBA TO COMPLY WITH THE WILL OF THE UN HUMAN
RIGHTS COMMISSION AND PERMIT THIS REPRESENTATIVE TO VISIT IN
ORDER TO HELP CUBA MAKE THE NECESSARY PROGRESS IN THE FIELD
OF HUMAN AND CIVIL RIGHTS.

----
3.   S/CT PRESS GUIDANCE , APRIL 19, 2002

-- ECUADOR: DEPUTY SECRETARY'S REMARKS --

Current Class: UNCLASSIFIED
```
```

UNCLASSIFIED

Current Class: UNCLASSIFIED
Current Handling: n/a

ALL POSTS FOR PAO, USSOCOM FOR POLAD

E.O. 12958: N/A
TAGS: OPRC, KPAO
SUBJECT: WHA GUIDANCE, APRIL 22, 2002

SUMMARY OF CONTENTS:
1. WHA PRESS GUIDANCE, APRIL 22 (VENEZUELA)
2. WHA PRESS GUIDANCE, APRIL 19 (CUBA)
3. S/CT PRESS GUIDANCE, APRIL 19 (ECUADOR)
4. TAKEN QUESTIONS, APRIL 19 (CANADA, VENEZEULA)
END SUMMARY.

----
1. WHA PRESS GUIDANCE, APRIL 22, 2002

-- VENEZUELA: AMBASSADOR SHAPIRO MEETING WITH
CARMONA/ASSERTIONS U.S. TOO CLOSE TO OPPOSITION --
UNCLASSIFIED

PAGE 03   STATE   075817 222122Z

Q: WHAT DID AMBASSADOR SHAPIRO SAY TO PEDRO CARMONA?

A: AMBASSADOR SHAPIRO SPOKE WITH PEDRO CARMONA TWICE IN THE
IMMEDIATE AFTERMATH OF APRIL 11. FIRST, ON APRIL 12 BEFORE
CARMONA SWORE HIMSELF IN, AMBASSADOR SHAPIRO PHONED CARMONA
AND TOLD HIM THAT ANY POLITICAL TRANSITION PROCESS HAD TO BE
CONSTITUTIONAL AND DEMOCRATIC AND URGED HIM NOT TO DISSOLVE
THE NATIONAL ASSEMBLY. ON APRIL 13, AFTER CARMONA HAD SWORN
HIMSELF IN AS THE &INTERIM PROVISIONAL PRESIDENT8 AND HAD
DISSOLVED THE NATIONAL ASSEMBLY, AMBASSADOR SHAPIRO MET WITH
CARMONA (AT MIRAFLORES PALACE) AND PROVIDED HIM A COPY OF THE
INTER-AMERICAN DEMOCRATIC CHARTER, URGED HIM TO RE-ESTABLISH
THE NATIONAL ASSEMBLY, TO MOVE TO ELECTIONS AS SOON AS
POSSIBLE, AND TO CONTACT THE ORGANIZATION OF AMERICAN STATES
(OAS) SECRETARY GENERAL TO WELCOME AN OAS DELEGATION.

DURING HIS MEETING WITH INTERIM PRESIDENT CARMONA, AMBASSADOR
SHAPIRO URGED CARMONA TO IMMEDIATELY RESTORE CONSTITUTIONAL
ORDER AND NORMALIZE DEMOCRATIC RULE IN VENEZUELA.

OUR MESSAGE TO ALL VENEZUELAN CONTACTS HAS BEEN CONSISTENT:
THE POLITICAL SITUATION IN VENEZUELA IS ONE FOR VENEZUELANS
TO RESOLVE PEACEFULLY, DEMOCRATICALLY AND CONSTITUTIONALLY.
WE EXPLICITLY TOLD ALL OF OUR VENEZUELAN INTERLOCUTORS ON
NUMEROUS OCCASIONS AND AT MANY LEVELS THAT UNDER NO
CIRCUMSTANCES WOULD THE UNITED STATES SUPPORT ANY
UNCONSTITUTIONAL, UNDEMOCRATIC EFFORT, SUCH AS A COUP.

Current Class: UNCLASSIFIED

UNCLASSIFIED

UNCLASSIFIED

Current Class: UNCLASSIFIED
Current Handling: n/a

ALL POSTS FOR PAO, USSOCOM FOR POLAD

E.O. 12958: N/A
TAGS: OPRC, KPAO
SUBJECT: WHA GUIDANCE, AUGUST 13, 2002

SUMMARY OF CONTENTS:
1. TAKEN QUESTION, AUGUST 12 (VENEZUELA)
2. WHA PRESS GUIDANCE, AUGUST 12 (VENEZUELA)
3. WHA PRESS GUIDANCE, AUGUST 13 (CUBA, COLOMBIA, MEXICO)
END SUMMARY.

---
1. TAKEN QUESTION - WHA PRESS GUIDANCE, AUGUST 12, 2002:

-- VENEZUELA: VISIT OF FOREIGN MINISTER ROY CHADERTON
(TO FROM 8-12-02 DAILY PRESS BRIEFING) --
UNCLASSIFIED

PAGE 03   STATE   155266   141703Z

QUESTION: IS A MEETING BETWEEN DEPUTY SECRETARY ARMITAGE AND
VENEZUELAN FOREIGN MINISTER ROY CHADERTON SCHEDULED? IF SO,
WHEN?

ANSWER: THE DEPUTY SECRETARY WILL MEET WITH VENEZUELAN
FOREIGN MINISTER ROY CHADERTON ON TUESDAY, AUGUST 20.

QUESTION: WILL THE SUBJECT OF THE VENEZUELAN SUPREME COURT'S
DELIBERATIONS ON THE QUESTION OF WHETHER TO CHARGE WITH
REBELLION FOUR SENIOR MILITARY OFFICERS BE ON THE AGENDA?
WHAT ELSE WILL BE INCLUDED ON THE AGENDA?

ANSWER: THE DEPUTY SECRETARY AND THE FOREIGN MINISTER
CHADERTON WILL DISCUSS A WIDE VARIETY OF ISSUES INCLUDING THE
CURRENT POLITICAL SITUATION IN VENEZUELA AND ISSUES OF MUTUAL
INTEREST TO OUR BILATERAL RELATIONSHIP.

---
2. WHA PRESS GUIDANCE, AUGUST 12, 2002:

-- VENEZUELA: REVOCATION OF VISAS --

Q: CAN YOU CONFIRM THAT PEDRO CARMONA AND MOLINA TAMAYO'S US
VISAS WERE REVOKED?

A: MESSRS. CARMONA AND TAMAYO'S VISAS WERE REVOKED UNDER
SECTION 214(B) OF THE IMMIGRATION AND NATIONALITY ACT, WHICH

Current Class: UNCLASSIFIED

UNCLASSIFIED

16. Department of State Press Guidance
August 12-13, 2002, p. 2

Current Class: UNCLASSIFIED
Current Handling: n/a

PROVIDES THAT FOREIGN NATIONALS ARE PRESUMED TO BE INTENDING

PAGE 04   STATE 155266 141703Z
IMMIGRANTS AND THEREFORE INELIGIBLE FOR A NONIMMIGRANT VISA
UNLESS THEY CAN ESTABLISH THEY QUALIFY FOR NONIMMIGRANT
CLASSIFICATION.

Q. WHAT WAS THE BASIS FOR THE DETERMINATION THAT THEY DIDN'T
QUALIFY FOR VISAS ANY LONGER UNDER SECTION 214(B).

A: VISA RECORDS ARE CONFIDENTIAL UNDER U.S. LAW, AND I
CAN,T PROVIDE ANY DETAILS ON THE UNDERLYING FACTUAL BASIS
FOR THE INELIGIBILITY FINDINGS.

----
3. WHA PRESS GUIDANCE, AUGUST 13, 2002:

-- CUBA: FORMER UN AMBASSADOR IN DEPARTMENT --

Q: WILL FORMER UN AMBASSADOR TO CUBA JORGE ALCIBIADES
HIDALGO BASULTO BE MEETING WITH ANYONE IN THE DEPARTMENT?

A: FORMER UN AMBASSADOR TO CUBA JORGE ALCIBIADES HIDALGO
BASULTO WILL MEET WITH STATE DEPARTMENT OFFICIALS, INCLUDING
ASSISTANT SECRETARY FOR WESTERN HEMISPHERE AFFAIRS OTTO J.
REICH.   WE LOOK FORWARD TO HEARING HIDALGO'S FIRST-HAND
ASSESSMENT OF THE SITUATION ON THE ISLAND.

-- COLOMBIA: "STATE OF INTERNAL DISTURBANCE" DECLARED --

PAGE 05   STATE   155266 141703Z
QUESTION: DO YOU HAVE ANY COMMENT ON THE PRESIDENT URIBE,S
DECLARATION OF A STATE OF INTERNAL DISTURBANCE? WHAT IS THE
STATUS OF THE EMBASSY? AMERICAN COMMUNITY? ADDITIONAL
TRAVEL WARNINGS ANTICIPATED?

A: PRESIDENT URIBE DECLARED A "STATE OF INTERNAL
DISTURBANCE" EARLY AUGUST 12, AS PROVIDED FOR UNDER THE 1991
CONSTITUTION. A "STATE OF INTERNAL DISTURBANCE" MAY LAST A
MAXIMUM OF 270 DAYS, AND ALLOWS FOR THE PRESIDENT TO ISSUE
DECREE LAWS, DECLARE CURFEWS MAKE SEARCHES WITHOUT WARRANT,
WHILE PROMISING THE PROTECTION OF HUMAN RIGHTS AND CIVIL
LIBERTIES. A RANGE OF COLOMBIAN POLITICAL LEADERS HAVE
SPOKEN OUT IN FAVOR OF THE DECREE.

WE ARE UNAWARE OF SPECIFIC NEW THREATS AGAINST EITHER THE

Current Class: UNCLASSIFIED

USAID $ 10 million Grant to DAI for Venezuela Program

SECTION C - DESCRIPTION/SPECIFICATIONS/STATEMENT OF WORK

C.1 STATEMENT OF WORK - VENEZUELA STATEMENT OF WORK
SPECIFICATIONS

1. BACKGROUND

USAID's Office of Transition Initiatives (OTI) was established in 1994 to respond to countries experiencing a significant and sometimes rapid political transition, which may or may not be accompanied by a social and/or economic crisis. OTI assesses designs and implements programs that have characteristics of being fast, flexible, innovative, tangible, targeted, catalytic and overtly political, focusing on the root causes of the crisis.

A political transition may occur as a result of military intervention like in Kosovo or Haiti; a change in presidency like in Indonesia or Peru; a peace agreement like in Guatemala or Mindanao, Philippines; or in support for peaceful resolution to political strife as in Colombia. OTI is often engaged in the most sensitive political issues of the US government's priority and high profile countries. It operates on the premise that fast, flexible, targeted, catalytic and overt political transition assistance can assist countries in moving away from crisis or other "at risk" situations to stability. Operating under the special authorities of the International Disaster Assistance (IDA) account funding, OTI's initial responses and set-up are rapid; its operations decentralized and streamlined, and its programs brief - normally about two years. Therefore, time is always of the essence in each phase of its program: assessment, deployment, operations set-up, grant making and phase-out or hand-off. With this OTI must have the ability to change, reorient or otherwise refocus its programs and/or respond to new crises in the country or region.

In the field, OTI works with organizations of various political dimensions, including indigenous groups; cooperatives; associations; informal groups; local, regional and national governments; private voluntary organizations (PVO's); student groups; media; international organizations; private sector and coalitions of these entities. Activities may include efforts to: promote reconciliation, conflict resolution and prevention; advance an economic recovery with employment and vocational training; promote independent media with journalist training and law reform; demobilize and reintegrate ex-combatants; increased land access with determining efforts; provide nation-wide training to regional and local elected officials; promote national messages using television, radio and newsprint; reactivate critical NGO's with start-up grants; promote governance with elections support; develop a strong civil society; and initiate rural infrastructure rehabilitation projects with community participation.

OTI frequently uses small grants (from $500 to under $100,000) with defined goals, objectives, deliverables, and reporting, to undertake these initiatives. The prototype grant involves some or all of the following:

broad and diverse community participation in the grant's design and implementation; community grant counterpart (e.g. in labor or materials); catalytic nature; near-term, high-impact; a media component to amplify the results; tangible visible benefits; and in-kind procurement. The types of grants may vary, but they focus on the root causes of the crisis. Because the grant aims to "advance peaceful democratic change," these grants may focus on issues of higher risk and/or activities not currently being funded by others. These grants are usually (or primarily) "disbursed" in-kind, but cash or cash advances are sometimes more cost effective and efficient depending on the country situation, grantee, grant amount and grant type. Depending on the country and program focus, in-kind assistance may include, but not limited to office equipment, printing materials, conference/seminar venues, agricultural equipment or building supplies.

While the Cognizant Technical Officer (CTO) is Washington-based, one or more U.S. Personal Services Contractors (PSC's) will be assigned in the field to manage, oversee and make day-to-day decisions regarding the contract management and implementation of OTI's country program. The senior OTI field representative (a USPSC) will provide overall programmatic focus, direction, and grant approval. The senior OTI field representative will also determine the types or range of organizations or grantees that will be funded. The country representative will make these decisions based upon U.S. foreign policy interests and in close collaboration with the U.S. Embassy.

Field staffing and administrative structures may also vary according to the demands of each country program and area. There may be one or more OTI regional offices, possibly with a coordinating office in the capital, US Embassy or USAID Mission. In addition OTI may be required to establish a regional program to respond to a crisis. For each program the number of offices and location of offices will be determined by the senior OTI field representative in consideration of the programmatic focus and cost effectiveness and efficiency. Although the country context may vary, OTI works closely in the design and implementation of programs, with the US Embassy, the USAID Mission and the Office of Foreign Disaster Assistance (when present in the country).

OTI often needs a contractor to provide support for all phases of the program. Depending on the program, the contractor will be responsible for administrative, logistics, procurement and finance aspects of the program. More specifically, the contractor will set up offices; purchase office equipment and vehicles; locate and hire staff; establish communications systems; develop and maintain a procurement and financial system; determine grant worthiness; develop and maintain the database; and monitor grant effectiveness and impact. The contractor will be expected to provide varying amounts of funds on short notice and in countries where there are no or limited banking institutions.

Contracting partners are critical to the success of OTI programs because they are expected to overcome the significant challenges posed by "war torn" or otherwise unstable countries in which OTI operates.

2. CONTRACT DURATION

The contract will be for a one-year period, with an option to renew for an additional year at the end of the first year. A six-day workweek is authorized for the first six months, thereafter, with advanced CTO approval.

3. COUNTRY BACKGROUND - VENEZUELA

Venezuela has operated as a functioning, although imperfect, democracy since
1958. Under an arrangement known as punto fijo, the country's two most
influential political parties, the social democratic AD (Accion Democratica)
and the Christian democratic COPEI, agreed on means to share and control
power. Low petroleum prices in the late 1980s produced national financial
crises and economic measures that resulted in public outcry over the problems
the country faced and the government's inability to mend the situation. The
economic stress and the government's sometimes-repressive response to public
reaction marked the acceleration of increasingly widespread dissatisfaction
with puntofijismo and a weakening of already fragile democratic institutions.

In 1998, Hugo Chavez was elected by an overwhelming majority of voters on a
platform to address the problems of the poor and address corruption, which
had become a hallmark of the puntofijismo. In recent months, his popularity
has waned and political tensions have risen dramatically as President Chavez
has attempted to implement several controversial reforms. The tensions came
to a head on April when several protesters were shot outside the presidential
palace.

Support for democracy remains the top foreign policy priority in the
hemisphere for the United States and the United States has a strong interest
in ensuring that it endures in Venezuela. For democracy to remain viable,
support is needed for the institutions that provide for checks and balances,
and ensure the protection of human rights and the free expression of ideas,
including, at both the national and local levels, by the media, civil
society, political parties, and government institutions.

Venezuela is at a critical juncture in its democratic history and targeted,
flexible assistance aimed at supporting democracy could make a difference. A
pillar of USAID's strategy is conflict mitigation, and OTI through the
contractor chosen through this scope of work will specifically focus on
program areas that seek to restore democratic balance and ease societal
tensions. The timing for an OTI program is perhaps more relevant today than
when the initial assessment was conducted.

4. PROGRAM DESCRIPTION

The contractor will establish a flexible, quick-disbursing small grant fund,
able to respond to the rapidly evolving political situation in Venezuela.
For the base year the value of the grants to be disbursed will be $3,500,000.
If the option is exercised, the value of the grants to be disbursed for the
option year will be $3,500,000. This fund will be managed by an OTI field
representative reporting to the U.S. Ambassador in Venezuela and supported by
the incumbent contractor or cooperating agency. The field representative
will maintain close collaboration with other Embassy offices in identifying
opportunities, selecting partners, and ensuring the program remains
consistent with U.S. foreign policy. The OTI field representative will
approve grants under $100,000. The contractor shall develop grant formats
that are subject to prior approval by the Office of Procurement/Contracting
Officer for each type of proposed grant under this contract (i.e. PIOs, U.S.
Organizations, and local, regional and national governments). The contractor
will develop a field grant guide and provide trained and experienced grants

241

managers for grants under contracts, and more specifically where grants will
be provided to U.S. Organizations, PIOs, and local, regional and national
governments. In accordance with OTI's approved Grants Under Contracts
deviation, dated 1/7/02, grants under this contract are authorized as
follows:

1) **U.S. Organizations:** The OTI field representative shall approve grants to
U.S. organizations up to $100,000. The Contracting Officer must approve
any such grants over $100,000.

2) **Public International Organizations (PIOs):** The OTI field representative
shall approve grants to PIOs as defined in ADS 308.7, up to $100,000. The
Contracting Officer must approve such grants over $100,000.

3) **Local, Regional and National Government Organizations:** The OTI field
representative shall approve grants to local, regional and national
government organizations, up to $100,000. Any such grants over $100,000
require prior approval of the Cognizant Technical Officer (CTO).

The minimum criteria for grant selection and approval will include, but not
be limited to:

- Consistent with US interests and objectives.
- Consistent with the OTI program areas (some of which are outlined below).
- Demonstrate potential for short-term impact, i.e., less than 6 months.
- Significant counterpart contribution.

The current situation augers strongly for rapid U.S. government engagement.
OTI, through its contractor, will act quickly to initiate non-partisan
programs that promote pluralism and a democratic society. It will include
the participation of all groups that seek to promote an inclusive democracy
in Venezuela. OTI will not provide assistance to any groups seeking to
unconstitutionally alter the political order. The OTI program will be part
of a coordinated approach by the U.S. government supporting democracy.

OTI is already working closely with the USAID's Latin America and Caribbean
(LAC) Bureau to ensure a successful handoff of the program. OTI anticipates
an initial focus on the following two program areas:

1) **Preserve Democratic Institutions and Processes** - OTI will work with
democratically oriented elements in labor, business, political organizations,
government and civil society to strengthen democratic institutions and
processes. OTI will also work with media institutions through journalist
training and other means to ensure balanced coverage of events and political
matters in Venezuela.

2) **Enhance Dialogue/Reconciliation/Conflict Mediation** - Deprived of effective
democratic means of expressing dissent, the opposition has been forced to
implement work stoppages and marches to express its grievances; the most
recent iteration ended in violence with over a dozen people killed and many
more wounded. President Chavez has promised to institute round-tables and
promote general dialogue among various societal groups to reduce tension. OTI
will work with NGOs that seek to promote dialogue on an inclusive social and
political agenda for Venezuela and open avenues of dialogue currently closed
due to the polarization of the population. Through public debates, town hall
meetings, and university sponsored conferences, for example, OTI will

Development Alternatives, Inc.
Calle Guaicaipuro con Calle Mohedano
Torre Hener, Piso 2. Oficina 2-B,
Urb. El Rosal 1060-Caracas, Venezuela

Venezuela: Iniciative para la
Construción de Confianza

(b)(6)

Ref: Grant agreement between Development Alternatives, Inc. (DAI) and   (b)(6)
              (b)(6)
              Grant Number G-3822-101-008

Ref: USAID Contract No. HDA-C-00-02-00179 VICC
              Venezuelan Confidence Building Initiative

Dear   (b)(6)

In response to your proposal dated 11/01/2002, Development Alternatives, Inc (hereinafter, simply VICC/DAI") is pleased to award   (b)(6)
, or "the Beneficiary"), with a grant, in kind, of up to $US 9946.85 to be paid in local currency, in support of its project **Diálogo Social y Formación de Ciudadanía** for the period between 12/09/2002 and 02/07/2003.

The grant is financed by the United States Agency for International Development (USAID) through contract # HAD-C-00-02-00179 with DAI. This grant is to support the activities of the project, according to the attached Program Description (Annex 1), Program Budget (Annex 2) and Standard Provisions (Annex 3). The final proposal, budget and standard provisions (Annexes 1, 2 & 3) are considered integral parts of this Grant Agreement.

All acquisitions made by DAI on behalf of the Beneficiary will be in accordance with USAID procurement regulations. The Chief of Party or designated Program Development Officer (PDO) will make the necessary decisions about any dispute arising from or related to this grant.

All materials produced under the terms of this agreement -- written, graphic, film, magnetic tape, or otherwise -- shall remain the property of both the Grantee and DAI. Both the Grantee and DAI retain rights to publish or disseminate in all language reports arising from such materials, unless otherwise specified in this agreement. The rights and duties provided for in this paragraph shall continue, notwithstanding the termination of the contract or the execution of its other provisions. The Grantee shall acknowledge the support of USAID in any report, audio or video materials, presentation, or document based in whole or in part on work performed under this Agreement. Such acknowledgments shall be as follows:

"This workshop program, documents, radio advertisement, etc. was prepared with funds provided by Development Alternatives, Inc., with financing from the U.S. Agency for International Development under Contract Number HDA-C-00-02-00179 Venezuela Confidence Building Initiative Project (VICC)."

The party receiving the grant has full responsibility for executing the project or activity being supported by the grant and for complying with the award conditions. Although the receiving party is encouraged to ask for the opinion and support of VICC/DAI about any specific problems that may arise, this suggestion does not diminish the responsibility of the party receiving the grant. The latter party must apply solid technical and administrative criteria. The grant award does not imply that the responsibility for operative decisions has been transferred to VICC/DAI. The party receiving the grant has the responsibility of notifying VICC/DAI about any significant problems associated with the administrative or financial aspects of the grant award. All information and documents pertaining to this grant must be made available for three years following the termination of this grant.

Final Report: The Beneficiary will present the Final Project Progress Report before **02/10/2003** or within fifteen days after the finalization of the last activity of the program should any delay occur during the implementation. The final report will include the accomplishment of the grant benchmarks or milestones for which the grant was awarded. The final report will consist of a technical report and a financial report.

The Beneficiary will send all reports to the designated Program Development Officer,   (b)(6) VICC/DAI Calle Guaicaipuro con Calle Mohedano, Torre Hener, Piso 2. Oficina 2-B, Urb. El Rosal 1060-Caracas, Venezuela.

Sincerely,

John H. McCarthy   Dec. 6, 2002   Date: 12/06/2002
Jack McCarthy, Director/DAI

Acknowledgement of receipt: (b)(6)

Signed by: _____ (b)(6) _____   Date: 12/06/2002

USAID Contract with DAI for $ 10 million for Venezuela Projects

AWARD/CONTRACT	1. THIS CONTRACT IS RATED ORDER UNDER DPAS (15 CFR 350)		RATING N/A	PAGE 1	OF PAGES 49
2. CONTRACT NO. (Proc. Inst. Ident.) RDA-C-00-02-00179	3. EFFECTIVE DATE 08-30-2002		4. REQUISITION/PURCHASE REQUEST/PROJECT NO. 12506-0129		
5. ISSUED BY CODE		6. ADMINISTERED BY (If other than item 2)		CODE	

5. ISSUED BY CODE

U.S. Agency for Intl. Development
M/OP/HRAM/DATI
1300 Pennsylvania Avenue, NW
Room 7.10.15, RRB
Washington DC 20523-7100

7. NAME AND ADDRESS OF CONTRACTOR (No., street, city, county, state and ZIP Code)

Development Alternatives, Inc.
7250 Woodmont Ave., Suite 200
Bethesda MD 20814

8. DELIVERY
[ ] FOB ORIGIN [X] OTHER (See below)

9. DISCOUNT FOR PROMPT PAYMENT
N/A

10. SUBMIT INVOICES ITEM
(4 copies unless otherwise specified) Sect G.3
TO THE ADDRESS SHOWN IN:

CODE | FACILITY CODE
11. SHIP TO/MARK FOR CODE

12. PAYMENT WILL BE MADE BY CODE
U.S. Agency for Intl. Development
M/FM/CMP/DCB-Room 7.07-133
1300 Pennsylvania Avenue, NW
Washington DC 20523-7100

13. AUTHORITY FOR USING OTHER THAN FULL AND OPEN COMPETITION:
[ ] 10 U.S.C. 2304(c) ( )   [X] 41 U.S.C. 253(c) ( )

14. ACCOUNTING AND APPROPRIATION DATA
See Sect G.6.

15A. ITEM NO.	15B. SUPPLIES/SERVICES	15C. QUANTITY	15D. UNIT	15E. UNIT PRICE	15F. AMOUNT
005	Basic - Year 1 : 08/30/02 - 08/29/03 - $5,200,607	1			
010	Option - Year 2 : 08/30/03 - 08/29/04 - $4,861,255	1			
	TOTAL ESTIMATED COST: $10,061,862				

15G. TOTAL AMOUNT OF CONTRACT $10,061,862.

16. TABLE OF CONTENTS	See Attached Table of Contents				
(X)	SEC.	DESCRIPTION	PAGE(S)	(X)	SEC.	DESCRIPTION	PAGE(S)

16. TABLE OF CONTENTS — See Attached Table of Contents

PART I - THE SCHEDULE

(X)	SEC.	DESCRIPTION	PAGE(S)
X	A	SOLICITATION/CONTRACT FORM	1-3
X	B	SUPPLIES OR SERVICES AND PRICES/COSTS	4-6
X	C	DESCRIPTION/SPECS/WORK STATEMENT	7-21
X	D	PACKAGING AND MARKING	22
X	E	INSPECTION AND ACCEPTANCE	23
X	F	DELIVERIES OR PERFORMANCE	24-26
X	G	CONTRACT ADMINISTRATION DATA	27-31
X	H	SPECIAL CONTRACT REQUIREMENTS	32-38

PART II - CONTRACT CLAUSES

(X)	SEC.	DESCRIPTION	PAGE(S)
X	I	CONTRACT CLAUSES	38-48

PART III - LIST OF DOCUMENTS, EXHIBITS AND OTHER ATTACH.

| | J | LIST OF ATTACHMENTS | 49 |

PART IV - REPRESENTATIONS AND INSTRUCTIONS

	K	REPRESENTATIONS, CERTIFICATIONS AND OTHER STATEMENTS OF OFFERORS	
	L	INSTRS., CONDS. AND NOTICES TO OFFER	
	M	EVALUATION FACTORS FOR AWARD	

CONTRACTING OFFICER WILL COMPLETE ITEM 17 OR 18 AS APPLICABLE

17. [ ] CONTRACTOR'S NEGOTIATED AGREEMENT (Contractor is required to sign this document and return ___ copies to issuing office.)

18. [X] AWARD (Contractor is not required to sign this document.)
Solicitation Number M/OP-02-1364

19A. NAME AND TITLE OF SIGNER
Anna Marie Scott
Director of Contracts and Grants

20A. NAME OF CONTRACTING OFFICER
Mercedes Eugenia (cb)

19B. NAME OF CONTRACTOR (Signature of person authorized to sign)
19C. DATE SIGNED 30 Aug 02

20B. UNITED STATES OF AMERICA BY (Signature of Contracting Officer)
20C. DATE SIGNED 30 Ag 02

STANDARD FORM 26 REV (4-88)

NATIONAL ENDOWMENT FOR DEMOCRACY

Grant Agreement No. 2003-548.0
between

Grantor: National Endowment for Democracy
1101 15th Street, NW, Suite 700
Washington, DC 20005

Grantee: Súmate, A.C.
Centro Empresarial Los Palos Grandes, piso 7
Av. Andres Bello, Los Palos Grandes, Chacao
Estado Miranda
Caracas, Venezuela

1. AUTHORITY

This Grant is awarded in accordance with the authority contained in P.L. 98-164, as amended (hereafter referred to as the "Act") and Grant No. S-LMAQM-03-GR-001 between the United States Department of State and the National Endowment for Democracy (hereafter referred to as "the Endowment").

2. PURPOSE

The purpose of this Grant is to enable the Grantee to carry out the project objectives shown in Attachment A, Program Description, which are consistent with the purposes stated in Section 502(b) of the Act.

3. GRANT AMOUNT AND BUDGET

The amount obligated under this Grant is $53,400, which is to be expended according to the Grant Budget shown in Attachment B.

The Grantee shall not use funds designated for Program Costs to pay Administrative Costs, nor vice versa, without prior written approval of the Endowment. The Grantee shall also obtain written approval from the Endowment prior to making an expenditure which would increase costs in a major budget category within either the Program or Administrative Costs budget by more than 15 percent or $5,000 (whichever amount is larger) above the amount budgeted for that category. Adjustments among budget categories shall not result in an increase in the total amount of the Grant. The Endowment will not fund costs in excess of the Grant amount shown above.

4. GRANT PERIOD

The effective date of this Grant is September 12, 2003.
The expiration date of this Grant is September 30, 2004.

All expenditures from Grant funds must be either for authorized activities that take place or for authorized obligations that are incurred during this Grant Period, unless otherwise stated in the Grant. Expenditures for costs incurred prior to the effective date or after the expiration date will be disallowed. Payments made after the expiration date for expenses incurred within the Grant Period are allowable.

If the Grant Period is insufficient for satisfactory completion of the project objectives, the Agreement may be amended to extend the period. The Grantee must request the extension in writing prior to the current expiration date, explaining the circumstances which warrant the extension. Requests for amendments may

CIA Answer to Jeremy Bigwood about Súmate

Central Intelligence Agency

Washington, D.C. 20505

24 December 2003

Mr. Jeremy Bigwood
3200 16th Street NW #806
Washington, DC 20010

Reference: F-2004-00521

Dear Mr. Bigwood:

This acknowledges receipt of your 5 December 2003 letter requesting records under the provisions of the Freedom of Information Act (FOIA). Specifically, your request is for records pertaining to "the Venezuelan organization called SUMATE (also called SÚMATE) from January, 2000 until the present." For identification purposes we have assigned your request the number referenced above. Please refer to this number in future correspondence.

With regard to information requested on foreign organizations or companies, it is the CIA policy to neither confirm nor deny the existence or nonexistence of any CIA records. Unless officially acknowledged, such information would be classified for reasons of national security under Sections 1.5(c) [intelligence sources and methods] and 1.5(d) [foreign relations] of Executive Order 12958. Further, the Director of Central Intelligence has the responsibility and authority to protect such information from unauthorized disclosure in accordance with Section 103 (c)(6) of the National Security Act of 1947 and Section 6 of the CIA Act of 1949.

Accordingly, your request is denied on the basis of FOIA exemptions (b)(1) and (b)(3). By this action, we are neither confirming nor denying the existence or nonexistence of such records. An explanation of cited FOIA exemptions is enclosed. The CIA official responsible for this denial is Robert T. Herman, Information and Privacy Coordinator. You may appeal this decision by addressing your appeal to the Agency Release Panel within 45 days from the date of this letter, in my care. Should you choose to do this, please explain the basis of your appeal.

Sincerely,

Robert T. Herman
Information and Privacy Coordinator

Enclosure

FREEDOM OF INFORMATION ACT APPEAL
F-2004-00521

Agency Release Panel
Office of Information Services
Central Intelligence Agency
Washington, D.C. 20505
December 31, 2003
Dear Agency Release Panel:

I am writing to appeal Robert T. Herman's 24 December, 2003 denial of my FOIA request that the Agency has numbered F-2004-00521 and which requested records pertaining to "the Venezuelan organization called SUMATE (also called SÚMATE) from January, 2000 until the present."

Mr. Herman's denial was framed as follows:

"With regard to information requested on foreign organizations or companies, it is the CIA policy to neither confirm nor deny the existence or nonexistence of any CIA records. Unless officially acknowledged, such information would be classified for reasons of national security under Sections 1.5(c) and 1.5(d) of Executive Order 12958. Further, the Director of Central Intelligence has the responsibility and authority to protect such information from unauthorized disclosure in accordance with Section 103 (c)(6) of the National Security Act of 1947 and Section 6 of the CIA Act of 1949.

Accordingly, your request is denied on the basis of FOIA exemptions (b)(1) and (b)(3). By this action, we are neither confirming nor denying the existence or nonexistence of such records. An explanation of cited FOIA exemptions is enclosed. The CIA official responsible for this denial is Robert T. Herman, Information and Privacy Coordinator. You may appeal this decision by addressing your appeal to the Agency Release Panel within 45 days from the date of this letter, in my care. Should you choose to do this, please explain the basis of your appeal."

Mr. Herman's response is essentially the notorious "Glomar response" backed up by an Executive Order, two Acts from the 1940s, of which constitute FOIA exemption (b) (1), and FOIA exemption (b) (3), the infamous "sources and methods" to protect CIA officers and agents from exposure. I should make it clear that I am not asking for information on CIA officers and agents, nor on the methodology of intelligence gathering.

However, I do take exception to the first line of the first paragraph quoted above which reads: "With regard to information requested on foreign organizations or companies, it is the CIA policy to neither confirm nor deny the existence or nonexistence of any CIA records." This is simply not true. The CIA, through its FOIA office has released me an abundance of documentation regarding several foreign organizations. Allow me to list some of them here, citing URLs where these can be viewed:

MRTA: http://jeremybigwood.net/FOIAs/MRTA/CIAonMRTA/index.htm
More MRTA: http://jeremybigwood.net/FOIAs/MRTA/MRTA_Hostage_Crisis/index.htm
EPL: http://jeremybigwood.net/FOIAs/EPL/index.htm
FARC, ELN: http://usfumigation.org/Literature/FOIA/Colombia_Insurgents_Drug_Trade-CIA/index.htm
FMLN: A large series of yearly analyses that I have not yet placed on the Internet.

Through its FOIA office, the CIA has given me a copious volume of information of all of the above foreign organizations. So what Mr. Herman says about CIA policy does not hold up to the test. And why, if the Agency is willing to give me all of this information on other Latin American organizations, is it not willing to give me information about Súmate?

The only difference I see between the listed foreign organizations I received responses on and Súmate, which was denied, is that none of the organizations listed above has been supported by the CIA. Furthermore, the refusal of the CIA to release the information I request on Súmate begs the logical question - what is the relationship between Súmate and the CIA? Am I being denied the information I seek for the same reason that CIA FOIA office used when it also denied me information on Vladimiro Montesinos (who was receiving CIA funding)? Such questions can only be answered by the rapid release of the information I seek.

Please reconsider your position and release me the documents I seek as soon as possible.

Thank you for your time and consideration,

Respectfully yours,

Jeremy Bigwood

Glossary

AFL-CIO: Appeared in 1955 when the two main U.S. unions active in Europe, the AFL (American Federation of Labor, re-presented by Irving Brown) and the CIO (Congress of Industrial Organizations, represented by Victor Reuther) joined forces to create the AFL-CIO, with the blessing of Averell Harriman, new Administrator of the Marshall Plan, together with his emissary in Europe, Milton Katz. Since its beginnings the AFL-CIO has directly participated in the destabilization of numerous countries in Europe and Latin America. It is the one organization that receives the most funding from USAID.

AIR FORCE INTELLIGENCE (AFI): According to its official description, its mission is espionage, surveillance and aerial reconnaissance. The planes, which formerly were equipped only with photographic cameras, are now veritable flying fortresses, equipped for electronic warfare. This Department is also responsible for the launching of spy satellites.

ALIANZA CÍVICA DE LA SOCIEDAD CIVIL (CIVIC ALLIANCE OF THE CIVIL SOCIETY): Supposedly an organism that unifies several civilian organizations for the defense of democracy in Venezuela. This organization signed a document which recognized the legitimacy of the insurgent Government of Pedro Carmona and it was one of the most active in approving the referendum recalling President Hugo Chávez. The organization's Coordinator is Elías Santana.

AMERICAN CENTER FOR INTERNATIONAL LABOUR SOLIDARITY (ACILS): An alliance of unions, governments and corporations in Latin America, fusing three international institutions: the African American Labor Center (AALC), the Asian American K-AAFLI (sic) and the AFL-CIO. The American Center for Workers' Solidarity, also known as the Solidarity Center, is headed by John J. Sweeney, the Secretary General of the AFL-CIO. The ACILS finances parties and social organizations to overthrow governments that are "enemies" of the United States. For example, in 2001 and 2002, through the mediation of this organization, USAID supplied salaried Cubans working for Washington with electronic communications equipment, books and other propaganda materials, also cash payments, to create unions "favorable" to the U.S.

AMERICAN INSTITUTE FOR FREE LABOR DEVELOPMENT (AIFLD): Financed by USAID and controlled by the CIA, the AIFLD was created in February 1962 to control union movements in Latin America. An Administrative Council made up of powerful businessmen with vested interests in Latin America determines priority activities of the AIFLD. The presidency is in the hands of the General Director of the chemical giant, the W. R. Grace Corporation, and the President of the North American Chapter of the Order of Malta, J. Peter Grace; the organization promotes the collaboration of classes and supports vertical unity between the labor unions and the bosses, mimicking a model common to fascist corporations.

AMERICAN POLITICAL FOUNDATION (APF): The APF was born in 1979 from the alliance of the U.S. Republican and Democratic Parties to strengthen the American bipartite system. Its first national President was a republican, William Brock, while a democrat, Charles Manatt, served as Vice-President in charge of finances. The APF took on the interchange between the two political parties in order to facilitate alliances with parties in other parts of the world. At the end of the seventies, once the political climate was modified, this organization created the Democratic Project, from which the NED emerged, to increase

U.S. commitment to the promotion of "democratic" values abroad.

ARMY INTELLIGENCE (AI): Army Intelligence is officially defined as one of the military espionage corps destined to facilitate strategic information to commando operatives. In truth, it is one of the minor departments within the Intelligence community, but it is the most trust-worthy whenever the U.S. is involved in armed conflict because its agents collect essential information on the spot.

CENTER FOR INTERNATIONAL PRIVATE ENTERPRISE (CIPE): It is another one of those centers for grant funds for the NED and acts as an affiliated and tax-free counterpart of the American Chamber of Commerce. This corporation was established in 1983 to support free trade policies and a number of business associations. Also, it is involved in the training of business leaders and their mobilization within political processes. In Eastern Europe, for example, CIPE directs support programs towards various business societies and it provides them with recommendations and assistance for legislative activities. Hungary, Rumania, Czechoslovakia and Poland were the recipients of this "advice." The Krakow Industrial Society was formed in Poland in an attempt to publish a national newspaper. This publication was a response to an interest in cultivating and promoting a free enterprise system, in what is known in Western business jargon as "good economic and democratic development." The Board of Directors is drawn from the business community. Included are William Archey and Richard Lesher of the Chamber of Commerce, Representatives of the conservative "think tanks" such as in the Heritage Foundation Robert Kruble and in the Hoover Institution Peter Dougnam. At the present time, it is directed by Thomas J. Donohue, President of the Chamber of Commerce, the "boss of bosses."

CENTRAL INTELLIGENCE AGENCY (CIA): The Central Intelligence Agency was created in 1947 under the National Security Law.

Its responsibilities go beyond the simple collection of information. It is also called upon to intervene in nations where diplomacy has resulted insufficient and a military action would be counterproductive or inconvenient. Its activities include, psychological warfare, financing pro-U.S. political parties abroad, provocations, actions against unions, parties or groups opposed to U.S. foreign policy, supporting and fomenting coups d'état, training mercenaries and armed groups. Secret special operations increased without limits during the early 1950s. The Iran-"contra" scandal (financing the "contras" in Nicaragua by illegally selling arms to Iran) and the Bank of Credit and Commerce International (BCCI) scandal, the preferred bank of the Agency but also of the Medellín drug cartel, placed the CIA in the eye of the hurricane. The CIA was later discredited by revelations made during the Clinton's Administration regarding the promulgation of torture techniques to diverse police, military and Intelligence organisms throughout the continent provided through manuals produced by the Agency (for example, Training Manual for the exploitation of human resources) and the atrocities committed by the CIA in Guatemala made public through hard evidence and documents (proof that the Agency utilized and protected torturers). At the end of the Cold War, because of the lack of enemies, the CIA oriented its actions towards the collection of economic information, protecting U.S. interests in emerging markets and waging the war against terrorism and drug trafficking. While throughout Latin America amnesty laws that protect the dictators of the past are being questioned and reviewed for legality, the CIA remains unable to escape or accept the past. In August 2000, the Agency denied the release of files proving its role in the coup d'état against Salvador Allende in Chile in 1973, at the hand of Augusto Pinochet.

CENTRO AL SERVICIO DE LA ACCIÓN POPULAR (CENTER FOR THE SERVICE OF POPULAR ACTION) (CESAP): This is characterized as a center at the service of social projects. It is financed by the United States and its directorship publicly justified the coup d'état against President Hugo Chávez in April 2002.

CENTRO DE DIVULGACIÓN DEL CONOCIMIENTO ECONÓMICO (CENTER FOR THE PUBLICATION OF ECONOMIC KNOWLEDGE) (CEDICE): Based in Caracas, it is characterized as "a non-profit civilian association whose chief aim is to publicize political and economic philosophies giving priority to the free actions of individual initiative and the analysis of organizations and conditions that permit the existence of free societies." Actually, it is an investigative center that is funded by CIPE and other American organizations in order to provide incentive for programs favoring the "democratization" of "beneficiary" countries and of incentives in the world economy.

COMMITTEE OF THE INDEPEPENDENT POLITICAL ELECTORAL ORGANIZATION (COPEI): The party founded by Rafael Caldera, on January 13, 1946 in Caracas. Its tendency is Christian Socialist and it also goes by the names of Christian Socialist Party, Christian Democratic Party or, simply, the Christian Democrats.

CONFEDERACIÓN DE TRABAJADORES VENEZOLANOS (CONFEDERATION OF VENEZUELAN WORKERS) (CTV): The CTV is the country's most powerful union organization, with more than a million members; it was one of the main organizers of the strikes and protests in the two months that culminated in the attempted coup d'état against Hugo Chávez in April 2002. The then Secretary General of this confederation, Carlos Ortega, was closely connected to the President of the coup's Junta, businessman Pedro Carmona Estanga.

CONSEJO DE EMPRESARIOS VENEZUELA-ESTADOS UNIDOS (COUNCIL OF VENEZUELAN AND U.S. BUSINESSMEN) (CEVEU): An organization that groups Venezuelan businessmen with commercial, financial and investment interests from the United States.

CONSEJO NACIONAL ELECTORAL (NATIONAL ELECTORAL COUNCIL) (CNE): The Electoral Power of the Bolivarian Republic of Venezuela which organizes and supervises everything related to popular elections, by way of universal, direct and secret voting. It also has the ability to organize the elections of unions and of civilian organizations, whenever they so request. Among its functions, it regulates the electoral laws and resolves any doubts or problems resulting from any omissions within these laws; it issues direction in financial and political-electoral matters and applies sanctions whenever laws have not been followed, and is able to declare null and void any election, either totally or partially.

COORDINADORA DEMOCRÁTICA (DEMOCRATIC COORDINATOR) (CD): An organization grouping the broad spectrum of opposition to Hugo Chávez, which collected signatures for the referendum to recall the Venezuelan President; it includes groups from the extreme right (Primero Justicia) and the extreme left (Bandera Roja), the parties that were in power during the period 1959-1999—the Christian Socialist COPEI and the Democratic Action, the Movement towards Socialism (MAS), and others.

COORDINADORA DEMOCRÁTICA NICARAGÜENSE (NICARAGUAN DEMOCRATIC COALITION) (CDN): Anti-Sandinista coalition financed by the United States which boycotted the 1984 Nicaraguan elections.

DCI STRATEGIC WARNING COMMITTEE: This Committee directs the entire protection and advisory warning system of the United States. It is made up of representatives of the CIA, DIA, NSA, State/INR and NIMA.

DEFENSE INTELLIGENCE AGENCY (DIA): It coordinates Intelligence information obtained by the various branches of the Armed Services (Army, Navy, Marines, Air Force, Coast Guard and Special Forces) and administers counter-measures (including the administration of security in the ultra-classified installations of the United States). It is the espionage department of the U.S. Army. Created in 1961, its chief mission is to facilitate Intelligence to the commanders of the Armed Forces.

DEMOCRATIC ACTION PARTY (AD): This party was founded in Caracas in 1941 by Rómulo Betancourt, with Social Democratic tendencies. The party has held power on six occasions under Presidents Rómulo Gallegos, Rómulo Betancourt, Raul Leoni, Carlos Andrés Pérez (twice), and Jaime Lusinchi.

DEPARTMENT OF STATE: It is the U.S. Department of Foreign Affairs and it has its own espionage service, but as in many cases, its agents are not exactly spies, rather, analysts and brainy specialists who deliver reports that enable the Secretary of State to "hear what must be known, not what would like to be known," as stated in its official description. This Department is intertwined with the rest of the Intelligence community in order to digest all the information produced, but they do not collect data on the spot, they basically receive the information sent to the Department of State by the other spy agencies.

DEPARTMENT OF THE TREASURY: This department is a part of the Intelligence community even though it possesses just a small division for the collecting of its own information. It is really fed by the Intelligence sent to it by the rest of the agencies related to the international economic policies of the U.S. It advises the U.S. Government when general economic policy decisions are to be taken, especially when they relate to international markets.

DEVELOPMENT ALTERNATIVES, INC. (DAI): Private consulting business firm used by businessmen and governments, with headquarters in the U.S. It was founded in Washington in the seventies and in recent years has been operating mainly in Afghanistan, Iraq and Liberia, using USAID funding. It supports the undercovert operations of the U.S. Government.

EMBASSY POLITICAL OFFICE (POLOFF): The political office in the Embassies of the United States throughout the world, headed generally by a CIA or other U.S. Intelligence officer.

FEDERAL BUREAU OF INVESTIGATION (FBI): The FBI is the spy agency with powers to execute activities within U.S. territory.

It really has the characteristics of a Federal Police Force—it can act in any of the States—but one of its prime missions is to generate Intelligence for decisions made on interior policies. It is the oldest of the Intelligence agencies. It was founded in 1908, even though it was not until 1935 that it received the name by which it is known today.

FREE TRADE OF THE AMERICAS ACT (FTAA): The area of free trade in the Americas, known in Spanish as ALCA. It appeared in 1994 and pretends to promote U.S. economic annexation of Latin America.

FREE TRADE UNION INSTITUTE (FTUI): This is the only basic nucleus of the NED—which preceded it—and it is the most complicated. It was created in 1962 as part of the Alliance for Progress initiative developed by President John F. Kennedy. It continued the work which the Free Trade Union Committee (FTUC) carried out with the CIA. This Committee had been founded in 1944 to fight the left wing tendencies of European unions. The Board of Directors is comprised of leaders of the AFL-CIO. The FTUI, a bipartisan group, supported President Ronald Reagan's Central American policies and channeled funds from the NED to the Nicaraguan opposition and, in 1986, for the newspaper *La Prensa*. It was a funnel for the grants that the NED set aside for union groups and for the "independent press" in the Soviet Union and other countries of Eastern Europe. The Department of International Affairs, to which FTUI belongs, is the nerve center for this organization's formation of foreign policy and for its global operations. From its inception, this Institute has been strongly liked not only with the Government of the United States but also with the multinational corporations that invest in Latin America, with the CIA and, since 1984, with the NED network. Among the many outstanding achievements of FTUI's interventionist activities, its participation in the elections of Ferdinand Marcos of the Philippines stands out. In 1984, the FTUI created headlines because of the transferal of funds made by the NED, using this Institute, for two French groups opposed to the policies of President François Mitterand.

FREEDOM OF INFORMATION ACT (FOIA): On March 12, 1997, the Committee on Government Reform and Oversight approved and adopted a report entitled *A Citizen's Guide on Using the Freedom of Information Act and the Privacy Act of 1974 to Request Government Records*. The Freedom of Information Act establishes the presumption that all persons have access to documents in the possession of the distinct agencies and departments of the U.S. Government by following FOIA regulations to request such documents and information. Supposedly, documents in the possession of other entities associated with the Federal Government are also subject to FOIA, including private entities that receive government funding. Nevertheless, FOIA also includes a series of exemptions that enable any agency or entity to deny the release or declassification of information in the name of national security, to protect the privacy of individuals or trade secrets, the functioning of the government or other important interests.

GLOBAL POSITIONING SYSTEMS (GPS): The GPS is a group of satellites—twenty-four to be exact—orbiting the earth, facilitating the location of persons, objects, buildings, etc., using portable receivers or stations.

GUARIMBA: Method used by the Venezuelan opposition to boycott government acts, consisting in violent occupation of the streets, destruction of buildings, firing weapons—all intended to incite a repressive governmental reaction. During tense moments, these activities, taking place particularly in areas of Caracas inhabited by the upper class, have resulted in the "enclosure" of the residents and thus generated hostile feelings.

INFORMATION AND TECHNOLOGY ENTERPRISE (INTESA): Enterprise that was composed of Petróleos de Venezuela S.A. (PDVSA) and the U.S. multinational Science Applications International Corporation (SAIC), to control all the information of Venezuela's State-owned oil company, PDVSA. It was a project prompted by the so-called "nomina mayor" of PDVSA and put into the hands of the SAIC, a façade for the CIA, all the information and Intelligence of the world's largest petroleum enterprise. Its initial investment was contributed by Venezuela, which had a right to only 40% of shares. Such a "business deal" was justified by the fact that this arrangement would drastically lower the costs of computer services: but this did not happen and SAIC charged its partner PDVSA around $80 million annually. INTESA not only controlled all of PDVSA's vital information, it could also manipulate it and even intervene at will and without scruples. Their servers housed all the financial, technical, budgetary and business data of the enterprise. During the oil industry strike of 2002-2003, INTESA was the principal participant in the sabotage of the petroleum industry. PDVSA decided not to renew the contract upon expiration and SAIC sued them for expropriation; this was ratified by OPIC, but not accepted by the Venezuelan Government.

INICIATIVA PARA LA CONSTRUCCIÓN DE CONFIANZA (INICIATIVE FOR THE CONSTRUCTION OF CONFIDENCE) (VICC): Officially a program of USAID and DAI in Venezuela. It commenced on August 1, 2002 with the goal of "providing opportune and flexible assistance in order to strengthen democracy in Venezuela."

INTERNATIONAL MILITARY EDUCATION AND TRAINING (IMET): This program is the backbone of collective professionalism and military education of the United States, outside of its borders. It offers opportunities for the professional development of very carefully selected soldiers and civilian candidates. It grants funds to military and civilian personnel in associated nations, so that they may attend professional development courses in U.S. military academies. Many of the graduates advance in their careers until they reach high-ranking levels in the directorships of their respective military and governmental institutions.

INTERNATIONAL REPUBLICAN INSTITUTE (IRI): The IRI is headed by Senator John McCain, who lost the 2002 primary election to George Bush, and who is now the main congressional defender for the global war against terrorism. It is the Republican Party section within the NED.

MARINE CORPS INTELLIGENCE (MCI): The MCI is specialized in rapid military intervention operations, from landings to invasions, using lightening attacks to rescue hostages, etc. The MCI is little more than a link in the network of espionage departments, especially in naval jurisdictions, but also related with the Air Force. Its analysts, above all else, draft plans for all possible scenarios so that, once the moment arises to execute a mission, everything is meticulously planned, to the point of routine.

MOVIMIENTO AL SOCIALISMO (MOVEMENT TOWARDS SOCIALISM) (MAS): Composed originally of members ousted from the Communist Party or from ultra-radical organizations, it became allied with traditional parties forming an opposition to President Hugo Chávez. It took part in the so-called Democratic Coordinator that demanded a referendum to depose Chávez.

MOVIMIENTO BOLIVARIANO REVOLUCIONARIO (REVOLUTIONARY BOLIVARIAN MOVEMENT) (MBR-200): Organized and led by Hugo Chávez, it was born on November 17, 1982, following the oath sworn by a small group of fellow soldiers, at Saman de Güere, a location that was once an encampment of Simón Bolívar. In 1997, it was transformed into Movímiento V República.

MOVIMIENTO V REPÚBLICA (MOVEMENT V REPUBLIC) (MVR): Founded on October 21, 1997 in Caracas, with Hugo Chávez as its General Director. It is the electoral version of the Revolutionary Bolivarian Movement-200, also created by Chávez in the eighties; it could not present a candidate in the elections because of legal impediments contained in the Political Parties Act, that prohibited the use of the name "Bolivarian" since this is a national symbol and Bolívar's name cannot be used for any party affiliations. For that reason, the name V Republic was adopted; in other words, it was hinting at the creation of a new republic and at the same time maintaining the already well-known combination of phonetics and initials, MBR and MVR.

NATIONAL DEMOCRATIC INSTITUTE FOR INTERNATIONAL AFFAIRS (NDI): This institute is headed by Madeleine K. Albright. It is the section of the Democratic Party within the NED and self-defines itself as "a non-profit organization for the consolidation and amplification of democracy in the world."

NATIONAL ENDOWMENT FOR DEMOCRACY (NED): Officially created on November 6, 1982, the NED was established by statute as a non-profit organization, yet its financing is approved by Congress and included in the chapter of the Department of State budget destined for the U.S. Agency for International Development-*USAID*. In order to maintain the illusion that it is a private organization, the NED also receives very small donations from three associations, which are also indirectly financed by federal contracts: the Smith Richardson Foundation, the John M. Olin Foundation and the Lynde and Harry Bradley Foundation. The majority of the historic figures linked to clandestine CIA actions have at some time been members of the Board of Directors or the Administrative Council of the NED, including Otto Reich, John Negroponte, Henry Cisneros and Elliot Abrams. The present Chairman of the NED Board of Directors is Vin Weber, founder of the ultraconservative organization Empower America, and campaign fundraiser for George W. Bush in 2000. NED's President is Carl Gershman, an ex-trotskist gone awry, and once a member of the Social Democrats, USA who later joined the growing club of neo-conservative and Reagan-Bush "hawks".

NATIONAL IMAGERY AND MAPPING AGENCY (NIMA): This used to be known as the National Geospatial-Intelligence Agency, belonging to the U.S. Department of Defense and developing, among many things, aeronautical map-making. Originally the

NIMA was a department within the Air Force Intelligence Agency until, in 1996, it left to become a new Intelligence Agency. From that time onward, part of the information obtained from the surveillance satellites (photographic) is later analyzed in this department, which receives the information to draft maps or to locate possible objectives.

NATIONAL INTELLIGENCE OFFICE FOR WARNING: The mission of this office is to advise and assist the CIA Director in all surveillance matters, and also to coordinate activities for national Intelligence. Its sources are located outside of the United States. This office is expected to directly alert the president and the National Security Council in the case of danger to national security.

NATIONAL RECONNAISSANCE OFFICE (NRO): This office is responsible for the enormous U.S. operation via satellite. It has been in operation since the sixties, but its existence was not revealed until 1992, when Washington declassified its name. Even though satellite launching depends on the Air Force, the control of all the satellites once they are in orbit corresponds to the NRO, which directs various other programs such as reconnaissance and surveillance satellites, and those that spy on defense signals or communications.

NATIONAL SECURITY AGENCY (NSA): Even though this agency is somewhat unknown, it spends nearly one half of the annual espionage budget of the United States. Founded in 1952 by President Harry Truman, the NSA is responsible for espionage of foreign communications. Its star program is called Echelon and has spy stations all over the world in order to intercept international communications.

NATIONAL SECURITY COUNCIL (NSC): The NSC is a group that designs policy for the Army and for the Intelligence services of the nation, concerning matters of national and international security. It answers directly to the president. It has a secret committee known as Committee 5412 which directs the "black" or undercovert operations and also a sub-committee (Sub-Committee PI-40) that directs and controls covert-up policies.

NAVY INTELLIGENCE (NI): It is the area of espionage used by the U.S. Navy. Its mission consists of providing vital information to the fleet, wherever it may be located. All U.S. naval bases in the world include a division of the Naval Security Group, whose fundamental mission is espionage.

NEW YORK POLICE DEPARTMENT (NYPD): The Police Department of the City of New York.

OFFICE OF TRANSITION INITIATIVES (OTI): It is an institution that is created in countries where the U.S. would like to exert its influence when faced with governments that have not yet acceded to U.S. interests. The web page of the Embassy of the United States in Caracas reads: "The OTI's have arisen to administer assistance programs in the countries of the former Communist Bloc who are in a transition phase towards full democracy and towards a free trade economy." Since 1994, they are established through the initiative of the USAID "to offer a response in countries that are passing through a significant and sometimes rapid political transition, which may or may not be accompanied by a social and/or economic crisis." The OTI "evaluates, designs and executes programs that are characterized as being expeditious, flexible, innovative, tangible, motivated, catalytic and openly political and which remove the root causes of crisis." The OTIs have been used in Kosovo, Haiti, Indonesia, Peru, Guatemala, the Philippines and Colombia, among other nations. Generally speaking, the USAID orientates its OTIs to put in place relationships with political organizations, communications media, and non-governmental organizations, and to supply the finances and training necessary to obtain the desired results. In Venezuela, it was created in July of 2002 in the United States Embassy in Caracas.

ORGANIZATION OF PETROLEUM EXPORTING COUNTRIES (OPEC): It was founded in Baghdad on September 14, 1960 and has its headquarters in Vienna. Its aims are the unification and coordination of petroleum policies of the member nations, defending their interests as producer countries. It arose as a reply to the decrease of the official price of petroleum, agreed upon unilaterally by the large distributing companies in August of 1960. Initially there were five member countries: Saudi Arabia, Iraq, Iran, Kuwait and Venezuela; it grew to include another six members: Qatar, Indonesia, Libya, the United Arab Emirates, Algeria and Nigeria. Ecuador and Gabon used to be members. Other important petroleum producing countries are not members of OPEC: Canada, Mexico, Norway, the United States, Russia and Oman.

PATRIA PARA TODOS (HOMELAND FOR ALL) (PPT): Born on September 26, 1997 during a public ceremony in the Radio City Theatre in Caracas, resulting from a division within the party, La Causa R. From inception, the PPT put all its efforts into the struggle against social exclusion and offered a humanist project whose central theme was the integral development of mankind (Declaration of Principles). Some of the members are Aristóbulo Istúriz, José Albornoz, Rafael Uzcátegui, Jacobo Torres, Xiomara Lucena, Rodolfo Sanz, Lelis Páez, and Vladimir Villegas.

PETRÓLEOS DE VENEZUELA (VENEZUELAN PETROLEUM), S.A. (PDVSA): It is the most important petroleum enterprise in the world and it belongs to the Venezuelan Government. Founded on January 1, 1976 with the aim of being in charge of the national petroleum industry and all its planning, coordination and supervision, it concluded the process of returning the hydrocarbon rights worked by the foreign companies on Venezuelan soil. At the present time, PDVSA produces more than three million barrels per day, it refines more than a million barrels daily and exports more than two and a half million barrels of hydrocarbons on a daily basis.

PLAN BOLÍVAR (THE BOLÍVAR PLAN): It was installed in 1999 upon the arrival in power of Hugo Chávez. It is an association of PDVSA with the National Armed Forces to contribute to the improvement of the social structure and standard of living; to offer complete services to the poorest of the population; in education, focusing on building repairs and maintenance; in the infrastructure, modernizing the public roads system; in housing, of great interest to the homeless; in alimentation, bringing within reach of those who most need it, sufficient quality coupled with reasonable prices.

POLO PATRIÓTICO (PATRIOTIC POLE) (PP): Political coalition composed of the Movement towards Socialism (MAS), the Republic V Movement (MVR), and Homeland for All (PPP) parties, all supporters of Hugo Chávez's candidacy in the presidential campaign of 1998 and resulting in victory.

SENIOR EXECUTIVE INTELLIGENCE BRIEF (SEIB): The name of the memorandum for executive officers in the principal U.S. Intelligence Services, with fairly broad distribution. It generally contains information summarizing Intelligence activities and has a tendency to be careful about protecting sources and the methods used to obtain the information. The precursor of this type of report, in the FBI and the CIA, was Richard Clarke, Coordinator of Antiterrorist Activities for the National Security Council (NSC).

THE "PUNTO FIJO" PACT: Faced with the proximity of general elections in 1958, and then with two attempted military coups, the presidential candidates of the Democratic Action Party, the Democratic Republican Union (URD) and the Committee of the Independen Political Electoral Organization, Rómulo Betancourt, Jóvito Villalba and Rafael Caldera, respectively, met on October 31 of that year in Caldera's residence, Punto Fijo Estate in Caracas, to sign a pre-electoral pact, that basically agreed to a system of alternating the power. Excluded from the pact, intentionally, was the Communist Party of Venezuela, even though it was part of the Patriotic Junta; likewise, left out was Republican Integration Movement, having as members many well-known personalities. In November 1958, the URD candidate, Rear Admiral Wolfgang Larrazabal Ugueto removed himself from the presidency of the Government Junta in order to dedicate himself to the presidential campaign. Only AD and COPEI stayed in the pact, agreeing to establish a government of "national unity," in which one of the signing pact members would have equal representation in the Executive Cabinet of the winner of the election.

THE SUPREME COUNCIL OF PRIVATE ENTERPRISE (COSEP): It was founded on February 16, 1972 with the name COSIP, supposedly a civilian non-profit association. It pulled together the Nicaraguan private big business sector and was the heart and nerve center of the CDN parties. More than any other social sector of the country, the COSEP was the one that has always had the closest and most direct ties with the U.S. Embassy: it united the class that ruled Nicaragua until 1979 with the U.S. Government and with the CDN parties, dominating them completely.

UNITED STATES AGENCY FOR INTERNATIONAL DEVELOPMENT (USAID): It functions as an instrument of CIA penetration into civil society, by enabling the "legitimate" funding of millions of dollars to promote U.S. foreign policy abroad and influence internal politics of foreign nations while avoiding congressional scrutiny.

UNITED STATES INFORMATION AGENCY (USIA): This agency is part of the U.S. Department of State. During William Clinton's presidency, starting precisely on October 1, 1999, after forty-six years acting as the organization of public diplomacy, the USIA ceased to exist as such and its functions were absorbed within the Department of State (the Ministry of Foreign Affairs).

UNIÓN NACIONAL OPOSITORA de Nicaragua (UNO) (Nicaragua NATIONAL OPPOSITION UNION PARTY) (ONE): It was founded on May 29, 1986, was composed of CDN members, among whom were former Somoza supporters and ex-communists. Their common ground was an anti-Sandinista point of view.

Eva Golinger is a Venezuelan-American attorney specializing in international human rights and inmigration law. Having grown up in the United States, Golinger moved to Venezuela in the mid-1990s to discover her Venezuelan roots. She lived nearly five years in the Andean city of Mérida, Venezuela, writing, teaching and singing in a band. Golinger studied music from the age of six and entered into the music department at Sarah Lawrence College in early 1991, majoring in vocal music. But during her university years, she switched her major to Political Science and Law and became particularly interested in the history of U.S. interventions in Latin America. Subsequently, she earned her Juris Doctorate from the City University of New York Law School.

Since Chávez won the presidency in 1998, Golinger has been writing about the social and political changes in Venezuela. Her articles are widely published on the Internet and in Venezuelan newspapers. In 2003 she began investigating U.S. involvement in the April 2002 coup against President Chávez and has uncovered more than US$20 million in financing to anti-Chávez groups from the U.S. Government. In October 2004, she obtained top-secret documents from the CIA, declassified under the Freedom of Information Act, demonstrating prior knowledge and complicity in the coup. Ms. Golinger's work has been covered by *The New York Times, The Washington Post, Newsday, Chicago Tribune, International Herald Tribune, The Wall Street Journal, Los Angeles Times* and other major media around the world. She currently resides between New York and Caracas, Venezuela. *The Chávez Code* is her first book.

IMPRENTA
ALEJO CARPENTIER

EVAGOLINGER@HOTMAIL.com